Rinsed

Rinsed

From Cartels to Crypto: How the Tech Industry Washes Money for the World's Deadliest Crooks

GEOFF WHITE

BUSINESS

PENGUIN BUSINESS

UK | USA | Canada | Ireland | Australia
India | New Zealand | South Africa

Penguin Business is part of the Penguin Random House group of companies
whose addresses can be found at global.penguinrandomhouse.com.

First published 2024

001

Copyright © Geoff White, 2024

The moral right of the author has been asserted

Set in 12/14.75pt Dante MT Std
Typeset by Jouve (UK), Milton Keynes
Printed and bound in Great Britain by Clays Ltd, Elcograf S.p.A.

The authorized representative in the EEA is Penguin Random House Ireland,
Morrison Chambers, 32 Nassau Street, Dublin D02 YH68

A CIP catalogue record for this book is available from the British Library

Hardback ISBN: 978–0–241–62483–8
Trade paperback ISBN: 978–0–241–62485–2

www.greenpenguin.co.uk

Contents

Introduction

Have you ever found yourself with too much money?

I'm not talking about discovering a forgotten banknote in a trouser pocket or feeling a bit flush after payday. I'm talking about serious cash. You see a luxury car and buy it on impulse. Pick out armfuls of designer clothes without a glance at the price tags. Pay for all your friends' meals at a Michelin-starred restaurant and don't even blink when the bill arrives.

The vast majority of us have never been in this situation, nor will we ever be. If we do have significant sums of money, they're usually locked away, perhaps in a property or pension or savings account, carefully managed and guarded behind layers of financial bureaucracy. They're not available to us as spendable funds to be thrown around like oligarchs' pocket money.

It's possible to fantasize about this situation, of course. You might win the lottery, one of those giant rollover amounts that make you instantly rich beyond your wildest imaginings. Many of us have daydreamed about the spending spree we'd go on if our numbers came up. But now, imagine what it would be like if you had to hide how you'd got the money. What if, instead of a lottery win, your wealth came from something you couldn't admit to – such as crime? You're faced with an excruciating dilemma. How do you enjoy your huge amounts of cash, but hide its origins to stop people asking awkward questions?

If you want to know why criminals launder their money, this is the ultimate answer: it's so that, when they buy the fancy car, the plush apartment or the expensive watch and the salesperson (or police officer or bank manager) asks them 'Where did you get this money?' they can provide a believable answer. To launder money is to change its history.

 Rinsed

Just to be clear: having too much illicit money is a problem that many crooks will never encounter. Take my mate Steve, for example. He was a drug dealer, which probably sounds quite edgy, unless you have actually met him. He was an intelligent, generally law-abiding person who during his college days had hit on a simple, low-level criminal scheme. He'd buy an ounce of cannabis and sell seven one-eighth portions to his friends. His profit would pay for the remaining eighth, which he'd smoke himself. Steve never had to disguise the money from his crimes because he never made enough to justify it. Money laundering is something even most criminals never have to do. But when you think of the person Steve bought his ounce from, and the person above them in the chain, and so on . . . eventually you come to someone for whom too much cash is most certainly an issue. It's a real problem for those at the very top of the criminal enterprise, the ones whose exploitation of others creates overwhelming profits.

This is why it's often hard to get people to care about money laundering. It's something that only happens when you have too much money (which most of us don't), and only if you acquired it illegally (which most of us haven't). To make matters worse, media coverage of money laundering can be perplexing. The headlines often feature huge sums, but when you read on you discover it's being washed through financial schemes too complex and abstract to grasp. There are occasional reports of eye-watering fines on big banks for money laundering, but very often they turn out to be for 'compliance failures'. Rarely does it feel like it's connected to tangible, comprehensible wrongdoing. Money laundering can feel totally ethereal – the ultimate victimless crime.

But make no mistake, without it, organized crime would grind to a halt. Laundering is the glue that holds the underworld together. As you'll see throughout this book, without avenues via which to wash their profits, criminals of many kinds simply cannot operate. The drug dealers in our nightclubs, the pimps in our backstreets, the fraudsters targeting our elderly relatives' bank accounts, all of them depend on a system of moving and hiding money. Without a reliable scheme to launder and extract their wealth, no one gets paid and the underworld falls apart.

This book will show you how this system works. And in order to demonstrate that laundering is absolutely not a victimless offence, I'm going to start by covering the crimes which generate the profits, before exploring the financial wrongdoing that follows. Some of the crimes are purely financial, such as fraud, others are physical, and some are deeply horrific, including the sexual abuse of both adults and children. Some of the stories in this book are painful and traumatic. But they're important to hear, because without a way to disguise the money that results from these crimes, much of this heinous behaviour would not be possible.

I'm also going to show you how technology is putting rocket boosters under the money-laundering industry.

As an investigative journalist, I've covered cybercrime for more than a decade. In some ways it's similar to money laundering; it's a subject many people would like to understand better, but it can seem complicated. I've tried hard to make the technicalities comprehensible, turning the cases into compelling stories and, where possible, telling the human stories at the heart of the hacks. Over time, as I continued to research cybercrime, I started to notice something unexpected. Like many, I'd initially regarded computer hackers as having god-like powers. They seemed like characters from movies, in which a shadowy figure wearing a hoodie would type a few lines of code and millions of dollars would instantly vanish. But as I investigated, I discovered it wasn't quite so clear-cut. Yes, hackers are very good at digitally breaking into places and getting their hands on money. But when it comes to actually moving, hiding and extracting those funds – money laundering, in other words – the hackers weren't necessarily as omnipotent as I'd thought. Time and again, I found that they were relying on other groups of people to handle the money. It felt like there were two worlds. There's the world of the hacker: immersed in code, scanning lines of program text for vulnerabilities and moving effortlessly through the computer networks of their victims. And then there's the world of the money mover: equally computer-literate but in a different way, able to create fake identities, marshal bank accounts and whizz funds around the globe in an instant. The two worlds are reliant upon each other, but from what I've seen, there's not that much crossover.

Then I started noticing these hi-tech money movers getting a new source of business: traditional crooks. Drug dealers, prostitution gangs and scammers of all varieties have clearly cottoned on to the benefits of digitizing their profits, which online crooks have always enjoyed. Compared to the headaches involved in using more traditional financial systems – trying to inveigle dodgy cash into a bank, for example – the modern, digital world of finance offers unprecedented and constantly escalating advantages of speed, flexibility and global reach. As you'll see in the following chapters, the emergence of entire new financial systems such as cryptocurrency has offered even more opportunity. It also helps the criminals stay one step ahead of the authorities, who sometimes struggle to comprehend these new and fast-moving tech finance systems, let alone regulate them. As a result of these trends, the boundaries between traditional, organized crime and cyber-crime are breaking down, and money laundering is the space where these worlds are crossing over.

This book will take you through the process of money laundering, detailing the steps involved in this shadow industry that have been honed over decades. It will show you how the tech industry is transforming each one of them – often unwittingly – by creating innovations that outpace traditional regulation. And finally it will give an example of how these advances in laundering create deeply dangerous consequences, allegedly enabling one of the world's most unpredictable regimes – North Korea – to develop weapons of mass destruction that threaten us all.

There's an old saying: 'a rising tide lifts all boats'. It's normally couched in positive terms – that overall economic improvement will benefit everyone. In the case of hi-tech money laundering, however, it offers a dark vision of the future. The better these launderers become at their work, the more crime of all types will be enabled. It's time to understand where the water is rising, before it washes over us all.

I.

Pablo's Problem

It was autumn 2017 when Nicolás first started having the visions. He was coming out of the garage beside his house when he saw a man wearing a hat, who strode calmly across the patio and then disappeared into the wall. Over the following weeks and months it happened again and again, always the same place, always the same apparition. Sometime later, the man was joined by a woman, who seemed to follow him in disappearing into the fabric of the building. Eventually, it was a whole family, with several children. 'They approached the wall, went through it and vanished,' Nicolás tells me. It was most peculiar, but he was unperturbed. 'Ghosts have never frightened me,' he says. 'To me, they are part of every-day life.'

Perhaps it was no surprise to find strange goings-on at this particular property. The house had an extraordinary history, and so does Nicolás. He's the nephew of the infamous cocaine baron Pablo Escobar, and the house in Medellin, Colombia, was one of the last hideouts his uncle used before his death in 1993.

These days, the city is trying to shake off its violent and bloody past as the heartland of Pablo's cartel. But remnants of its most famous son abound, from street murals to tourist trinkets bearing his image. Whereas these are just echoes from the past, in the giant house where Nicolás was living, he was about to come face to face with a much more visceral and direct legacy of his uncle's drug-dealing career.

After spending several months watching ghosts walking into the wall, Nicolás's curiosity got the better of him and he decided that he had to investigate: 'So, I took a metre ruler and started measuring.'

He discovered that the dimensions of the house didn't add up. Somewhere behind the wall into which the ghosts were disappearing was an unexplained void space. His curiosity was irrepressibly piqued. Nicolás called in a colleague and they decided to knock a hole in the wall to see what was afoot.

It didn't start well. 'We needed superhuman strength to bring the wall down. It was reinforced with concrete and there was no way to get in,' he says. Finally, however, their sledgehammers started having an impact, and Nicolás managed to smash a hole big enough to fit a hand through. Immediately they were hit with an awful smell. 'The stench was so unpleasant it was impossible to breathe, even though we were standing in an open space,' remembers Nicolás. Finally, the whiff subsided enough for them to push a mobile phone through the gap and film what was inside. That was when they realized they'd stumbled upon an old hiding place built for Pablo Escobar, ready to shield him as the net of law enforcement closed in. Nicolás and his helpers knew they'd have to move carefully. Such hideaways were often rigged with booby traps to catch pursuers. 'There could have been an explosive or some kind of way to prevent people from entering the place,' he says.

When they finally worked out that it was safe and managed to get inside, they found a fully kitted-out hideaway, complete with toilet, sink and shower, as well as an intricate access system which automatically triggered lights that would guide Pablo to the safety of the hideout. And then, in a separate chamber, they found a dusty package. It was an unexpected time capsule from before his uncle's death more than two decades before, and would bring Nicolás face to face with the past. What he found inside would demonstrate the immense wealth of Pablo's drug empire, and perfectly illustrate why money laundering is at the heart of every successful organized crime gang – something his uncle learned from his earliest days in crime.

Pablo Escobar's formative years were marked by two phenomena that would go on to exert considerable influence over his future life:

violence and poverty. For a decade from 1948, a conflict raged in Colombia that was so brutal it became known simply as La Violencia. Innocent people were killed by the thousand, their bodies sometimes mutilated in deeply sadistic ways.[1] Escobar was born into this horror in 1949. His family was also struggling constantly with money; Pablo's father scraped by smuggling liquor, and as Pablo came of age, he learned to hustle too.

Medellin was a smuggling hotspot, and the son soon moved into his father's trade, running contraband cigarettes and learning the underground routes through the country. Bizarre as it may seem, Pablo apparently got into cocaine because it was safer than smuggling cigarettes. According to his brother, Roberto (Nicolás's father), Pablo felt that the risk of arrest was lower. Roberto Escobar also recalls that once, as a test, his brother gave cocaine to ten people to try and 'almost all of them liked it better than marijuana'. With this piece of ad hoc market research under his belt, Pablo set about building a cocaine-smuggling empire.[2]

His motivation was simple: money. Escobar vowed that he would either become a millionaire by the age of twenty-two or commit suicide. It was a twist on the mantra of many youngsters desperate to escape from poverty and exclusion: get rich, or die trying. Money also bought safety in a perilous world. Pablo and his brother were able to buy off judges to escape imprisonment, something they seemed to consider a regular business expense. 'Pablo and I grew up knowing that all the rules were for sale,' Roberto writes in his memoir.[3] This extended to buying political power too. When Pablo decided to run for Congress as a deputy candidate, he would hand out wads of money at his rallies, winning the people's affection with drug cash. He funded local improvement projects. Partly as a result, Pablo is still regarded as a heroic figure by some in Colombia, especially in his home city of Medellin. As he quickly discovered, however, even the power of money has some limits. Once elected to Congress, his attempt to be simultaneously a politician and a drug smuggler came under inevitable fire from his opponents. In the end he quit the job, feeling snubbed and wounded.

Rejected from politics, Escobar doubled down on his drug-smuggling business, and the key market was the US. By the time American authorities realized the scale of the cocaine trade flooding across its border, it was far too late. Escobar had already become rich enough to stay one step ahead. So rich, in fact, that he made the *Forbes* billionaires list seven years running.[4] The money was used in part to fund his endless, dizzying innovations in smuggling. Drugs were hidden in hollow walking sticks, inside nuns' outfits and stitched into shoes manufactured at a factory run by an associate of Escobar's gang. His chemists later learned how to create liquid cocaine, which was mixed into everything from jeans to religious statues. The cocaine could then be extracted once the product had been shipped to its destination (with the added bonus that the jeans, statues and so on could be shipped cheaply as regular cargo rather than smuggled illicitly at greater cost). The gang's drug lab on the Venezuelan border was reportedly so advanced, it had a runway that was disguised beneath houses on wheels that could be moved aside whenever a plane needed to land.[5]

By the time the authorities finally rose up against him, Escobar had a massive war chest with which to fight back. Despite having the resources of one of the world's richest countries, America seemingly struggled to outspend and outsmart the cartel boss. When the US sent up costly surveillance planes to track his drug shipments, Pablo simply paid a US Customs agent $250,000 for information to evade them.[6] This constant battle to stay ahead was fuelled by drug profits. But as Escobar's empire expanded, those profits became problematic.

When we think of the drug trade, we tend to see it from one direction – the flow of narcotics into somewhere like the US. We often don't consider the reverse flow – of money travelling back to trafficking centres like Colombia. But this is where laundering comes into the picture, and where Roberto would become increasingly entwined in his brother's story.

Roberto became the cartel's accountant, and therefore the incoming flow of money was his problem. 'Most of our money came back to Medellin as straight cash,' he writes. This threw up an immediate logistical headache because, ironically, the thing that made cocaine such a great product – its packageability and profitability – also made it challenging. The cartel's planes could carry 1,200kg of cocaine in one load. But that was then sold for $60m, and even in large denomination notes, the Escobar gang couldn't fit all that money into the same plane in one load. As Roberto writes: 'Cash took more space than kilos of coke, and there was so much more of it. Getting cash back from America to Colombia was as difficult as getting the drugs into [America]. Maybe even more difficult.'

But having banknotes was essential, partly for pay-offs. For example, Escobar's brother claims that when a Peruvian intelligence chief had to be bribed to allow drug planes to land, he demanded $100k for each one, in cash.[7]

As a result, Roberto and his colleagues had to become as innovative with cash stashing as they had with cocaine smuggling. They built a network of *caletas*; homes belonging to Pablo with masses of banknotes hidden behind fake Styrofoam walls. Cash was squirrelled away on farms, in dustbins and inside sofas. They used coffee beans to hide the musty smell of notes so the stashes wouldn't be discovered. Roberto famously claims to have spent $2,500 per month on rubber bands just to hold it all together.[8]

Roberto and his accomplices were encountering the issue faced by any successful street drug operation: they were drowning in cash. But one person's problem is another's opportunity. By the 1980s the cocaine trade was in full flow, having expanded exponentially from Pablo Escobar's humble beginnings in Medellin a decade or so earlier. And the huge volumes of cash it generated created a need for professional laundering services – a need that could be exploited by both friends and foes, as one savvy lawyer was about to discover.

As the 1980s came into view, things weren't going well for Ken Rijock. He'd lost interest in his career as a lawyer for the banking industry and his marriage was on the rocks. But luckily for him (or unluckily, depending on how you look at it), Rijock happened to be living in what was fast becoming the beating heart of the US drug boom: Florida.

The supply of cocaine into the south-eastern US from the likes of Pablo Escobar was supplemented by the arrival of Cuban criminals, who sneaked into Florida among those escaping the regime of Cuban leader Fidel Castro. The result was an explosive combination of paranoia-inducing narcotics, big money and organized crime. It was the era of the 'cocaine cowboys', and thanks to its proximity to both South America and Cuba, southern Florida found itself the new Wild West.

Once again, cash was the inevitable by-product. *Time* magazine reported in November 1981 that Miami's Federal Reserve bank branch had a currency surplus of $5bn, 'mostly in drug-generated $50 and $100 bills'.[9] For Rijock, all this ready money would furnish a lucrative business opportunity.

One day in the early 1980s, a ship's captain came to Rijock with a prickly problem. He'd made $6m in cash from a marijuana deal. He knew Rijock was a smart lawyer. Could he help the skipper handle the money?

Through his career in the finance industry, Rijock had experience in long-term planning to protect the assets of the vastly wealthy. And so when the ship's captain came to him with $6m of drug money, Rijock considered it a challenge. Usefully for us, the system by which he laundered the cash is a step-by-step introduction to the basics of the trade: Money Laundering 101, if you like. There are three classic stages: placement, layering and integration.

Placement means getting the money into the financial system so it's safe, and not stashed in the walls of apartments like some of Pablo Escobar's cash. The problem for Rijock was that no US bank was ever going to accept the skipper's fishy $6m. For such large sums, banks are obliged by law to ask awkward questions about where the money came from. So Rijock had to get creative.

He found a solution on the tiny Caribbean island of Anguilla, a British Overseas Territory on the edge of the North Atlantic, with a population of less than 20,000. After winning a battle for independence from its larger neighbour Saint Kitts and Nevis, in the early 1980s Anguilla's government was seeking new economic opportunities. With little in the way of natural resources, beyond tourism, its options were limited. So Anguilla had, like many of its island neighbours, begun offering financial and corporate services as a way to make money.[10] But the world was already full of far larger, more experienced countries offering banking and company registration schemes. Why would anyone choose Anguilla? The tiny island needed an edge, so it offered secrecy. As Rijock discovered, the money held in Anguilla's banks and the identities of the people behind the companies registered on the island would be hidden behind a veil of bureaucracy. Other nations' courts and law-enforcement agencies would therefore struggle to get any information about those who put their money into the island's financial system. Brokers in Anguilla sold these services at a premium to anyone who wanted secrecy – perfect for people like Ken Rijock.[11] Anguilla would be the placement stage of his laundering plan. It would be the hole through which he would insert the skipper's $6m into the financial world.

To smuggle the cash out of the US, Rijock recruited a motley crew of accomplices, swapped their beach clothes for smart suits and gave them each a briefcase full of money. They would fly together with him to Anguilla, posing as property investors.

Handily, once they arrived in Anguilla they discovered that the island had, quite literally, a shopping mall full of banks ready to receive the money. And unlike the banks most of us use, these institutions were stunningly lax when it came to ID checks. Rather than signing his name, the skipper used a rubber stamp bearing the image of Mickey Mouse (try doing that in your local HSBC branch and see how far you get). As Rijock waited in the shopping mall of banks, the clerk ran his client's money through their counting machine. 'It's fair to say I'd never once wondered how long it would take to count $6m in cash,' he wrote. 'In reality it takes an eternity, especially when you're itching to get on a plane back home again.'[12]

Meanwhile, Rijock sat nervously on the edge of his seat – as he had done since leaving the US laden with banknotes – only relaxing when the bills had finally been accepted and deposited.

With the skipper's money now in the care of an Anguillan bank, the placement stage was complete. The next step in the laundering process is layering, which means moving the money around to make it harder to trace, and to break the connection between the money and the crime that created it. After all, if you leave it in the bank, there's a chance it can be tracked and recovered, even in a high-secrecy jurisdiction like Anguilla. So Rijock created a number of shell companies on the island, helped by a corrupt local lawyer, whose secretaries signed their names as the businesses' sole shareholders.[13] Rijock then got the bank in Anguilla who'd received the skipper's money to send it on to these companies. Even if the US authorities could trace the $6m drug money to Anguilla and even if they could pierce the banks' secrecy laws to discover the shell companies, they'd never be able to find out that it was actually Rijock and his new criminal accomplices behind those companies.

To further muddy the trail, as his money-laundering skills developed Rijock sent money to Switzerland, France and Taiwan. He changed some of it for cheques. He moved some of it into special secrecy-preserving shares. Anything to throw investigating authorities off the scent. Having cracked the placement stage of his scheme, Rijock was now becoming ever more adept at the layering aspect too.

All this was illegal activity, and Rijock knew it. He points out, however, that at the time he and many others he knew believed that drugs would be decriminalized and didn't see their use as a major crime. From that perspective, laundering money from the trade didn't seem too big a problem for Rijock. In addition, he was beginning to enjoy the excitement of his illicit work. He was a Vietnam veteran, and he believes that coloured his outlook. 'If you've grown up in a place where you are at risk, and you manage to survive, then going back to the nine-to-five world sometimes can be a little too mundane,' he tells me. As if laundering drug money wasn't risky enough, Rijock was doing all this while dating a woman who worked as an economic crime detective in the Florida police force. He even moved in with her. 'Risk can be very addictive,' he admits. But it wasn't just risk that motivated him. Rijock earned a hefty fee every time he successfully laundered. 'The monetary gains from legitimate commerce were minimal; the gains from laundering were obscenely high,' he writes.[14]

With the skipper's money successfully placed (entered into the financial industry via Anguilla's banks) and layered (moved around between the shell companies and through different countries and assets), it was time for the final stage of the money-laundering process: integration. This is the most fun part for criminals, because they actually get to spend their ill-gotten gains, which have by this point been cleaned of any connection to crime. But rather than indulging in some hedonistic splurge, the wise move is to spend the money on some kind of business or asset that's going to give you an income even when your criminal days are behind you. You might want to go for property (which is what Roberto Escobar ended up doing with a lot of his brother's drug cash), or perhaps high art (if you choose wisely, it'll go up in value). The advantage of such purchases is that, even if you get convicted for your crimes, the authorities won't be able to seize the properties or the artworks (because, thanks to the layering work, they can't link them to the crimes). So when you come out of prison, your penthouse pad or Picasso painting are still waiting for you.

In the skipper's case, he and some of his colleagues used their newly washed drug money to buy a glamorous restaurant in Miami. This wasn't just a fun hang-out. The restaurant also gave them a couple of advantages: firstly, because it was a cash-intensive business, when the skipper got more drug money he could wash it through the restaurant's tills, potentially avoiding having to take it to Anguilla. 'In its first year so much of their narco-profits were being pumped into the venture that the diner became the sixth-highest grossing restaurant in the entire US,' remembers Rijock.[15] And secondly, the restaurant was ostensibly a legitimate business (albeit secretly acquired with criminal money) so the skipper could pay his taxes like a regular businessman, thereby avoiding the risk that the Internal Revenue Service might get suspicious.

After assisting the skipper, Rijock continued laundering and, as his expertise grew over the following years, word spread, and others beat a path to his door. Soon he was handling many more millions of dollars, making regular cash-smuggling trips to Anguilla's banks and his suite of businesses.

The three-stage system used by Rijock doesn't just apply to drug cash. Whatever crime is committed, and however the proceeds are manifested, they still need to be finagled into a financial system, washed of their connection to the crime and extricated for long-term gain. It's the bedrock of any successful laundering operation.

But Rijock's luck wouldn't last long. He wasn't the only one who'd spotted how vital financial services had become to the booming drug trade in places like Florida. As the cocaine cowboys partied into the 1980s, the sheriffs started circling. Law-enforcement agencies realized that the barons' mountains of cash created a possible way to take them down. They had the laundering activity of the likes of Rijock in their sights, and would begin an audacious operation to infiltrate it.

Like Pablo Escobar's brother Roberto, Bob Mazur could have easily ended up with a regular desk job if his life had gone in just a slightly different direction. Smart and with a head for figures, Mazur had trained in the accountancy industry, but then became intrigued by a career in law enforcement, eventually joining the US Customs Service. By chance, like Rijock, Mazur ended up in South Florida just as the cocaine boom took off, and watched as the *Miami Vice*-style antics of the organized crime gangs became ever more brazen. Also like Rijock, Mazur would become an expert in money laundering, but as a US Customs agent his goals would be the polar opposite of Rijock's. Mazur wanted to track and destroy the drug gangs' money flows, depriving them of their lifeblood. He understood that getting under the skin of the laundering industry would require immense patience and persistence. So he went undercover as Bob Musella, a wealthy businessman who ran a legitimate financial consultancy, but who was open to some shady business in exchange for the right fee – in short, the perfect contact for a drug dealer in need of some laundering help.

Mazur's first target was a small-time drug dealer and launderer called Gonzalo Mora Jr. Originally from Colombia, Mora and his family had set up shop in LA and Miami, selling ten kilos of coke at a time to dealers keen to get their hands on the must-have drug. But as the sales mounted up, Mora faced the same problem as Pablo Escobar: shipping all those bulky US dollars back to Colombia to buy more cocaine was difficult, hazardous and expensive. So, instead, Mora used a different system.

Mora would distribute the incoming drug cash between his friends and family, who would deposit it, $3,000 or less at a time, into their own bank accounts. Breaking it up into smaller chunks in this way made it less likely the banks would ask awkward questions. It's what's known in the laundering trade as 'smurfing', because this army of low-level cash handlers evokes images of the swarming little blue cartoon characters.[16] Mora had access to his smurfs' accounts. Once their deposits added up to a certain amount, say $50,000, Mora would write a blank cheque on their account for the same sum. His next task was to find a Colombian businessman who had pesos, but wanted to buy dollars. Why would they want to do that? Mazur explains: 'If you were a Colombian businessman and you wanted to buy something outside Colombia, you needed dollars, which gave you two choices. You could buy them through the Colombian government and lose as much as 40 per cent to taxes, duties and fees, or you could go to a black-market broker and pay a fee of 10 per cent or less.'

Mora was one of those black-market brokers. Once he found a Colombian businessman keen to buy dollars, Mora would give him the cheque drawn on his US smurf's account. The businessman could then cash that cheque to buy goods overseas in dollars. In return, the businessman would give Mora an equivalent amount in pesos back in Colombia, which Mora or his accomplices could then use to buy more coke to export and sell. And so the cycle continued.

This is called the Black Market Peso Exchange. It became a linchpin laundering tactic for the drug trade in the 1980s and was hugely lucrative for the launderers. That's because Mora could potentially make 20 per cent on the deal: he could charge 10 per cent to the businessman for turning his pesos into dollars, and could then charge 10 per cent to his drug-dealing accomplices back in Colombia as a fee for moving their American dollars into Colombian pesos. So for every $50,000 he laundered, Mora could potentially pocket an additional $10,000.

But there was a snag: the smurfs. Unlike the giant army of blue cartoon creatures, Mora had only a tiny network consisting of a couple of family members and a trusted friend. In terms of Ken Rijock's three-stage system, Mora was struggling with the first step: placement. He was making so much money, he was finding it hard to enter it into the financial system without raising alarms. 'Gonzalo [Mora] couldn't safely move more than $50,000 in drug cash per week,' writes Mazur, 'before he met us.'[17] By 'us', Mazur means his alter ego Musella, and his fellow undercover law-enforcement associates. Mazur offered to let Mora use his front companies to launder the money, thereby massively increasing Mora's cash-moving ability. With the help of 'Musella', Mora's laundering increased tenfold.

Mora was Mazur's ticket into the hidden financial realm of the cartels' operations. Like Rijock, as word of his abilities spread via Mora and others, Mazur moved up the ranks and was introduced to bigger and bigger players, eventually including those working directly with Pablo Escobar. For crooks looking to achieve the first stage of the laundering process – placing the cash into a financial system – Mazur was a hero.

For his cover to be convincing, he had to look the part. One of his contacts, a cartel hitman, told him: 'Movers and shakers in the business have money coming out their ass, and spending $1,000 on a suit is an everyday thing for them.'[18] So Mazur shelled out, living the high life, staying in five-star hotels and travelling on Concorde (all paid for, conveniently, out of the drug dealers' own profits that they were paying to Mazur to launder). The lifestyle may sound glamorous, but ultimately it's about protection. The drug gangs Mazur was working with were immensely paranoid and reflexively violent. A member once told Mazur that he'd rumbled an undercover agent just by the way he leaned next to his car. To survive, Mazur had to play the part.

'When you're doing the kind of work that a long-term undercover agent does, you've got two brains moving at the same time,' he tells me. 'You've got to stay outwardly appearing to be this person you're claiming to be, but you still need to manage where you're going in your conversations in your agent brain because you're not there just to bullshit, you're there to get information and you've got to be able to coax the conversation. I was so busy trying to manage that, that I missed a lot of the things I could have enjoyed, like being in the best restaurant in Paris.' Mazur had his fair share of nail-biting moments, notably when his expensive, custom-built briefcase fell apart in a meeting with a cartel boss – almost exposing the tape recorder hidden inside.

As Mazur's involvement with the cartels deepened, the amounts of cash he was laundering were going up to eye-watering levels. At one point, a single part of his multifaceted undercover operation was picking up $3m per week. As always, dealing with the physical logistics of handling so much money was taxing. On one occasion, two of Mazur's undercover colleagues were tasked with collecting boxes of drug cash in New York. The money would eventually end up in Mazur's laundering network, but first it had to be counted so US authorities could log it as part of the investigation. However, when they opened the boxes they discovered that about $99,000 of it was in $1 bills, a huge quantity, triggering a heated argument over how much overtime it would take to count it all.[19]

Cash, cash, cash. Reams of it were now flooding through the streets of the US. It was the drug gangs' lifeblood, but also their

Achilles heel. It all needed to be cleaned, moved and returned to the drug barons whose profits it represented, and that allowed the likes of Bob Mazur to penetrate their operation. But it wasn't just in the economic sphere that the drug cartels' empire was being attacked. Back in Colombia, a full-blown street war was about to break out.

As Pablo Escobar rose to power, there was one existential threat he seemed to fear above all others: extradition for trial in the US. 'I prefer to be in the grave in Colombia than in a jail cell in the United States' became his rallying cry. Perhaps a big reason for this was that Escobar knew that in the US, unlike in Colombia, he wouldn't be able to buy his way out of prosecution by bribing judges and so on.

In April 1984, the Colombian justice minister was assassinated. His death was attributed to Pablo Escobar; it was seen as an effort to intimidate the government out of its support for an extradition law. But the murder had the opposite effect. The outrage it sparked spurred the government to pass the legislation. Escobar was furious, and from then on, his conflict with the Colombian authorities (and as a result, with the US) became an all-out battle. There were hundreds of bombings. Kidnapping became a key weapon. Nearly a hundred people were killed during a raid on the Palace of Justice in 1985, which destroyed evidence that could have seen Escobar and others extradited. The Colombian government hit back hard, creating the Search Bloc, a specially trained police team tasked with finding Escobar. Its heavy-handed tactics in the backstreets of Medellin actually increased sympathy for the fugitive among some of the public.

Meanwhile, Roberto Escobar became a target for arrest too. Even years later he seems to struggle to comprehend why, claiming he was only pursued because he was Pablo's brother. He doesn't seem to consider his role in laundering millions of dollars of drug cash to be a crime.

In the end, Roberto, Pablo and other members of the cartel agreed with the government to surrender, but only on the condition they be incarcerated in a prison of their own making. The 'Cathedral', as they called it, has a strong claim to being the cushiest jail ever built, complete with jacuzzis, two private chefs, a stack of Elvis records and a ready supply of women smuggled in inside specially converted vehicles.[20] Conveniently, the Cathedral also helped to keep out Escobar's domestic enemies who were still at large outside the prison such as cartel rivals, the numbers of which were increasing.

But when the government wanted to move the inmates to another prison, they rebelled and fled in the middle of the night. Life on the run became increasingly fraught for Pablo. The net was closing in; his communications were being monitored, his safe houses surveilled. In the end, though, there would be no arrest, and Escobar would not face his dreaded extradition to the US. Instead, the world's most infamous drug baron died from gunshot wounds on 2 December 1993 as he fled across the rooftops in Medellin, racing to evade capture from the police.

Meanwhile, Bob Mazur's undercover work as a high-rolling money launderer was continuing to accumulate evidence against the cartels, including Pablo's network. But it couldn't continue for ever. At some point, the hammer had to fall. That time came in October 1998 in an incredible sting operation, in which Mazur – who by this point had been undercover for several years – told his criminal accomplices he was getting married, luring them to the 'ceremony' where they were arrested en masse. Mazur's story was eventually made into the Hollywood movie *The Infiltrator*, in which Bryan Cranston played the role of Mazur/Musella.

Several years before Mazur's sting, justice had finally caught up with Ken Rijock's money-laundering activities too. US authorities had at last managed to pierce the shield of secrecy around his Anguilla companies, worked out who really owned them and what they were being used for. Rijock pleaded guilty and cooperated with the prosecutors. He served two years in a federal prison and is now a financial crime consultant. He says he feels obligated to help investigators tackle the very crimes he once committed, partly because he knows he could have received a much longer sentence if the prosecutors hadn't been willing to strike a deal on his sentence.

When his brother died, Roberto Escobar was also in prison, having surrendered the previous year. While there, he was targeted with a letter-bomb attack which severely and permanently damaged his sight. Meanwhile, Pablo was buried at Monte Sacro cemetery in his beloved Medellin. The tombstone was once inscribed with 'Here Lies the King', but the text was later scrubbed off (according to Roberto, on government orders).[21] It's an illustration of the mixed feelings in Colombia surrounding his legacy: was he a benign Robin Hood character who battled for the people against an uncaring government, or a venal smuggler who used drug money to corrupt the world to his whim?

Whatever the truth of his political legacy, the financial lessons from Escobar's escapades – and those of Rijock and Mazur – are clear: criminals are constantly in need of assistance to launder their illicit income, and placing it into some kind of financial system is a vital first step in that process. When this isn't possible, the consequences can be immensely costly – something Pablo's nephew was about to find out in his uncle's old house in Medellin in 2017.

Nicolás Escobar and his helpers had been crawling through the smelly, dusty hiding place they'd discovered after they finally managed to smash through the reinforced concrete wall – the one through which the ghosts had disappeared. Inside, they found a long-deserted bathroom and a cache of items left by Pablo before his death: a camera, tape recorders, a two-way radio and a huge stack of crumbling paper. As Nicolás rummaged through it he realized what he was touching: the remnants of approximately $18m of cash. Thanks to the ghosts, he'd discovered a sizeable example of one of Pablo's legendary money stashes. It sounds like the stuff of daydreams: poking around at home and finding millions left by a long-deceased relative. But for Nicolás this would not be a life-transforming windfall – the money was useless. 'It had decomposed,' he tells me. 'The bags resembled the way we would package money, but there really was no money.'

However, Nicolás was always far more interested in the other items he found inside the Medellin hideout. The idea of uncovering some long-lost photos or recordings of his uncle was exciting. But he was to be disappointed: when he developed the film, it was blank. And when he played back the tapes, there was nothing on them.

The story of Nicolás's discovery and its spooky genesis was broken by Juan Carlo Giraldo and Fabián Forero of the Colombian news outlet Red+ Noticias. Nicolás was interviewed by the press and the tale went round the world. Global media was predictably intrigued by the man who discovered millions of Escobar's drug money, but they missed the wider picture. The strange tale of Nicolás Escobar's find also perfectly illustrates one of the key reasons *why* organized criminals launder money. When your illicit enterprise gets so successful that you're making serious amounts, it's vital that you find somewhere safe, lucrative and long-term to put it. Because if you don't, there's a good chance your money will simply disappear in any one of a myriad number of ways: nibbled by rats, diminished by inflation, stolen by rivals, seized by the cops, or just eaten away by time, like the decaying notes that crumbled in Nicolás's hands in Medellin.

And if you're going to launder the money, you're best to fall back on the tried-and-tested, three-stage plan followed by lawyer-turned-launderer Ken Rijock, along with generations of other professional money movers: placement, layering and integration. Now you understand the basics of money laundering, it's time to explore how technology is enhancing each of the stages in the process. The tactics may be old, but the industry itself is constantly evolving. Launderers are eager to embrace the potential of any financial innovation to advance their schemes, and digital technology is no exception. Modern laundering has become a hi-tech business – something that's being embraced with gusto by today's would-be Pablo Escobars.

2.

From Bury to Bitcoin

Meet the Din sisters: 43-year-old Shazia and 45-year-old Abia. To the outside world, they were a couple of well-to-do middle-aged women working hard to make their way in the cut-and-thrust world of online commerce. In 2010 they'd set up the Beauty Booth, a website offering all manner of lotions and unguents from blemish control kits to Billion Dollar Brows pencils (a snip at £20), all run out of a commercial unit in an ordinary suburban street in Bury, in the north of England.

A third sister ran a beauty salon, a separate business but located immediately next door. Customers would pop in for a facial or a pedicure, and perhaps a good chinwag. All in all, it looked like a female-led, family-run community of businesses. The Din sisters were 'lovely people', according to those who worked with them.

But there was something unusual about Shazia and Abia. Even for two women who worked in the beauty trade, they were conspicuously lavish in their tastes. They had Rolex watches, diamond rings and a wardrobe full of designer labels that would have made a fashion correspondent green with envy: Yves Saint Laurent, Louis Vuitton, Gucci, Hermès, Mulberry and more. Then there were the cars: a silver E-Class Merc for Shazia and a BMW X6 for Abia. People must have wondered: how on earth could they afford it all, running an online cosmetics business from behind their sister's salon in Bury?

In reality, Shazia and Abia Din were leading a double life. Outwardly, the pair may have looked like successful Internet entrepreneurs. But behind the scenes, they were at the heart of a giant drug-smuggling empire, feeding a hungry market with millions of pounds' worth of cocaine, amphetamines and heroin. And in contrast to their hi-tech, e-commerce business, the drugs were sold the traditional way: on the streets, for cash. Which, of course, created a logistical overhead. The Dins needed couriers to shuttle the drugs to the dealers, and to deliver the resulting cash back to them. This river of money would ultimately leave the Dins' operation fatally vulnerable to police investigation. Like Pablo Escobar, Shazia and Abia were about to discover that cash is the bane of any successful large-scale drug operation. But unlike Escobar, the Dins had a hi-tech solution. As their operation expanded, the Dins' wider network would turn to the cutting edge of financial tech to put their profits beyond law enforcement's clutches.

On the outskirts of Manchester, surrounded by retail parks, is a bland four-storey building called Nexus House. Driving past, you might think it was a local council department, or a big accountancy firm. But as you get closer, you realize this isn't any old office block. There are multi-layered security gates, high, hefty fences and a disproportionate amount of CCTV. In fact, this is the headquarters of Greater Manchester Police's Serious Crime Division. It was here in late 2018 that Detective Inspector Roger Smethurst and his team got a tip-off that Shazia Din was involved in dealing Class A drugs.

It wasn't exactly a bolt from the blue. Her sister Abia had been jailed in 2014 for drug dealing around Manchester and Salford. Other family members had been involved too. Their brother Mohammed got nine years. Another brother was wanted in connection with different drug offences.[1] Abia had only got out of prison in May 2018, and now, within months, her family was back on the police's radar.

By December, Smethurst and his team at Manchester Police had Shazia Din under surveillance, keeping careful watch on who was turning up at both her business and her home, a swish apartment in a modern complex a few minutes' walk away from the Beauty Booth. This is how the next piece of the puzzle fell into place. One of the cars that turned up at Shazia's house was linked to a man named Peter Wrafter. That was another red flag for the police: Wrafter had a long criminal record and had been jailed for ten years in 2008 for conspiracy to supply cocaine.[2] The fact that the two were meeting and potentially working together was an intriguing – and concerning – revelation.

Smethurst's team started to piece together the network, which they referred to as the Din OCG – Organized Crime Gang. The partnership with Wrafter made commercial sense. Shazia and Abia clearly had strong links in the Manchester area to distribute their drugs. Wrafter lived in Doncaster in South Yorkshire, fifty miles to the east. Working with him gave the Dins access to a whole new market.

The police put Wrafter under surveillance too, under what was now being called Operation Heart. But here they hit a snag: Wrafter and Shazia Din were communicating using a special type of mobile phone that made things very difficult for the police. The handsets were manufactured by a French company called EncroChat with one clear objective in mind: to protect their users from any type of snooping whatsoever. They were remarkable devices. On the surface they looked like ordinary mobiles using Google's Android software, but under the hood, they'd been specially modified. They used encrypted communications apps, meaning no one – not even the police – could access the messages. Even if the phones got seized, the contents would be scrambled. Unsurprisingly, the handsets were a big hit with the criminal community. EncroChat would eventually be cracked thanks to a joint operation by Dutch and French law enforcement, but at the time Manchester Police were investigating Shazia Din and Peter Wrafter, the phones were a closed box.[3] That meant Roger Smethurst's team had to fall back on traditional, physical surveillance. It was time-consuming and resource-heavy, but it gradually started to yield results.

In January 2019, the police saw Peter Wrafter handing a package to a man called Lewis Yates, who they suspected was one of the gang's couriers. The police believed the package contained money from the drug deals. If they could question Yates, it might yield valuable information. But arresting him presented Smethurst with a dilemma: 'What do we want to disclose and what do we not want to disclose?' he says. 'At that point, I'm not wanting to disclose to Lewis Yates the fact that we have seen him meet with Peter Wrafter, because if I do, all it's going to do is alert Wrafter to the fact that the police are aware of his presence.'

Instead, the police pulled in Yates on a routine traffic stop. Of course, they then found large amounts of cash in the car – enough for them to question him. After all, it's not exactly normal behaviour. 'Ordinarily if you've got to move cash to somebody, you do it by way of bank transfer, or you might do it by banker's draft or whatever,' says Smethurst. 'You don't physically go into NatWest and get a carrier bag for the £10 and £20 notes and then drive it ten miles to go and drop it off.' Once again, the conspicuously cash-intensive nature of large-scale drug dealing was proving hazardous to the criminals, and providing police with a way in.

In the end, Smethurst's team carried out a limited interview with Yates, gleaned what they could, and released him pending further investigation, hoping this wasn't enough to tip off Wrafter and the Dins. But the investigation into Wrafter was about to move up a gear. The police got word that he might have a gun. This time, there was no dilemma about tipping him off: they had to move in on Wrafter as soon as possible. Sure enough, when they pulled him over near his home on 7 January, they found a revolver and ammunition stashed in his van. As they searched his home they found yet more incriminating evidence: 26kg of amphetamines and 2kg of heroin.[4]

Wrafter was arrested, sending a shock wave through the Din OCG. The police couldn't access the messages on Wrafter's Encro-Chat phone, but as they had the physical phone itself they could see who was calling who. They watched as Shazia made multiple frantic efforts to contact Wrafter, but to no avail: he was now in police custody, and wouldn't be getting out for a long time. The man in charge of the Dins' major distribution network was out of the picture. It was a headache for the sisters, but also for the police. 'He's charged and he's out of the equation,' says Smethurst. 'Which sets us back a little bit because we then have to work out how Shazia is operating.' The answer turned out to be quite a surprise.

On 5 February, Shazia Din visited Doncaster prison, where Peter Wrafter was being held pending his trial. With her was Wrafter's 31-year-old daughter, Natalie, who'd brought her toddler along. On the surface, it looked like a standard prison visit by a worried relative and a concerned business partner (albeit a partner in crime). What the two women didn't know was that there was a police surveillance team in the prison car park. They watched as the pair came out of the jail and went to the boot of Shazia's car. Natalie rummaged in her handbag before unloading several packages. Shazia watched on, holding the child in her arms. Remarkably, it seemed that the pair were doing some kind of deal in the car park, perilously close to the jail's CCTV and prison officers and (unknown to them) under the watchful eye of the police surveillance team's cameras.[5] It was a pretty brazen stunt. It also indicated that Natalie Wrafter was part of the operation. And as the police began to discover, she was far from a minor player.

'We start to do some work around reviewing her telecoms and who she's in contact with,' says Smethurst. 'We then realize she's now running the Doncaster side of the operation while her dad's in prison.'

There were changes within the Din OCG side too. Shazia's son Hassan had entered the picture. 'Peter Wrafter had been doing the day-to-day leg work, and I think because he drops off the scene they needed someone to do that instead,' says Smethurst. 'Somebody who's going to count the money, who's going to move stuff around for them.' This was Hassan Din, and it was his involvement that would give police their next lead.

Like generations of organized criminals before them, the Din OCG needed to launder their money, and as illustrated by cartel launderer Ken Rijock in the previous chapter, the vital first step in the process is placing it into some kind of financial system. The Din gang were about to do just that. But rather than trying to sneak it into a shady bank on some Caribbean island as Rijock did, they'd found a new, hi-tech method to get all their cash off the streets. They'd discovered there was a whole industry of tech-savvy money washers ready to assist them, and as an added bonus, it would vastly increase their profit margin.

By the early part of 2019, the Din OCG had recruited a network of couriers to move the drugs and cash back and forth across the Pennines, the range of hills that separates Manchester and Lancashire in the west from Doncaster and South Yorkshire in the east – the Wrafters' territory. According to police, some of these couriers were small-time drug dealers themselves, while others were simply contacts of the gang keen to earn some ready cash with no questions asked. It was this network police were targeting with the arrests of people like Lewis Yates, and they were about to have a significant breakthrough.

On 27 February, Hassan was seen leaving the Dins' apartment in Bury carrying a holdall. From past experience, the police were pretty sure it contained drug money, so they kept their eyes on it as it was handed from courier to courier. It ended up in the boot of a hired Vauxhall Mokka, being driven by a 31-year-old man named Arjan Bedesha. From the outskirts of Manchester he headed south, seemingly making for the M6 motorway. Police believed he was on his way to London. Again, Roger Smethurst had to make a quick decision: intervene and seize the bag, potentially tipping off Hassan and the rest of the Din OCG, or sit tight and potentially lose track of the evidence? In the end, the decision was made to stop Bedesha before he reached the motorway, in a little village called Mere. There, in the boot of the car, hidden in the spare-wheel compartment, they found almost £175,000 in cash. It was the largest money seizure of the whole operation, leading Smethurst to believe they'd intercepted a big deal.

'I've been involved in these kind of operations for seven or eight years, and you might get £30,000, £40,000, £50,000 cash recoveries,' he says. 'But £175,000? That is major. If you're getting £30k to £40k that would equate to a smaller customer paying off a bill to an upstream supplier. To get £175k says to me this is somebody who's sat really high up in the food chain, who is paying ultimately for a large amount of drugs that they have had at some stage.'

Alongside the cash, the police also found two mobile phones, and this time they were in luck: they were not the super-secure Encro-Chat variety. After Bedesha handed over the passwords, the police unlocked the phones and discovered a string of messages to and from a character calling themselves 'Kem Dog'. (The messages were sent using encrypted apps like Telegram and WhatsApp. These apps protect communications from being intercepted and read as they travel to and from the recipient, but of course they don't protect you if the person you're corresponding with decides to reveal the contents, as happened here.)

It was clear enough from the messages that a discussion about money was being had: what was to be done with this £175,000 of drug cash? But to the untrained eye, large parts of the conversation are gibberish – just long strings of seemingly random letters and numbers. Could it be a code? Some private system devised by the gang to further obfuscate their communications?

In fact, the strings of letters and numbers in the messages were the IDs of Bitcoin wallets. Faced with how to move this large haul of drug cash, it seems the Din OCG had hit upon the potential of cryptocurrency. Arjan Bedesha was on his way to hand over the £175,000 in cash to Kem Dog, who was to change it into Bitcoin.

In their laundering process, what the Din OCG were working on was a more effective method of placement: transferring the money into a financial system where it could be moved, cleaned and eventually extracted. Taking £175,000 to a bank would obviously have raised a lot of questions. By contrast, Kem Dog was happy to receive the loot and change it into cryptocurrency; in exchange for a decent fee, of course. Thereafter, as digital money it could be whizzed seamlessly and instantly worldwide much faster than many banks could manage, and with no questions asked. By creating Bitcoin, the tech industry had inadvertently built a tool for helping criminals place their dirty funds into a financial system, and now the Din gang had discovered this digital money-laundering trick.

The discovery of the phone messages opened up a new line of enquiry in Operation Heart. Piecing together the messages and investigating the cryptocurrency transactions could potentially reveal a lot more about the gang's wider network. While police forces increasingly have the ability to do this in-house, they still often rely on private companies' expertise for the fine-grained work. So, the case ended up on the desk of Phil Larratt, director of investigations at a company called Chainalysis. Their name will come up elsewhere in the course of this book: they're one of the world's biggest cryptocurrency-tracing firms, and tasks like trying to work out what the Din OCG were up to with their Bitcoin shenanigans are their bread and butter.

Larratt started investigating the messages (he also used to work at Manchester Police, so cases like this were very familiar to him). Just a few Bitcoin wallet addresses might not seem like much to go on, but actually, Larratt was able to rummage out plenty from those breadcrumb traces, thanks to how cryptocurrency works.

To say that Bitcoin is a virtual currency makes it sound quite complex and technical. But if you think about it, almost all currency these days is virtual. When you transfer money from your bank account to someone else's, it's all done electronically; the numbers update on the screen and hey presto. It's not as though some poor employee from your bank has to physically take your banknotes over to the branch of your payee. It's similar with purchases – when you pay using your card at the till, the shop electronically instructs the bank to transfer the money from your account. Bitcoin, and other cryptocurrencies, are the same: the transfer of funds from one party to another is done electronically.

The difference, of course, is the authority that sits behind the transaction. In the case of a bank or a shop dealing in traditional (so-called 'fiat') money, there is an army of employees running the computer systems and checking that the transfers have really happened. If it goes wrong, you can complain to the bank or the shop. If it goes really wrong, you can complain to the police. You could use the courts to try and sue for your money. And, of course, the ultimate guarantor of this fiat money is the government, so they have a hand in making sure it's stable and well regulated. In other words, traditional currency is undergirded by layer upon layer of officialdom.

Bitcoin and other cryptocurrencies have none of this. They are created, policed and run by their users. There is no higher power to appeal to if it goes wrong; no government standing behind it. So how can people trust it? The answer is that, unlike a bank, Bitcoin makes the entire ledger of everyone's accounts publicly available.

Here's how it works (in very simplified terms): the Bitcoin software gives each user the login details for a unique digital wallet containing one or more addresses, which function a bit like bank account numbers. In order to send a Bitcoin, you have to log in, specify the wallet address you want to use, the Bitcoin you're sending, and your recipient's wallet address. So let's imagine my address is ABC, I want to send you 12 Bitcoins, and your address is DEF. The transaction can be represented as ABC12DEF. Now let's imagine you want to transfer six of those Bitcoins to another person whose wallet address is XYZ. That transaction can be represented as DEF6XYZ. And so it goes on, each transaction linked to the previous one. These transactions are published online for all to see, in order to create trust in the system. When I send you the coins, it shows up on the record – along with the history of all the other transactions in and out of our wallets. There's no room for doubt. And if I try to pull a fast one and, for example, try to send my 12 coins to two different people simultaneously, the system spots it and the transactions ultimately fail. All the transactions are eventually bundled up into a publicly available record called the blockchain.[6] It's an unchangeable, ever-growing ledger of transactions. The wallet addresses themselves are anonymous – just strings of random-looking letters and numbers. But if you can link any of them to a real person's identity, you can start to de-anonymize the chain. And for Phil Larratt at Chainalysis, this would throw up some intriguing information about the Din drug gang and their use of cutting-edge tech to launder their drug cash.

From the information the police found on Arjan Bedesha's phones, Larratt could discern that Kem Dog had agreed to receive the cash, turn it into Bitcoin and send it on to a Bitcoin wallet address specified by the gang. Thanks to the blockchain and its publicly available record of transactions, Larratt could check the Bitcoin going in and out of that wallet. Sure enough, around the time Bedesha was couriering the money, the wallet address did indeed receive £174,900 worth of Bitcoin.[7]

Kem Dog, it appeared, had already sent the money to the gang's wallet. But that was potentially a big problem for Arjan Bedesha, who was meant to be taking him the £175,000 cash to fund the transaction. Because that cash was now in the hands of Manchester Police, and Bedesha had been arrested and charged with money laundering. As a result, someone – Kem Dog or one of his accomplices – was therefore short of a fat stack of money, and they probably weren't happy about it.

Naturally, I wanted to get Arjan Bedesha's side of the story. After his arrest he was sentenced to three years four months in prison, but had been released by the time I was researching this book.[8] I managed to find him on social media, but he didn't want to talk to me. So it was quite a surprise when, the next day, I got a call from his dad.

Jack Bedesha was ringing me from his home in Dubai, and wanted to explain the circumstances of his son's conviction to me. According to Bedesha Senior, Arjan had no idea of the origins of the cargo he was carrying. He was deeply surprised when he was stopped and questioned, and he immediately cooperated with the police, who seized the £175,000. If Chainalysis's research is correct, this would have left Kem Dog and his associates with a big hole in their finances. When I asked if the seizure of the £175,000 had caused his son any trouble in prison, Bedesha Senior said: 'He didn't have a good time while he served his time, so from that answer, you can make your own judgement.'

Jack Bedesha insisted Arjan thought he was just helping some associates by driving a bag from one place to another. It's hard to square that, however, with the facts on the ground. Arjan had access to two phones on which messages had been sent and received about what was to happen to the bag of money. And as police dug further into the messages, they discovered evidence indicating that the same phones had been used for other laundering jobs. There were conversations on the encrypted app Telegram with other crypto-currency brokers, giving information about exchange rates, fees and so on. As Chainalysis dug even deeper into the blockchain record, they found that wallets provided by Bedesha to the UK broker had received approximately $1 million of BTC.[9] In other words, according to the investigators, Arjan was very far from just an unwitting delivery driver.

His father didn't mention any of this on our phone call. And that wasn't the only detail he left out. Jack Bedesha turned out to be Jas-binder Bedesha, who has a ten-year conviction for fraud and fled the UK owing £14m to the government. The story goes back to 2005, when Britain's tax authority, HMRC, discovered a massive scam involving VAT, the UK sales tax. Inspectors found that a network of British companies was fiddling the system. They would import mobile phones and computer parts from Dubai, pretend to charge VAT on them, export them, and then fraudulently claim back the VAT payments from the UK government.

Jack Bedesha was, according to investigators, the Dubai end of the operation. It's called 'carousel fraud'; a complicated scam that is hard to pull off, but once you get it going it can be very lucrative indeed. In this case it earned the gang £38m.[10] And that was just the start. In the end, the criminal network was believed to have profited by almost £170m, partly by providing laundering services to other crooks. As one article stated: 'Armed with an easy way to move money around the world, the plotters also offered out their services to launder cash from organized crime gangs.' Much of the money was laundered through Birmingham casinos.[11]

Bedesha was arrested when he entered the UK, jailed for seven and a half years and ordered to pay just over £14m. He declined to do so, and so in 2013 he got an extra ten years' jail time.[12] On his release in March 2018 he left the country, still owing the money.

None of this came up in our initial chat, so I phoned Bedesha back to ask about it. He told me he felt the HMRC case against him was unfair, and insists he does not owe the UK government any money. He says he served his time in prison, and is now trying to make a new life for himself in Dubai, where he says he works for a real estate company.

'What more can I do?' he asks. I'm sure the UK government's answer would be: repay the money. Thanks to interest charged at £3,000 a day, HMRC now puts his bill at around £25m.

All of which led to the obvious question: given his criminal history, was Jack Bedesha somehow involved in the offences for which his son was convicted? Was he part of the hi-tech Bitcoin laundering scheme? Absolutely not, he says. But UK authorities disagree.

According to Manchester police, it appears Jack Bedesha wasn't just a concerned father whose son got mixed up in something way over his head. Instead, their information suggests Arjan was actually couriering under the instruction of Jack Bedesha. As they traced the path of the cryptocurrency transactions from the Din OCG, UK investigators found evidence linking the drug proceeds with cryptocurrency investments of £119m apparently controlled by Bedesha Senior. If proven, this would make him potentially a significant player in the operation to launder the Din gang's drug money. As it stands, however, no charges have been announced against Jack Bedesha, and he firmly denies any involvement in his son's wrongdoing.

The story doesn't end with Arjan Bedesha's arrest, however. In the ensuing six months, more and more couriers were pulled in by Smethurst's team, some carrying cash, others with drugs. Manchester Police were circling ever closer to the centre of the Din OCG. In March, police raided their safe house – a luxurious flat in a modern housing development in Bury. Not the sort of place you'd expect to find a drug-dealing hideout (it was 'really good cover', as one officer described it to me). Inside, they found all the kit you'd need for a large-scale drug operation, including a cash-counting machine, weighing scales and vacuum-packing equipment.[13]

In May they raided a garage in Manchester and found 1.5kg of heroin. The garage owner had been making encrypted calls to

Shazia Din; he was later caught with a huge haul of 28kg of heroin, with a street value of £3m.[14] The seizures were getting bigger, and the trail was leading ever closer to the Din sisters themselves.

Finally, on 24 July 2019, Shazia and Abia were arrested at their home, just down the road from their beauty business premises. Notably, they were never caught red-handed with drugs themselves. But in the end it didn't matter – the seven-month police operation had accumulated enough evidence to convict the sisters and many of their accomplices. Between them, eighteen members of the gang got nearly 140 years' jail time. Abia Din got eighteen years, Shazia fifteen and Hassan fourteen. Peter Wrafter got twelve years and his daughter Natalie eleven years and three months. Lewis Yates got a twelve-month suspended sentence. (The third Din sister, who ran a nearby beauty salon, was not arrested and there is no suggestion she was involved in any wrongdoing.)

Even the convictions weren't the end of the case. During the surveillance operation against the Din sisters and their network, Roger Smethurst's financial investigation team had been carefully keeping a track of the women's trappings of wealth. Now, with the Dins behind bars, they went after it, seizing anything they could link back to the drug dealing. Cars, watches, clothes, jewellery, property, bank deposits – they grabbed the lot. It's an indication of how badly the gang fared in the second stage of the laundering process: layering. Had they done a better job of washing their profits before going on their shopping sprees, the financial investigators would never have been able to link the purchases to the crime, and wouldn't have been able to seize them. As it was, the gang's possessions were sent over to an auction house in Northern Ireland where they fetched just over £39,000. The Rolex watches alone sold for more than £10,000.

Among the bling and designer brands there was one thing conspicuously missing from the seizures and the sales, though: cryptocurrency. While much of the Din OCG's criminal profits existed in the physical world, it's obvious that a significant proportion was also making its way into cryptocurrency along with other suspicious transactions. At least £1m, according to Chainalysis, had been washed through the system of crypto brokers with whom Arjan Bedesha was in touch. None of that was recovered in the police operation. In other words, by using hi-tech finance the gang had successfully achieved the first two stages of laundering: the cash had been placed into crypto and layered so effectively that it was beyond the authorities' reach. Roger Smethurst believes there may be records of other crypto transactions hidden on the gang's encrypted EncroChat phones. Now that the encryption has been cracked it might be possible to discover the details, but frustratingly, with Manchester Police's operation over, there's no chance to go back and revisit them. And it seems those behind the Bitcoin laundry, like the mysterious Kem Dog, were never caught.

The Din sisters and their accomplices will be in prison for a long time. But thanks to their canny use of cryptocurrency, it's very possible that when they get out there'll be a significant pile of drug money waiting for them, ready to spend and enjoy, which, after all, is one of the key goals of money laundering. And given crypto's long-term growth curve, it may well have gone up significantly in value – another important consideration in long-term laundering.

Meanwhile, Chainalysis's research into the digital money trail threw up one other fascinating detail about the gang's laundering activity. Thanks to their ability to analyse the blockchain records, Chainalysis was able to calculate the fee taken by Kem Dog. Apparently, he was charging just 4 per cent for brokering the drug cash into Bitcoin. That's an astonishingly low figure. Because of the risk they take, money launderers traditionally charge way more than that (I've seen numbers as high as 60 per cent). It seems the Din gang had bagged themselves a bargain. No wonder they were so keen to push their cash into crypto – doing so would have saved them hundreds of thousands of pounds in fees. In commercial terms, it was a no-brainer.

The low broker fee wasn't the only advantage for the drug dealers in adopting this new, hi-tech laundering system. Previously, the gang would have had to connive a way of getting their cash into the bank, or failing that, bundle it up and somehow send it overseas to pay off those supplying them with the drugs. With Bitcoin, the money could be sent internationally, instantly, without risking awkward questions from the banks, or infiltration from narcs like Bob Mazur, the US Customs agent mentioned in the previous chapter. And there's a whole army of people – the likes of Kem Dog and Arjan Bedesha among them – standing ready to help the drug gangs swap their cash for crypto and marshal it around the blockchain.

Manchester Police may have had limited success in grabbing the missing Bitcoin in Operation Heart, but others have had more luck. In January 2022 it was revealed that twelve UK forces had between them confiscated £322m worth of crypto proceeds in the previous five years.[15] The Metropolitan Police alone pulled in almost £180m in one operation in 2021.[16]

You might think that such seizures would make criminals think twice about using cryptocurrency for money laundering. But while they may sound like big numbers, the sums nabbed by the police are pretty modest compared to the total amount of criminal money sloshing through the UK. The crime gangs show no signs of abandoning crypto as a tool for money laundering. The Din network was far from alone in adopting such hi-tech solutions. A senior banker recently revealed that UK police have found more than 80 per cent of credit-card crooks arrested have cryptocurrency wallets stored on their mobile phones.[17] When the encrypted EncroChat phones were finally broken open, according to Roger Smethurst, much of the correspondence concerned crypto transfers. Digital currencies have become a vital and widely used tool for criminals at all levels, from street-level dealers to the kingpins who oversee global rackets.

This new world of virtual money has been embraced with gusto by a whole range of crooks, who see its usefulness for avoiding the scrutiny of traditional finance, making international transfers with ease and cutting down on fees. It's a potentially far easier and more lucrative way to achieve the first stage in the laundering process: placing dodgy funds into a financial system. The Din gang used to place hundreds of thousands of pounds from Class A drug dealing into Bitcoin. But now we'll look at a case in which similar tactics were used to place millions of dollars of income, and used it to facilitate even more horrific crimes.

3.

Crypto Pimps

A warning: this chapter contains references to trafficking, rape and sexual abuse, including of children.

Some people can pinpoint the exact date and time when their life changed for ever. For Melanie Thompson, it was in New York, late one night in 2010. She was on her way home from the cinema with her two best friends. They were in sixth grade, Thompson was twelve. They ran into two boys they knew from school who were sixteen and seventeen.

'We ended up just going back to their house and hanging out,' she recalls. 'They invited us for drinks, and you know, when you're kids, you play spin the bottle and all of those games and such. So, at first it was really innocent, and we were just kind of having a good time, and then I remember drinking a lot and I blacked out.'[1]

When she woke up, she was being raped by one of the older boys. Terrified, she tried to escape, and things suddenly escalated.

'When I was running up the stairs to leave the house, that boy ended up coming back down the stairs with an older man, someone I didn't know. And I remember him saying to me, "Where do you think you're going? Huh, where you going?" It was like he was playing with me, like it was a joke.'

But it was deadly serious. The man took Thompson to an abandoned house nearby. 'I was held captive . . . locked in from the outside, in a house with no running water or electricity. It was a room, and a mattress that had bed bugs and no sheet.'

As the hours ticked by, Thompson's mum began to search for her, unaware she was being held captive in the same neighbourhood. In time, she put up missing posters, desperately trying to find her daughter. But Thompson wasn't coming home. Her kidnapper had now become her pimp. Initially, he was trafficking her on the streets. But after a few months, he hit upon a new method of exploitation. 'He was like, "We need to put you on the Internet, 'cause that's where the money is,"' says Thompson. For her exploiter, this may have been simply a commercially motivated change. For Thompson, it meant a horrific increase in the scale of abuse.

'When I was outside on the street, it would be, you know . . . a couple of people a night maybe. Online it was at least fifteen people a day – and that was on a slow day,' she tells me. In the online adverts he placed, Thompson's exploiter would give her physical details. 'It would describe my measurements; so my bust size, my hip size, my pant size and my bra size.' He would then give Thompson a different name. 'Mimi, Tammy, Jennifer . . . anything that he thought would appeal to different demographics.'

For her exploiter and others like him, the process seems to have been treated almost like listing an item on eBay. But in this grim trade, the product was people, and young girls in particular. And for this modern generation of pimps, one website was the go-to place of business: Backpage.

The site would become infamous, a battleground over freedom of speech at the cutting edge of the Internet. Melanie Thompson's story would be woven throughout it, along with many others'. And in the war that would be waged to bring down Backpage, hi-tech money laundering would be at the very centre of the conflict.

Backpage was born in the fires of dissent at a particularly turbulent time in US history, and was the progeny of two iconoclasts. The son of a construction worker, Michael Lacey was at Arizona State University in 1970 as campus demonstrations raged against the Vietnam War. Lacey quit college to set up a newspaper in opposition to what he called the 'ultra conservative local media's coverage' of the protests.

Two years later he joined with fellow Arizona dropout James Larkin to create a chain of weeklies.[2] By 2001, the pair owned eleven papers, making more than $100m a year,[3] and in 2005 they merged with the *Village Voice*, the New York-based icon of liberal counterculture.

Lacey and Larkin pushed for spiky investigative stories that held power to account. They wore their pugnacity on their sleeves – or in Lacey's case, on his knuckles, where he has the phrase 'hold fast' tattooed in capital letters. He told one interviewer: 'As a journalist, if you don't get up in the morning and say "fuck you" to someone, why even do it?'[4]

Their belligerence repeatedly landed them in court, but they fought hard and often won. 'I didn't get into this racket to be told what to publish,' Lacey said. 'By anybody.'[5] In the years that followed, their combination of aggressive defence of freedom of speech and courtroom savvy would prove very handy indeed, as they pushed into the emerging world of online publications.

In 1995, a shy computer science graduate living in San Francisco named Craig Newmark launched Craigslist, initially a homespun index of local events, which mushroomed into a giant national listings service and eventually spread to seventy countries. Seemingly without realizing it, this unassuming techie had created a behemoth that began eating away at many newspapers' revenue model. Advertisers who'd previously used the papers' classified sections to punt their wares began instead flocking to Craigslist, and media ad execs started to panic. Lacey and Larkin's empire wasn't immune. Craigslist was described in 2005 as 'the biggest single crisis the *Village Voice* has faced in its whole 50 years'.[6]

Never ones to shirk a challenge, Lacey and Larkin fought fire with fire. They launched their own version of Craigslist, with the help of a man who'd become pivotal to their business. His skill, cunning and technical acumen would ultimately triumph over their rival. Advertising executive Carl Ferrer had been with the *Village Voice* group since 1996. He saw the way Craigslist was upending the business, and lobbied hard for Lacey and Larkin to move online. He also saw a chance to seize some power in the fast-growing company. In 2004, he proudly launched backpage.com as an alternative to

Craigslist for classifieds.[7] It was to be Ferrer's fiefdom. But eventually it would bring them all crashing down.

Among the ads for second-hand water beds, wigs and woodworking tools was an adult section featuring listings for masseurs, escorts and more. Taken at face value, that wasn't particularly controversial. Around this time, I was working for a local paper in the UK which had a similar classified ads section that included adult services. It was the cause of occasional titters in the newsroom and, like many at the time, I never stopped to think too deeply about the legalities of the whole thing. And yet it is a subject which justifies reflection, because in the case of Backpage the legal nuances would have huge implications that would lead its bosses into financial manipulation and hi-tech money laundering.

Prostitution is illegal under state law almost everywhere in the US, apart from a few spots in Nevada. It's usually defined as engaging in, or offering, sexual conduct for a fee. Assisting it is generally what's meant by 'pimping'. But what exactly is meant by 'sexual conduct'? When it comes to sexual assault offences in the state of New York, for example, the types of illegal sexual contact are quite clearly defined (anal, oral, vaginal and some others too grim to go into here). Yet in its prostitution laws, there's no such handy definition of what exactly constitutes sexual conduct.[8]

This means that, across the US, there is a massive grey zone of people selling sexual services who believe (or, at least, can argue that) their activities don't count as prostitution; massage parlours, phone sex chat lines, dominatrices and more. Some such services are a fig leaf covering up conduct that's unquestionably illicit, but others are arguably legal under the law. It's often left to the courts to resolve.

This was the grey zone in which Backpage's adult ads section was operating. And it was far from alone: Craigslist also had adult ads (initially called 'Erotic Services'), and being the much larger site it had many more of them, some of which seemed to be pretty thinly disguised prostitution businesses. As a result, Craig Newmark's site found itself under increasing pressure to crack down on illegal practices. Eventually, Craigslist pulled its adult section, briefly replacing it with a 'censored' banner before ditching it altogether in 2010. Backpage, under the stewardship of the canny Carl Ferrer, spotted a giant opportunity. But its execs warned it was also 'a time when we need to make sure our content is not illegal'.[9] Over the ensuing years, that warning would be heeded less and less. The siren song of profit would soon overcome any notes of caution about illicit content, and many, many people would be irrevocably harmed as a result.

Backpage is sometimes described in media reports as a 'sex advertising website'. While that wasn't originally the case (at its outset in 2004 there were only a few hundred adult ads, as opposed to a few thousand for apartment rentals), by 2011 that situation had dramatically altered. By then there were 700,000 adult ads, attracting a billion views per month.[10]

There was a hard economic logic to this. Backpage allowed users to post most ads for free (something that helped seal the fate of newspapers' paid-for classified sections), but it charged a fee for adult ads. As a result, adult ads accounted for only 15.5 per cent of Backpage's overall listings, but generated an astonishing 93.4 per cent of its paid ad income.[11] From $29m in revenue in 2010, Backpage more than doubled to $71m in 2012, partly thanks to the influx of adult ads from those no longer able to use Craigslist.[12]

Backpage was now a giant cash cow, and its ad execs became ever more proactive and creative at chasing leads, especially for the paid-for adult section. They would even google prostitutes advertising on other sites and offer them a free ad on Backpage.[13] One sex worker said that, when her ads on Backpage began to go out of date, its salespeople would email her offering freebies to entice her back to the site.[14]

The money was pouring in, but so were the potential legal problems. As well as navigating state-level prostitution law, Backpage also had to contend with US-wide federal legislation on sex trafficking, defined as: '. . . the recruitment, harboring, transportation, provision, obtaining, patronizing, or soliciting of a person for the purpose of a commercial sex act . . . induced by force, fraud, or coercion, or in which the person induced to perform such act has not attained 18 years of age.'[15] In other words, if any of the people being advertised on Backpage for sex were being forced into it or were underage, Backpage could be accused of assisting a criminal offence.

Deciding whether someone has been forced or coerced into sex isn't always as easy as you might think. In cases such as Melanie Thompson's, it's very clear. Other examples, however, are more nuanced. For instance, if a person struggling for work decides to sell sexual services to make ends meet, can you say they've been 'forced' into it? If so, by whom? It's an area of intense debate.

By contrast, the issue of whether someone is aged under eighteen is black and white. And in the case of Backpage, it was quickly becoming obvious that there were many children being trafficked via its adult ads section, all of whom were at very high risk of enduring the kind of abuse suffered by Melanie Thompson.

As its name suggests, the National Center for Missing and Exploited Children (NCMEC) is America's main agency dealing with trafficked kids. In 2017 it revealed that Backpage was involved in 73 per cent of all cases reported to it by the public.[16] As the Center pointed out, Backpage required advertisers of boats, motorcycles and pets to provide a phone number to prevent scam ads. Yet the same rule did not apply to its escort ads section. As NCMEC concluded: 'Backpage does more to protect customers from scam pet ads than to protect children from being sold for sex.'[17]

As criticism mounted, Backpage insisted it was trying to tackle the problem, proactively reporting suspect ads to NCMEC and even hiring someone who used to work for the Center to advise the company in-house. But on the ground, it was painfully clear that Backpage was failing to tackle the problem, and was reaping profits as a result. NCMEC disclosed heartbreaking messages from parents who'd found their missing children on Backpage, only to get short shrift when they tried to contact the site's administrators.

One parent wrote: 'Your website has ads featuring our 16-year-old daughter, posing as an escort . . . I have emailed the ad multiple times using your website, but have gotten no response . . . For God's sake, she is only 16.'[18]

Backpage's dirty secret was out. Headlines were mounting. A petition calling for Backpage to follow Craigslist in axing its adult section was signed by members of rock band REM and singer Alicia Keys.[19] *The New York Times* ran a series of hard-hitting exposés, interviewing children who'd been advertised on the site (Melanie Thompson, using a pseudonym, was among them).[20] Given the history of Backpage's founders, Michael Lacey and Jim Larkin, and their bullish colleague Carl Ferrer, their response to the controversy probably won't surprise you. They hit back at their critics, insisting their protection policies were robust and even using their media empire to debunk some of the trafficking claims made by their detractors.

But the battle against Backpage wasn't just happening in the court of public opinion. Prosecutors were circling and, following the high-profile negative publicity, they had Backpage firmly in their sights. One woman in particular would spend years of her life pursuing it.

Tuesday, 7 December 2004, was a pretty typical day for Maggy Krell. A deputy district attorney only a couple of years into the job, she was confronted by a depressingly familiar scene when she turned up for work at the San Joaquin County Superior Court. The local police had led a prostitution sting operation the preceding weekend, and those swept up had now filtered down into the judicial system for processing. 'All the defendants were women. And they were all young, many of them teenagers. Almost all were African American,' wrote Krell.

For their pimps, the women were commodities to be traded. And having fallen foul of the law, those same women now seemed resigned to being shunted through the court system. 'They stared blankly into space and looked numb and lifeless,' observed Krell.

Krell knew the women were connected by a common thread. They'd all been arrested at the same motel, somewhere that had become a regular target for police prostitution operations. Krell had an idea. 'What if, I wondered, we could target that motel?'[21]

She pulled together a case, and it worked. The motel owner pleaded guilty to conspiracy to commit prostitution and pimping, and the place was shut down. So when, years later, she started hearing about Backpage, Krell thought she might use the same tactic. After all, she figured, wasn't Backpage's adult section just the online equivalent of the motel?

So once again she assembled a case, but this time the court disagreed. Krell's case failed – and it was far from the only one. In summer 2009, a girl who'd been listed by her pimp on Backpage aged thirteen tried to sue the site for damages, without success.[22] And in 2014, three women who'd been advertised for sex on Backpage when they were children also tried to sue. Again, they failed. When they tried to appeal, the judges' comments combined sympathy with cold rejection: 'This is a hard case . . . the law requires that we . . . deny relief to plaintiffs whose circumstances evoke outrage.'[23]

Despite the lawyers' best efforts, none of the attempts succeeded. In the face of so many cases, so much compelling evidence of children's suffering and so much outrage, Backpage's adult section 'held fast', just like the message on Michael Lacey's knuckles. How?

Backpage's resilience came thanks to a few thousand words that have provoked many hundreds of hours of debate. Section 230 of the Communications Decency Act (CDA) gives US websites immunity from prosecution by states and local courts. No matter what people post on a forum or website, the owners can't be sued at state or local level. That's totally different to the situation for newspapers, magazines, radio broadcasters and TV stations, which have to vet every piece of content before it gets published.

In fairness, without this legislation the online lives many of us enjoy would come to a grinding halt. Imagine if Instagram or X (formerly called Twitter) had to vet every post before it went live (as newspaper editors must do with articles). Your holiday selfies would be stuck in a near-infinite queue.

Section 230 of the CDA helps the modern Internet function, but it has also created huge problems as the World Wide Web has become the dominant information conduit for many people. And when it comes to the issue of prostitution, it has created a uniquely agonizing situation for abuse victims and those seeking to protect them. Because while prostitution and pimping are illegal at state level, Section 230 of the CDA applies at the federal, national level. This meant that every time someone tried to go up against Backpage on state-level pimping or prostitution-related charges, Backpage played their federal-level trump card, rolling out the CDA which would, once again, give them immunity from prosecution.

In October 2016, there was yet another attempt, this time by Kamala Harris (who was then California's Attorney General and would go on to become Vice President). Backpage boss Carl Ferrer was arrested on charges of pimping a minor as he landed at Houston airport. Lacey and Larkin were similarly charged with adult pimping offences. The company's HQ was searched; Maggy Krell was part of the team, and hoped the moment was close when she'd see Backpage shut down for good. She even managed to get a quick photo of Carl Ferrer, holding up his arrest card as he was processed through the court system.[24] On his face is a smug smile. It turned out he had every right to be cocky. On 9 December 2016, a judge threw out the attempted prosecution, once again ruling that the CDA was a 'complete shield' for Backpage's conduct.[25]

In the courts, things were stymied. Public opinion didn't seem to be changing much – even with the likes of REM joining the fight. Backpage flourished behind its CDA shield. But their safety wouldn't last much longer. The money they were raking in would prove to be their downfall. Financial crime experts were sharpening their daggers, and Backpage's flank would soon be fatally exposed.

Backpage's founders weren't the only ones taking careful note of the site's ballooning revenue. In June 2015 Tom Dart, Sheriff of Cook County, Illinois, spotted a chance to hit Backpage where it counted: in the wallet. He wrote to the chief executives of Mastercard and

Visa, who as the world's biggest payment companies were ultimately processing the purchase of many of the ads on Backpage. He had a simple message for them:

> Your [credit] cards have and will continue to be used to buy ads that
> sell children for sex on sites like Backpage.com . . . It has become
> increasingly indefensible for any corporation to continue to willfully
> play a central role in an industry that reaps its cash from the victim-
> ization of women and girls across the world.[26]

Predictably enough, Backpage lawyered up and sued Dart, arguing he'd over-reached his position and breached their freedom of speech rights. They won, but it was a hollow victory; two days after receiving Dart's missive, Mastercard and Visa stopped processing payments for adult ads on Backpage. This was seriously bad news for the site; the world's two biggest card companies were freezing it out. With the threat of financial starvation looming, Backpage would take a series of rash decisions that would eventually bring the entire site crashing down for good.

In reality, the company's money problems started long before Sheriff Dart's intervention. In the days when Backpage was part of Village Voice Media, its transactions with banks and card companies could be channelled through the newspapers' accounts. That meant these financial providers didn't necessarily know what the money had been used to pay for. But in 2012, as the group's weekly papers had struggled with revenue, they had been sold off and Backpage spun out as a separate commercial entity. That meant it could no longer hide its transactions behind the group's other publications. Banks and card companies knew full well that Backpage's money was coming from ads, and since the vast majority of them were for adult services, potentially including prostitution and trafficking, the financial companies started turning them down.

Carl Ferrer was painfully aware of this. As early as August 2013, he forwarded an array of emails from Backpage customers who were complaining that their credit card companies had refused

49

payments for Backpage ads. Ferrer was therefore faced with the same problem encountered by drug gangs like the Dins and even Pablo Escobar – he somehow had to figure out how to keep Backpage's money flowing into the financial system, obscuring its origins. He needed a plan for that vital first stage in the laundering process: placement.

Unlike the Dins, Ferrer didn't have the headache of dealing exclusively with cash. But, nonetheless, the task of placing Backpage's money would still present him with enormous challenges.

Ever the schemer, Ferrer had a plan to keep the money pumping: he would set up shell companies with no apparent connection to Backpage, channelling the money through these front companies to fool credit card firms into thinking the cash was coming from transactions on different websites.[27]

Early in 2015, Ferrer was told that American Express would stop processing transactions for his site after 1 May.[28] In response, he and his colleagues set up a website called postfastr.com. On the surface, it had no connections to Backpage whatsoever. It was mainly advertising blue collar jobs, especially in trucking. However, at the bottom of the page was a link labelled 'buy credits' – and it was here that the secret tunnel to Backpage began. Users of postfastr.com could log in to the site, use their Amex cards to buy credits on postfastr.com, then if they used the same login details to access backpage.com, the credits they bought would magically appear and could be spent buying ads. But as far as American Express was concerned, they were processing money from the apparently legitimate site, postfastr.com. It seemed a neat fix, but for Ferrer the problems were actually about to get far worse, driving him deeper into the illicit world of money laundering.

After Visa and Mastercard backed out in July 2015 following Sheriff Dart's intervention, Backpage was confronted with a cold, hard truth: those who pay the piper (or at least process the piper's payments) call the tune. The card companies had decided Backpage was supporting illegal activity, and they were calling time.

Once again, Ferrer and his team scrambled to keep the money

moving into the financial system. They set up a new company to accept cheques from advertisers, then sent the money via yet more shell companies to Backpage's coffers.

It wasn't long before Ferrer, as a skilled techie and financial wizard, hit on Bitcoin as a potential solution to the company's financial woes. Like the Din gang, he'd discovered that technology had unwittingly created a back door through which illicit cash could be finagled into the financial system. Backpage offered customers the chance to pay with the new cryptocurrency, and were soon routing money via big crypto companies like Coinbase, GoCoin, Paxful and Kraken (companies which, thanks to Ferrer's intricate shell game, may have had no idea where the money was coming from).[29]

The methods became increasingly complex and ingenious. At one point, a Backpage employee suggested that customers could use prepaid credit cards to pay for ads. Rather than route the money directly to its bank accounts, Backpage would instead use it to buy Bitcoin, and then give the customer credits to spend on ads. This would allow Backpage to profit without having to run the money via banks or card companies, but its customers would be none the wiser. 'From the user's perspective they just input their card and get their credits or purchase,' read the email.[30]

One can imagine that Backpage staff thought these strategies were very clever, and believed that with enough shell companies and crypto-tricks, they could run rings around the banks and card companies and keep placing their millions of dollars of revenue into the financial system. But, in fact, they were digging their own hole. The tactics Carl Ferrer had adopted had crossed the line into money laundering. Every new trick he tried was gradually stripping away the armour that had protected Backpage for years. And it wasn't long before the people pursuing Backpage spotted it.

December 2016 was a bleak time for Maggy Krell. Despite all her work, the California Attorney General's Office had lost its case against Backpage. The judge had once again ruled that Section 230 of the Communications Decency Act protected the site, and there was nothing he could do about it. 'Congress has spoken on this matter, and it is for Congress, not the Court, to revisit,' he said.[31] 'I spent the two weeks after the case dismissal in dismal silence at work,' wrote Krell.[32] Then she hit upon a new idea. Looking through the evidence they'd gleaned in the previous, unsuccessful prosecution, she alighted on the financial information that had been uncovered, and it opened the door to a new prosecutorial tactic, one that had been touted before but so far remained unused: targeting Backpage's money and Ferrer's use of increasingly hi-tech money-laundering methods.

It was a potentially perfect way to get around the Section 230 shield that had sheltered Backpage for so long. To achieve a conviction for money laundering, the prosecution has to prove that the defendant tried to hide money from a crime (the so-called 'predicate offence'), but crucially, they don't need to prove the initial crime itself. So, all those failed attempts to sue Backpage for facilitating prostitution didn't matter. So long as the prosecution could convince a court that prostitution had happened, and that Backpage had tried to wash the resultant money, they stood a chance of getting a conviction. 'Rather than focusing on the website itself and the defendants' advertising, we would be focusing on their sources of money and how they conducted their illicit business,' Krell wrote.

The idea of going after the cash made perfect sense to Melanie Thompson. She'd seen from the inside how pimps utilized and profited from Backpage. Her abuser had eventually been caught and sentenced to four to twelve years in prison for trafficking, kidnapping and other offences,[33] but her nightmare was far from over. The path of her life had been irreversibly altered that night back in 2010. She'd subsequently been through a series of detention and residential centres, and mental health hospitals, and was finally placed with a foster family. However, she says that one of her foster carers resumed the abuse, trafficking her once more.

By the mid 2010s, Thompson says, the online trade had pretty much taken over. 'We didn't even do street walking or anything any more. I think that when people saw how much money you can generate online, and that anonymity component, it just became a no-brainer for sex buyers to only go on the Internet.'

To get the money-laundering charges to stick, Krell would have to disentangle the complex financial and corporate web Ferrer and his team had created, and demonstrate how criminal money had been placed into the banks. On the plus side, they had no shortage of material. 'Simultaneous with the arrest of the defendants and search of Backpage headquarters back in October [2016], we served search warrants on major banks that Backpage had done business with,' wrote Krell.

On the downside, the amount of data threatened to become overwhelming. 'Certain types of payments went through so many processors that they became impossible to trace. This was money laundering at its most successful,'[34] she wrote. In addition to the bank data, they had tens of thousands of emails from the company's staff. Krell needed help combing through it all. And that's when she reached out to someone who would go on to become an unlikely hero in the battle to take down Backpage.

Bassem Banafa started life as a forensic accountant working for private companies, including a stint at top consultancy firm Ernst and Young. His career was taking a stolidly corporate path, with a focus on insurance fraud cases. But the prospect of spending his days saving insurance companies millions of dollars was deeply unappealing to Banafa. He'd got into forensic accounting because he wanted to set the world to rights; to fight the good fight. So he joined the Contra Costa County District Attorney's office. Working side by side with cops, he suddenly found himself surrounded by sweary, straight-talking people, many of whom carried guns. Compared to the slick, corporate world of Big Four accountancy, it was quite an eye-opener.

As part of his work for the DA's office, Banafa began looking into a website for massage parlours that many suspected was a front for people trafficking. Some of his law-enforcement colleagues felt that such sites were actually a useful resource: yes, they could be sinkholes for criminality, but at least it was clear where the criminality was and police officers could use such sites to investigate it. Some even felt the same about Backpage. But Banafa disagreed. All he saw was a website enabling abuse, and he wanted to stop it.

Banafa asked Krell for help, but when he reached out, she told him they were working on a much bigger case. When Banafa found out they were investigating Backpage, he took one look at the site, scanned the plethora of companies behind it, and immediately decided he wanted in on the investigation. He told me that part of the attraction was the level of obfuscation Backpage's bosses had put in place around its financial set-up, including the spider's web of shell corporations. The very thing that would make most people run a mile in the opposite direction was the thing getting Banafa's juices flowing. He and Krell began wrangling the mountain of data and, slowly but surely, assembling their case.

Krell's office in Sacramento was emptying out in the run-up to Christmas, but she was still hard at work. 'Fueled by peanut-butter pretzels and making my way through a [six-pack] of Diet Coke, I spent hours and hours uninterrupted in my Backpage cave drafting a new complaint based on a new theory supported by new evidence,' she wrote. Meanwhile, about 100 miles south in Milpitas, Banafa was also beavering away, fuelled by an equally unhealthy diet largely reliant on an energy drink called Mountain Dew Amp. He had computer monitors balanced precariously on top of boxes and papers, and spent hours obsessively poring over Backpage's data.

'He worked like a mad scientist,' as Krell puts it. 'Bassem was mildly friendly, severely quirky and smart beyond any human I'd ever encountered. If I could only filter his smartness into translatable and usable information, the sky was the limit.'

Sure enough, Banafa's hard work paid off and he hit the jackpot. He discovered that Backpage had built a computer system to funnel the money through its various shell companies. The computer system was stored in the cloud, on servers owned by Amazon. The prosecution team had got a copy of the system as part of its investigation into Backpage. It was potentially a treasure trove of evidence for the money-laundering case, like discovering the secret ledger books of a corrupt banker. But there was a problem: the system was custom-built by Backpage. Banafa would have to painstakingly take it apart in order to figure out how it worked. And, of course, he wouldn't be getting any help from those who'd developed it. It was like unloading the dishwasher in a stranger's kitchen: he had to open every drawer till he worked out where things went.

'I sat for days just changing every single setting in every possible combination that exists to get it to open,' he recalls. Then one day, eventually, he hit the right combination, and the system unlocked. 'I screamed and ran around the house,' says Banafa. At last, he could see large parts of Backpage's financial network, and how it was manipulating the money flow from the site via its network of shell companies and seemingly unrelated websites.

The prosecution team also discovered Ferrer's trick of trying to fool the banks into thinking that money wasn't coming from Backpage by diverting it via other businesses. This could be interpreted as an attempt to defraud the banks, and if so, that would open him up to yet another money-laundering allegation, the predicate crime being bank fraud rather than enabling prostitution. Two days before Christmas, Ferrer, Lacey and Larkin got an unwelcome gift: new charges. They still included pimping allegations, including pimping of children. But now there were dozens of money-laundering charges too. The rap sheet covered millions of dollars of criminal proceeds, all listed down to the last cent, largely thanks to the financial records that Banafa and Krell had cracked open.[35] For all their hi-tech scheming, Backpage's once-impregnable defences were starting to crumble. And things were about to get much, much worse for them.

When Melanie Thompson was being trafficked on Backpage, she knew that the site seemed to have rules about what could be posted in an ad. 'Sometimes if you would write, you know, "sexy teen" they wouldn't allow you to move to the next page to post because they would say you have to check what the words are in your ads.

So you have to switch it to a code word. Instead of saying "sexy" or "sex", you would change the E to a dollar sign. Or instead of saying "teen", you have to put "green" or "naïve" or something like that to let it go through.' Nonetheless, it was clear to Thompson that, even with these euphemisms, clients knew exactly what they were getting, and she says it would trigger an influx of calls to her pimp. '"Naïve" is a code word for young. Those code words that identify underage were always the ones that got the most phone calls.'

As Backpage's advertising business grew, so did the number of ads that clearly involved trafficked women and children. This led Backpage to a conundrum. On the one hand, the morally right thing to do was to reject such ads. But on the other hand, the advertisers (even the traffickers) were Backpage's cash cows, and rejecting them was bad for business. To resolve the dilemma, Backpage told its staff to tweak the ads instead, to make them suitable for the site.[36]

But this created an issue for Backpage: if its staff not only knew that ads for illegal services were being attempted, but even went to the extent of sanitizing them, then Backpage could be accused of editing the ads, therefore making it a publisher rather than just an Internet platform. If so, the site's protection under Section 230 of the Communications Decency Act might disappear.

So Ferrer, ever the resourceful techie, came up with a solution called 'Strip Term From Ad'. It was a piece of software that would automatically remove problematic words from the text of an ad before placing it on the site. The words it removed left little doubt about the original intent of the advertiser: 'lolita', 'rape', 'fresh', 'little girl' and so on. Eventually, this automated system took over, and manual editing was phased out.[37] And it wasn't just a handful of adverts that were being edited. By late 2010, Backpage was tweaking 70–80 per cent of all ads in the adult section – an indication of just how rife such material had become on the site.[38]

At the same time as Maggy Krell and Bassem Banafa had been sorting through their mountain of data to assemble the money-laundering charges, the US Senate Permanent Subcommittee on Investigations had also been looking into Backpage. They were probing for information about how the company policed its advertising, including through using systems like Strip Term From Ad. On 10 January 2017, the subcommittee went public with their findings in a damning fifty-three-page report entitled 'Backpage.com's Knowing Facilitation of Online Sex Trafficking'.

The game was up. The day before the Senate committee released its report, Backpage removed the adult category from all its sites, claiming censorship (just as Craigslist had initially done). But if Carl Ferrer and his colleagues thought that was enough to save themselves, they had another thing coming. In California, Maggy Krell's case was still pending, threatening another hammer blow to Backpage.

Krell had endured a frustrating wait after filing the new charges, including money laundering, in December 2016. The judge needed time to consider whether they could go ahead. Finally, on 23 August 2017, Judge Brown was ready to announce his decision. Everyone filed into court, and the defendants' legal teams were given paper copies of his ruling first, before Krell. 'I was staring at the defendants,' she wrote. 'From their sour faces, I knew what the ruling was.'

The pimping charges had been dismissed: once again, Section 230 protected Backpage. But the money-laundering charges could go ahead. 'I sat quietly, showing no emotion while secretly doing back-flips inside,' remembers Krell.[39] Carl Ferrer's financial wizardry was coming back to haunt him, and his hi-tech money-laundering schemes had caught him out. There's a photo of him in court that day. This time, there's no smug smile. He, Lacey and Larkin look deathly.

In addition to Maggy Krell's state-level investigation, federal agencies had also been circling Backpage, and on 6 April 2018 they moved in to take down the entire website, not just the adult section. Forensic accountant Bassem Banafa was still part of the investigation and got a ringside seat as US government officials fought to kill the site. 'I was in a hotel room with US Postal Inspectors and the IRS (Internal Revenue Service) in San Francisco,' he recalls. 'We were trying to take the site down, but [the Internet Service

Provider] kept putting it back up. They didn't know what was happening. I was shaking, like, "We cannot mess this up!"' Finally, the site went down, to be replaced by a seizure notice that remains in place to this day.

Once again, Ferrer, Lacey and Larkin were arrested, and this time round, Ferrer pleaded guilty. Not just to four of the money-laundering charges, but also to conspiracy to facilitate prostitution. And beyond prostitution, Texas had also launched a case against Backpage for trafficking. Backpage pleaded guilty, with Ferrer, as CEO, signing on behalf of the site.

At the time of writing, Ferrer is waiting to be sentenced and facing a maximum of five years in prison. After all the years of trying to prosecute Backpage for its prostitution ads, it was arguably the introduction of money-laundering charges that really toppled him. And that's what potentially awaited his colleagues Michael Lacey and James Larkin, who, along with other former Backpage staff, were facing federal charges. But despite the financial aspects of the prosecution, at the heart of the case, Lacey and Larkin saw this as a new front in their lifelong battle for freedom of speech.

'They didn't do it for greed,' Larkin's lawyer told the court. Rather, he said, Lacey and Larkin spent 'fifty years as journalists standing up for the right of everyone to speak legally as long as it was legal speech. That's why they did it.'[40]

The prosecution's first attempt ended in dismal failure. In September 2021, the judge declared a mistrial, owing to the fact that prosecutors repeatedly referred to child sex trafficking, despite the fact that the charges did not relate to minors. A retrial was scheduled for August 2023. But just days before the case was due to be heard, there came shocking news for those following the legal action. James Larkin committed suicide, aged seventy-four. 'I had a four-decade friendship with a wonderful man. Now I have only his memory,' Lacey was quoted as saying.[41] After a short delay, the trial went ahead. Once again, lawyers for Lacey and other former senior Backpage employees argued that the site did not enable ads for prostitution, and criticized the prosecution as an attack on freedom of speech. It seems the jury agreed – at least in Lacey's case. They could not reach a verdict on eighty-four counts against him related to facilitating prostitution. But in a bombshell verdict they found him guilty on one, highly significant charge: money laundering. After years of pursuing Backpage's founders, the prosecution finally triumphed by using the financially focused tactics pioneered by Krell and Banafa. At the time of writing, Lacey is awaiting sentencing, and faces a maximum of twenty years in jail.[42]

(My requests for comment from lawyers for Lacey, Larkin and Ferrer – made prior to Larkin's death – went unanswered.)

Meanwhile, Melanie Thompson managed to escape the life of abuse that scarred her formative years. She joined a theatre collective and, through that, began working with support groups and non-profit organizations, helping others avoid the situation she'd found herself in. She's now a lived experience expert, advising policy makers and charities on sex trafficking. And the legal case against Backpage's former staff rumbles on, with its former CEO Carl Ferrer as a key witness. As the Texas authorities wrote: 'As part of the plea agreement, Ferrer . . . agreed to testify against all pending defendants, turned over the identities of the top 3,000 buyers of Backpage.com advertisements, and is assisting in identifying all company and codefendant assets for seizure.'[43]

But for all the discussion over Backpage's immense wealth, and the efforts to trace its bank accounts and shell companies, there's one aspect of this that gets little attention: cryptocurrency. As traditional finance turned away from Backpage, the site's managers increasingly pivoted to Bitcoin to keep money coming through the door. It was a key means to achieve that vital first stage of laundering: placement – funnelling illicit earnings into a financial system.

One investigator I spoke to reckoned that, towards the end, around a third of the site's transactions were conducted in Bitcoin, which means that many millions of dollars were washed as cryptocurrency. Authorities did manage to seize some of it, but not without a few technical headaches, as Bassem Banafa remembers. He says that the night before the takedown of Backpage's website, law enforcement realized that in order to seize the site's Bitcoin, they needed a particular type of computer flash drive. They didn't have one, so in a moment of supreme irony, they turned to . . . Craigslist, where they found one for sale. 'I didn't go with them [to pick it up],' says Banafa, 'but I just had this mental image of someone trying to sell this flash drive, and armed federal agents showing up to hand over cash, taking it and just leaving.'

The Feds weren't the only ones struggling with the crypto side of Backpage's shadow financial set-up. As Maggy Krell was putting together the money-laundering charges in California, she found they were dealing with so much data that it was easier to concentrate on the traditional finance stuff, despite the prevalence of cryptocurrency in Backpage's laundering schemes. 'Many of the payments at this point were cryptocurrency, like Bitcoin, and to simplify our case, we were focusing on specific commercial banks and filtering out cryptocurrency,' she wrote.[44]

Arguably, had Ferrer and his colleagues managed to do more with cryptocurrencies like Bitcoin, they could have hidden much more of the laundering that eventually brought down the site. But even Carl Ferrer couldn't run a purely cryptocurrency operation to launder all the site's money. Most of its customers were making payments using traditional finance – credit cards and the like. Placing all that money into Bitcoin was a challenge: crypto was still a nascent industry and moving large sums around was hard work. Going back to Ken Rijock's three-stage process – placement, layering, integration – Backpage struggled with finding technological methods to crack that first step: placement. But as crypto tech has progressed, others have easily leapt that hurdle. In the next chapter we'll meet a group of people so well versed in this world that they created an entirely virtual crypto-laundering operation, and used it to fund activity even darker and more harmful than what was happening on Backpage.

4.

Welcome To Video

A warning: this chapter contains coverage
of child sexual exploitation.

In the mid 1990s, the US military and intelligence establishment faced a conundrum. The Internet and World Wide Web were booming, Amazon and eBay had launched and youngsters were swapping Hotmail addresses in bars and cafés. For government spooks, the new technology offered a golden opportunity not just for surveilling people's communications, but also for allowing spies and sources all over the world to relay information back to their handlers. But there was a snag: the Internet wasn't built to keep secrets.

For example, if you visit the Penguin website page for this book, the traffic from your computer to the site is bounced through a series of Internet intermediaries as it snakes its way around the globe towards Penguin's computer servers. Any of those intermediaries can see your IP address (the unique number your computer is assigned when it connects to the Internet), and the IP address of the Penguin site you're visiting. Those IP addresses can very often be used to identify you, and the site you're trying to reach. Now imagine you're a CIA operative in the US, trying to gain intelligence by visiting a jihadi website in the Middle East. You don't want every online intermediary to see what you're up to, and you certainly don't want the website owner to know who's knocking at their virtual door.

So, a bunch of gifted computer scientists at the US Naval Research Laboratory came up with a solution. They called it 'onion routing', because it works by wrapping your Internet traffic in layers of encryption. Each time your website request is bounced through an intermediary computer as it makes its way towards its destination, just one layer of encryption is peeled back. As a result, none of the intermediaries can ever see the full picture of where the traffic came from and where it is going. They can't connect your identity with the site you're eventually trying to reach. The US government had invented the dark web.[1]

To use this encryption trick, all you need to do is install a special web browser called Tor (short for The Onion Router). Not only does it disguise your traffic as you surf the Internet by wrapping it in layers of encryption, but it also allows you access to a set of websites that are only viewable to visitors using Tor (if you try to load up these web-sites on a normal browser like Chrome or Firefox, you get an error message). These websites have long, seemingly random addresses. Instead of ending with .com or .co.uk, they end with .onion. These are the shadowy dark web sites you may have heard about in the news. Traffic to and from these sites is automatically cloaked in Tor's encryption. As such, they're an invaluable tool for anyone who needs secrecy. This can be for perfectly legitimate reasons such as anti-government protesters living under repressive regimes, or journalists working with whistle-blowers. But because of their secretive nature, they're also a repository for all the vile and criminal things that catch the headlines: drugs, hacker forums and child sexual abuse, besides other offerings.

But whatever you're using your dark web site for, it still needs to be hosted on a server, just like a normal website. That means that all the images, text and so on need to be stored on an Internet-accessible computer. When someone visits your site, this computer 'serves up' the site's content, hence the name. Most people use a professional server company for this, called a 'host'.

If you want to set up a dark web site selling, say, hard drugs, this presents a problem. If you try to host your website on a server run by a legitimate company, the police will simply come along with a warrant and the company will shut your site down. So as a criminal dark web site owner, what you need is a company that'll host your site, no questions asked, and won't respond to queries from the cops. This is what's called 'bulletproof hosting'.

Over the years, an entire industry has sprung up to serve the hosting needs of the dark web's crooks, and in July 2008, an important new player entered the scene: Freedom Hosting. At first glance, its terms and conditions sounded quite morally upstanding: 'We do not give permission for upload of any illegal files' (*sic*). But the terms continued: 'If you chose to do so anyway, we are not responsible for your actions.'² And with that, Freedom Hosting's bosses washed their hands of any responsibility for the sites they were harbouring, creating an online Wild West with no sheriff. As a result, their service fast became a sinkhole for the Internet's most depraved content: bestiality, the promotion of sex tourism and the sexual abuse of children.

By 2011, Freedom Hosting's role in enabling such depravity caught the attention of the Anonymous hacker movement. Having emerged from the shadows of a free-wheeling Internet forum called 4chan, these Guy Fawkes-mask-toting iconoclasts provoked mixed reactions. Some regarded them as Internet terrorists, others as online Scarlet Pimpernels fighting for justice on the web. They specialized in hitting their targets with swarming, decentralized digital attacks, often combined with headline-grabbing wit delivered via Twitter.

On 15 October 2011, they launched #OpDarknet, striking Freedom Hosting with the intention of overwhelming its sites with extremely high numbers of visits, forcing them offline. But Freedom Hosting lived up to its bulletproof reputation; within just two hours, its sites were back up and running.³ And over time, Anonymous's crusade had the opposite of its intended effect. In the wake of the attacks, one of the sites hosted by Freedom Hosting, Lolita City, claimed a ten-fold increase in the amount of child sexual abuse material on offer, and a similar growth in members, who now numbered 15,000. 'Rather than kill them, Anonymous had publicized them,' wrote the journalist Patrick O'Neill.⁴

As Anonymous waged war on Freedom Hosting, one 4chan user watched with interest, following the battle keenly. He used the online nickname 'Lux', but his real identity was shrouded in mystery. Instead of joining the takedown, Lux found himself increasingly intrigued by the paedophile sites themselves. He began to believe he could create versions that would be even more appealing to this community.

To justify his work, he fell back on the freedom of speech defence, taking the libertarian ideals of Michael Lacey and Jim Larkin, the Backpage publishers covered in the previous chapter, and stretching them almost to breaking point. Of the horrific content he set out to host, Lux told O'Neill: 'If anyone had ever done such a thing to any of the kids I know, I would put a bullet in their head. Given that, I still think that people who have interest in such things should have a place where they're able to voice their opinions and desires.'[5] Lux was also after infamy, and pursued it by creating in February 2013 a truly disturbing site. Hurt2TheCore was set up on Freedom Hosting and dedicated to 'hurtcore' material: sadistic abuse not just of children, but of adults and animals too. In fact, anything that pushed at the very limit of horror. The site quickly caught the eye of a British man who, even in the realm of such abhorrent behaviour, would take things to an unprecedented level. He was a predator who used social media to trick and trap his victims; a technique he'd honed to a devastating level of efficacy.

In April 2013, Beatrice, a 15-year-old British schoolgirl, was trying to earn some pocket money by advertising as a babysitter on the classified ads site Gumtree. She was approached by a woman calling herself 'Liz'. The pair got chatting over email, and soon Liz offered her a different proposal. Liz claimed to be a life-drawing artist, something she said she'd taken up to help with depression. She asked Beatrice to send an intimate but relatively modest photo of herself that Liz could draw from, in exchange for £800. Beatrice thought it through, and eventually decided to help Liz out by sending a photo.

But as soon as the picture was sent, Liz suddenly changed from being a caring artist to a vicious blackmailer, threatening to send Beatrice's compromising photo to her family and friends unless she supplied more. 'I felt stupid and trapped. The idea of people seeing me topless made me feel sick. I knew I couldn't let it happen,' Beatrice said.

She began to comply with Liz's requests, sending her hundreds more naked photos over the next two months. Liz forced her to photograph herself doing humiliating tasks. 'I didn't know who "Liz" was or why she was doing this, but felt I had no option,' said Beatrice.

She wasn't alone. A 16-year-old girl had almost exactly the same experience after advertising as a babysitter on Gumtree. Separately, a 15-year-old girl placed an ad on the site looking to buy a pet dog. Again, Liz responded, using the same tactics to trick the girl into sending a topless image, before bullying and blackmailing her into sending increasingly degrading pictures. 'I will do everything I can to make your life awful,' Liz told her.

It soon became obvious where these images were ending up. In one request, Liz told the victim to hold up a sign mentioning a particular website: Hurt2TheCore.[6] It seemed Liz was exploiting teens to provide material for the site created by Lux.

Several of the victims reported their ordeal to their local police forces across the UK. But the officers weren't able to make much headway. They could see the email addresses that Liz was using to communicate, but the email providers were secrecy-focused companies who prided themselves on guarding users' privacy, similar to the bulletproof mindset of Freedom Hosting. There was no way they'd answer police queries. And besides, each police force believed it was working on an individual, one-off case: they couldn't see the full scale of Liz's offending.

These devastating instances of blackmail and sexual exploitation turned out to be just the opening moves of a four-year campaign of relentless abuse. The person behind the Liz persona was in fact a man, who would use dark web technology to evade law enforcement across the world. And he would eventually lead them to a site which would be a test case for hi-tech money-laundering investigation.

As Liz was carrying out her child grooming on Gumtree, the FBI had started to look into Freedom Hosting, the bulletproof server provider that was harbouring Hurt2TheCore and other similar sites. Using a top-secret technique, the Bureau had managed to discover an IP address for the site that led to a server company in France called OVH.[7] It appeared Freedom Hosting was sub-letting servers from the company. OVH was not a bulletproof provider, but a regular, legitimate firm, ready and willing to comply with police requests. Information from OVH revealed that Freedom Hosting's server space was paid for using a credit card, which enabled the FBI to track the card owner to an address in Dublin. On 29 July 2013, Freedom Hosting's secretive boss, 'the largest facilitator of child porn on the planet', as the FBI described him, was arrested and revealed as 28-year-old Eric Marques.[8]

Freedom Hosting was finally destroyed. The FBI identified 200 child exploitation websites enabled by Marques's service, and found a staggering 1.97 million pictures and videos that were previously unknown to law enforcement. Now would begin the painstaking work of trying to identify the children in those images, locate them and, if possible, rescue them.[9]

In the wake of the Freedom Hosting takedown, in late 2013, the FBI began sharing its insights from Marques's network of sites, including Hurt2TheCore, with other law-enforcement agencies around the world. One user, who went by the nickname Inthegarden, appeared to be from the UK. His posts, along with the scant details in his profile, suggested he was somewhere in England. As such, his details were forwarded to the National Crime Agency (NCA), the FBI's UK equivalent. The NCA looked through his profile and found the output of a vicious, sadistic individual. Inthegarden had posted explicit, humiliating photos of a teenage girl, whom he was blackmailing into providing images on demand. He had even solicited suggestions from other Hurt2TheCore users about what he should get the girl to do next.

The girl in the pictures was Beatrice, the 15-year-old who'd fallen into Liz's trap on Gumtree after advertising her babysitting services.

But at the time, the NCA didn't know that the cases of Beatrice and the other Gumtree victims were being investigated by separate police forces at a local level. The NCA was looking into Inthegarden and Hurt2TheCore at a national level. They were hunting the same offender, but digging in separate ground, and it would take years for the connection to be made.

Meanwhile, the NCA was working hard to identify the girl in the pictures that Inthegarden had posted, and to work out who he really was. But making headway was hard. Inthegarden was an extremely clever and meticulously careful offender. Added to that, the site on which he was originally active, Hurt2TheCore, had already been taken down by the FBI. This presented a challenge for the NCA. Sometimes, in order to unmask a secretive offender, the agency will set up a fake persona and chat to them, hoping the culprit will slip up and reveal some critical personal detail. But with Hurt2TheCore gone, the NCA was working with Inthegarden's historic, archived identity, not his current, live one, so their investigative options were limited. Time marched on, but no breakthroughs came.

Two years later, in April 2015, the NCA started investigating a new dark web site which covered gruesome territory similar to its precursor, Hurt2TheCore. There they discovered the profile of a man believed to be in the UK, using the handle Evilmind. And then, something caught their eye. Evilmind was claiming ownership of the same set of images that had made Inthegarden infamous on Hurt2TheCore two years previously. It seemed the same offender had popped back on their radar with a new ID. To make matters worse, Evilmind had posted images of a girl he claimed was his daughter, and was soliciting suggestions for her imminent abuse. The clock was ticking. Every day that passed could mean more suffering for the girl in the photo.

The NCA reached out to local police forces across the country – could anyone help identify the girl? And, eventually, they found out about the Gumtree cases. There were six, at least, including Beatrice. They went to Gumtree's owners, who tried to help, but Liz had been canny: after initially contacting her victims on Gumtree, she'd moved the conversation to email, using around twenty different addresses. Most of the email providers behind those addresses were the kind of bulletproof, secrecy-focused services that had stymied previous investigations. But one of the email firms did cooperate, providing the NCA with access to one of Liz's inboxes. That's when the agency learned that they weren't dealing with just half-a-dozen UK victims – the man behind the Liz persona had approached more than 300 people, from all around the world. Liz was just a front identity for one man's giant, global campaign of devastating grooming and abuse.

For the NCA, everything was starting to click into place. The man pretending to be 'Liz' had groomed the teenagers on Gumtree, gaining their trust and tricking them into surrendering intimate photos. He would then blackmail them for more, which he would post to Hurt2TheCore and other sites, using the handles Inthegarden and Evilmind. It turned out these were just a few of the IDs he used. In total there were around seventy.

The police realized they were up against a prolific, experienced and deeply sadistic global abuser who was using every technological trick in the book to stay hidden. In August 2015, a task force was set up bringing together the NCA, GCHQ (the UK's signals intelligence agency), Homeland Security in the US, Europol, the Australian Federal Police and others. Somehow, they had to tempt Evilmind out into the open, away from the secrecy-preserving networks he inhabited.

'All we needed was one instance where he emerges from the shadows, and we see him,' Matt Sutton, senior investigating officer for the NCA, told me. It would take more than a year for that breakthrough to happen, and as well as technical means, it would require careful, patient use of psychological acumen.

Undercover officers started contacting Evilmind via the sites he used, striking up conversation, pretending to be part of the same community of abusers. Eventually, in March 2017, they tricked him into letting slip his IP address (the NCA would not be drawn on the specific tactic, wanting to preserve it for use against others). The IP led to an address in Birmingham, central England, and a 29-year-old academic named Matthew Falder.

He was a geophysicist working at Birmingham University. Part of his specialism was deciphering images of swirling vortices of water in the middle of the Atlantic Ocean. He used high-powered computers which generated mesmerizing patterns of red and blue on a background of white. To the uninitiated it looked almost like modern art.

Falder wasn't just any academic. As one of his former colleagues told me: 'Even among Oxford and Cambridge academics and a wide selection of very clever people, he shone as far smarter. He was one of those people who could have excelled in almost any field. He was very funny, very quick off the mark, and very popular. Everyone liked him, because he was smart and personable. He was the person in the office who, if you were visibly having a bad day, would say "Are you all right?" and crack some jokes. He was that sort of guy.'[10] To his colleagues, there was nothing to indicate his secret, depraved alter ego.

The NCA put Falder under surveillance, following him as he travelled, trying to build up a picture of their suspect without tipping him off. On 21 June 2017, they finally made their move, arresting Falder in his office at the university. On the NCA's video recording, Falder can be seen wearing a yellow T-shirt and glasses, and with a frizzy shock of blond hair. 'What was it I've done . . . ?' he begins to ask, before interrupting himself, 'What was it I'm supposed to have . . . ?' The police officer then reads out a list of child sex abuse offences. Falder listens for a while. 'Sounds like the rap sheet from hell,' he quips.

News of the arrest spread like wildfire across the campus, and further afield. One of Falder's former colleagues told me: 'Because he was popular, everyone was suddenly asking "What the hell's going on?"'

Meanwhile, Falder was being grilled by the NCA. He was videoed, arms folded, sitting in the corner of the interview room wearing the same yellow T-shirt as he had been when he was arrested.

He repeatedly answers 'no comment', something he kept up for three days of questioning. Eventually, however, he admits to being the man behind the Evilmind accounts. It had taken more than four years to bring him to justice since UK police had first learned of Inthegarden and his alter ego, Liz.

Contrary to his comments on the abuse sites, Falder didn't have a daughter. The photo of the girl he'd used had also been connived via Gumtree. Within hours of receiving it he'd made it his profile picture, pretending it was his daughter and asking for ideas for what he could do to her. The NCA was able to track her down and ensure she was safe.

Falder's offending stood out not only in terms of its duration, but also its breadth and scale. As well as blackmailing strangers for images online, he'd targeted his friends in the physical world too. Falder attended Clare College, Cambridge University, where he started a natural sciences degree in 2007. While there, he'd installed hidden cameras in bathrooms at the university's accommodation as well as at his parents' main home and holiday home.[11] (There was talk of stripping Falder of his Cambridge University degrees, including his PhD, but it came to nothing. A spokesperson for the university told me that academic penalties can only be applied for academic misconduct – not the kind of crimes committed by Falder.)

As the news reports emerged, they revealed more and more of the scale of Falder's sadism and abuse against people of all ages, including his friends, colleagues and strangers. Those who knew him were stunned. 'The overall reaction was abject horror,' the former colleague told me. 'He never talked about the dark web, even when it came up in conversation. In hindsight he gave away nothing, and didn't mention that he'd ever been on it, let alone that he had an entire separate identity where he was spending all his time on it.'

Eventually, Falder pleaded guilty to 137 criminal charges. But the shock waves from his case were far from over. This horrific offender would lead the authorities to yet another child abuse site. This time, however, investigators would have a vital weapon in their fight against the abuse it facilitated. Digital money laundering would once again prove pivotal in the case.

In summer 2017, shortly after Falder's guilty plea, the National Crime Agency received a visit from Jonathan Levin, one of the co-founders of Chainalysis.[12] The company had by this point become one of the global leaders in cryptocurrency tracing, working with law-enforcement agencies and others around the world who were racing to keep up with this fast-evolving, high-tech financial world.

As part of the Falder investigation, the NCA had stumbled across another child sexual abuse site he was using, called Welcome To Video. In terms of the material on offer, it was depressingly similar to many of the other abuse sites the police had come across. Except for one crucial detail: Welcome To Video was charging money for access.

Many of the other sites and services utilized by paedophiles are run on a largely non-commercial basis. Lux didn't charge for Hurt-2TheCore, for example, and Eric Marques seemed to consider his work on Freedom Hosting as almost a charity. 'The admin covers [the cost] himself as a service to the pedo community,' he wrote to another user.[13]

Around the fringes of the paedophile community there is money changing hands between creators and viewers, but it's not the core of the industry. As the NCA's Matt Sutton observes: 'Their currency is not money. Their currency is the images which they share.'

Welcome To Video was different. Visitors to its dark web site could create a free account with a username and password and browse previews of the videos on offer. But to download them, users had to pay.[14] All of this of course required a financial infra-structure, and for this, Welcome To Video had turned to Bitcoin.

The crooks in previous chapters, like the Din OCG drug dealers and Backpage's Carl Ferrer, struggled with the initial placement stage of laundering, as they battled to turn their criminal income from cash and credit cards into digital currency. As a 'crypto-native' business, Welcome To Video faced no such hurdles. The money

71

from its customers came straight into the business as Bitcoin. Perhaps this gave the site's owner an impression of security. But even in this hi-tech financial set-up, the site's owner made fatal errors in the laundering process that would eventually lead to his downfall.

Through their analysis of Matthew Falder's case, the NCA had uncovered an important lead: they'd discovered one of the Bitcoin wallets into which Welcome To Video users could pay their money. When Jonathan Levin visited the NCA, they showed him the address, and asked if he might be able to do anything with it.[15] Luckily, the answer was yes.

As all Bitcoin transactions are published permanently in blockchain, there had to be wallet addresses for both payers and payees of all Welcome To Video transactions somewhere. The NCA showed Levin the wallet address that Welcome To Video had used to receive payments. Thanks to the blockchain, he could track back all the payments that had been made into that wallet, and see the addresses that had made those payments. It led to a spiralling map of Bitcoin addresses, all of them belonging to users of this site. But in terms of finding the actual offenders, this list of abstract wallet addresses wasn't much use. Chainalysis somehow needed to use this data to reveal the real-world identities of the people willing to pay to watch child sex abuse videos.

As Levin peered deeper into the charts, he spotted something striking about the addresses that had sent money to Welcome To Video. Many of them tracked back to cryptocurrency exchanges. These are businesses where, just like any currency swap shop, users can change dollars and pounds into crypto. Once they've done so, the cryptocurrency exchange can set them up with a wallet address and deposit their cryptocurrency into it. When people want to pay for something, they can simply transfer it straight out of their wallet at the exchange. And, of course, that transaction will be recorded, like all the others, in the blockchain. That's what Levin was looking at.

It seemed that, when they wanted to purchase credits to view material on Welcome To Video, many customers had paid directly from their crypto exchange accounts. And Levin was seeing it all. 'Many of this child abuse site's users . . . had done almost nothing to obscure their cryptocurrency trails. An entire network of criminal payments, all intended to be secret, was laid bare before him,' writes journalist Andy Greenberg, in his book on cryptocurrency tracing, *Tracers in the Dark*, which details the US side of the Welcome to Video investigation that followed.[16] In other words, Welcome To Video was failing at the second stage of the laundering process: layering. The site's users weren't doing enough to break the chain connecting the crime with the money.

This was very good news, because Levin knew that some of those crypto exchanges would keep records of their customers. Increasingly, mainstream exchanges are asking users to provide ID, such as a passport, if they want to set up an account (in some countries, there's legislation requiring them to do so). If the exchanges had kept such records in this case, and if they would cooperate and give them to law enforcement, they could potentially link the Welcome To Video payments to a real person.

This was helpful in tracking the site's users, but it didn't help identify the people behind the site itself. For that, Levin needed to use the blockchain to trace the money onwards from Welcome To Video's recipient wallets, looking at where it flowed next: to the site's owners. And that was a problem, because Welcome To Video had created 1.3 million recipient addresses.[17] That's not as hard as it might sound. Because Bitcoin is a digital currency that exists entirely through computer software, fresh addresses can be made with the click of a mouse. It's like what would happen if your bank could create a new account number for every online purchase you make. Welcome To Video had created a blizzard of crypto transactions. Unlike the site's users, who had made little effort to disguise their money trails, on the face of it, it looked like Welcome To Video's owner had successfully mastered the second stage of the laundering process, layering the transactions through hundreds of thousands of wallets. By using so many Bitcoin addresses, they'd worked hard to break the chain that could connect any one wallet to a specific crime. But Chainalysis had a trick up its sleeve for just such occasions, a technique for lumping together disparate, seemingly separate addresses.

If, for example, I have two wallets, both containing one Bitcoin, and I want to pay someone two Bitcoins, I can combine my two addresses to make the transfer. These are called 'multi-input' transactions. The downside is that anyone watching on the blockchain now knows that my two addresses are linked together, so it further chips away at Bitcoin's much-vaunted anonymity.

This is what Chainalysis did with Welcome To Video's 1.3 million recipient addresses: they looked out for transactions where two or more combined together. As they did so, they started to see the flows of money converge. As Greenberg writes: 'Someone seemed to be continually using large, multi-input transactions to gather up the site's funds.'[18]

The site's attempts at layering its illicit funds were being gradually unpicked. The digital money-laundering scheme was falling apart. Following that crypto flow onwards, Levin could see that, once again, it converged on a handful of cryptocurrency exchanges, where it was swapped for traditional currency – 'cashing out', as it's called in the money-laundering business. Significantly, two of the main exchanges being used were based in South Korea. If the crypto payments coming out of Welcome To Video were ending up as cash in the country, it was a strong indication that the site's owner – or at least, someone very closely connected to them – was based there.

Levin took his findings to the Criminal Investigation department of the US Internal Revenue Service. It may seem an odd choice, taking a South Korean child sex abuse case to the American tax authorities. But when you think about it, the IRS is a fairly natural destination for a money-laundering investigation. After all, criminals aren't exactly famed for their willingness to pay tax on their ill-gotten gains, so the IRS ends up investigating a lot of financial crime. On top of that, the IRS's Criminal Investigation team had made significant breakthroughs in previous crypto cases, notably Silk Road, a giant dark web marketplace specializing mainly in drug sales.

As a result, two of the IRS-CI agents in particular had become highly skilled in using crypto tracing to nail suspects. Chris Janczewski and Tigran Gambaryan had never worked a child protection case before – possibly because most child abuse sites hadn't had such a well-developed financial architecture. To crack the case they were going to have to follow the money, just as Chainalysis's Levin had done. But before they did so, they needed to take a look at Welcome To Video to see what they were dealing with. Creating an account was free, so Janczewski and Gambaryan registered and logged in. They were understandably horrified by what they saw. The site listed the most popular keywords users had entered. Top of the list was an abbreviation for 'one-year-old'. The second most popular was an abbreviation for 'two-year-old'.

The site claimed to have been running since March 2015, and to have had more than a million downloads of material. It contained at least 200,000 videos, and a prominent warning instructing users: 'Do not upload adult porn'.[19]

A key goal for Janczewski and Gambaryan was to find the site's IP address: the golden nugget of information that had cracked open previous online abuse sites, and which might give the IRS investigators the location of the computer server hosting Welcome To Video's content. At a minimum, they could get the site unplugged. And the server might even lead them to a real-world perpetrator, as it had done with Freedom Hosting.

As we have established, law-enforcement agencies have developed all sorts of coveted and secretive ways for revealing these IP addresses. But in this case, it was so stunningly easy that law enforcement had no need to keep it under wraps.

If you go to any website and right-click on a page, you'll see an option to 'view page source'. This reveals the code that creates the site, including the computer server addresses for each of the page's individual components; the pictures, graphics and so on. If you try this trick for a dark web site, though, the components' addresses are normally all hosted on the dark web – hidden behind layers of encryption – which doesn't help you work out the physical location of the server or the person behind it. But in the case of Welcome To

Video, the site's builder had apparently made a huge mistake. When agent Gambaryan tried right-clicking on the site, he discovered that while most of the components on the site had indeed been hidden inside the dark web, the pictures on the page were stored on a normal server, not a dark web one. Gambaryan couldn't believe his luck.

What's more, when they checked the IP address for the server hosting the pictures, they discovered that once again it tracked back to South Korea, just like the cryptocurrency payments.[20] It was a hot lead, but not necessarily the highest priority for the wider investigation team, who had more pressing concerns. Having gained entry to the site, the team had to work quickly to identify as many users as possible, suss out which ones had access to children, and prioritize chasing them in the hope the child could be rescued.

Tracing the culprits meant watching videos from the site – something Janczewski described in terms that brought to mind the scene in Anthony Burgess's book *A Clockwork Orange*, in which one of the characters is made to watch a stream of distressing videos, his eyes forced open.[21]

Meanwhile, the team had started to get responses from the cryptocurrency exchanges that Welcome To Video's members had used to make their payments to the site. As Greenberg writes:

> They began to collect the names, faces, and photos of hundreds of men – they were almost all men – from all walks of life, everywhere in the world. Their descriptions crossed boundaries of race, age, class, and nationality. All these individuals seemed to have in common was their gender and their financial connection to a worldwide, hidden haven of child abuse.[22]

One man turned out to be an assistant high school principal living with his wife and two children in a middle-class suburb on the outskirts of Atlanta. He was eventually charged with sexual assault of minors. Another was a Border Patrol agent within the Department of Homeland Security living in Texas. His wife had a young daughter, and the man had posted on social media that he hoped to adopt her. But as they delved into Welcome To Video's material, the investigating team discovered that the man was in fact filming his abuse of the same girl and uploading it to the site. He was also pulled into custody.

Gradually, the highest-priority suspects were brought in and – more importantly – the children they'd targeted were rescued from further abuse. Now the team could start to look at pursuing the site's owner, who they strongly suspected was in South Korea, given the IP address data Gambaryan had found on the site and the fact that so much of its cryptocurrency was cashed out at exchanges in the country. The investigators targeted those exchanges in the same way they'd approached the exchanges used by Welcome To Video's members – requesting the registration information that had been used to set up the accounts. The answer came back from one exchange – they sent the IRS team the account holder's photo and ID. It was a man based in South Korea. The next step in the investigation was a flight to Seoul.

In February 2018, an international team working on the Welcome To Video case arrived in South Korea. It included IRS agent Chris Janczewski and members of his team, US Homeland Security Investigations, as well as the UK's National Crime Agency and German Federal Police, who'd also been pursuing Welcome To Video.

As the IRS Criminal Investigation team had delved deeper into the IP address for the server hosting Welcome To Video's images, they realized something surprising. This wasn't a server operated by a professional company: it seemed to be just a personal computer. And its physical address matched the address given by the person who'd created the cryptocurrency exchange accounts through which the Bitcoin was cashed out. All roads led to an apartment in a province several hours' drive south of Seoul. On 5 March 2018, the international police team set out for the suspect's apartment. When they arrived, the South Korean police team moved in. The foreign contingent weren't allowed to join them – under Korean rules, only local law enforcement could enter.

As a result, Janczewski followed the search of the apartment through FaceTime video instead. On his phone's screen, he watched as the police entered the apartment, searched from room to room, and eventually reached the bedroom where they found a computer tower. It looked like the kind of thing you see buzzing away under innumerable desks in offices around the world. Yet this was the heart of Welcome To Video. This small rectangle was the repository for hundreds of thousands of videos of abused children, a digital Pandora's box, filled with the very worst things that human beings can do. Also in the flat was the computer's owner, 22-year-old Son Jong-Woo, the mastermind who had created Welcome To Video and administered it from his bedroom in Seoul.

With the raid over, US agents were eventually allowed to analyse the server, where they uncovered a trove of records of Bitcoin payments to Welcome To Video. Some members had even given their website usernames in the Bitcoin transactions, allowing investigators to directly link their payments to the videos they consumed. They compiled a list of the transactions. On the one hand, it looks like the kind of mundane payment records kept by any e-commerce website: lists of IDs, amounts, dates and orders. But then you remember that each of these represents an individual, somewhere in the world, actively seeking out child sexual abuse footage, and in some cases abusing children who trusted them in order to create more. The US Department of Justice team found that 45 per cent of the clips contained new images that were not previously known to law enforcement. Once again, the urgent, harrowing task began of identifying and locating as many children as possible. As of October 2019, twenty-three had been rescued in the US, Spain and the UK.[23]

Having seized a copy of the Welcome To Video server from Son's bedroom, the IRS team could construct a complete database of the site's members and their activity. They could then combine that with the real-world identities they'd received from the cryptocurrency exchanges through which the men had made their payments. The map of offenders stretched from Australia to the Czech Republic. The IRS team sent out details of those suspects to police forces in their respective countries. Janczewski and his colleagues would sometimes have to explain to less experienced officers in other countries how Bitcoin worked, so they understood why the men were being accused based on 'funny Internet money'.[24] In the end, 337 people from at least eighteen countries who used Welcome To Video were arrested and charged, and 223 of them were South Korean.[25]

With Son in custody, the trial soon began and all eyes were on South Korea. How would its justice system deal with the young man behind one of the world's most prolific paedophile websites? In 2018, Son was sentenced to two years in prison, suspended for three years. He then appealed, hoping for an even shorter sentence. In the meantime, he got married, and part of his appeal case was his need to support his new family. Perhaps as a result, his sentence was then cut to eighteen months. He's subsequently reported to have annulled the marriage.[26] Predictably, the court's treatment of Son was met with howls of anger in the press and also among the wider public. The outcry worsened when the South Korean courts refused to extradite him to the US, where he faced a longer sentence, on the grounds that it would hamper South Korea's own investigations.

And so, Son was released from custody and walked free. News photographers were there to greet him when he did, though his face was blurred out in the coverage – apparently thanks to South Korea's media laws – a courtesy he and his fellow offenders didn't extend to their many victims. If, like many, you're dismayed at the treatment of Son, there's better news when it comes to the various other abusers and enablers covered in this chapter.

Eric Marques, who ran Freedom Hosting and provided a home for sites like Hurt2TheCore, pleaded guilty to conspiracy to advertise child pornography and was sentenced to twenty-seven years in September 2021.[27]

Lux, the man behind Hurt2TheCore, was also eventually caught, and revealed to be Matthew Graham, a nanotechnology student living in a quiet suburb just outside Melbourne, Australia. He'd set up the site when he was just eighteen. In September 2015, Graham pleaded guilty to thirteen charges, and was later sentenced to fifteen and a half years in jail.[28]

And in the UK two years later, the Birmingham academic Matthew Falder, the man behind the Inthegarden and Evilmind handles, was sentenced to thirty-two years in prison.[29] On appeal this was dropped to twenty-five, of which he'll serve a minimum of sixteen years.

It's hard not to see parallels between the cases of Graham and Falder, beyond their shared Christian name. Both were bright young men trained in the sciences, both outwardly polite and seemingly brought up in nice, middle-class families. To the outside world, there was nothing unusual about their lives, no giveaway of their horrific alter egos. Graham lived in a normal residential home in a sleepy little suburb in Victoria with his parents and his sister. But, of course, we can never truly know what lies behind the public appearance. When new owners moved into the Graham family house, for example, they reportedly found a small piece of graffiti scrawled inside a bedroom wardrobe which read: 'Parents should be afraid of raising children like us.'[30]

The insidious nature of such crimes – the idea that they can be going on in any household, among your neighbours, your colleagues – can have a corrosive and long-lasting impact on anyone they touch. Matthew Falder's former colleague tells me that after Falder's conviction he read every single media report that he could find on the case. 'I wanted to understand how I'd missed it,' he said. 'You wouldn't believe the number of nights this has kept me awake. Even in hindsight, I still can't pick out even a single time that I can be like, "I should have known from that". When I think back about him, I can think of a whole bunch of examples of kindness, generosity. In hindsight, all of those occasions of being nice, was that part of the act? Was all of that an act? It undoubtedly made me distrust my own judgement of people forever after.' But as he points out: 'It was a million times less for me than for any of his actual victims, I had nothing compared to them.'

Beatrice, the 15-year-old whom Falder groomed on Gumtree and blackmailed into supplying ever more photos of herself, will be in her twenties at the time this book is published. She has been profoundly harmed by his actions. She feels she can't talk about what happened to her, even with those closest to her.

Worryingly, research from Chainalysis, the cryptocurrency-tracing firm that helped track the Welcome To Video money, indicates that the child sex abuse industry is growing and that cryptocurrency and related laundering are a contributing factor. In 2019, crypto payments for such material rose by an astonishing 32 per cent, to almost $1m. That may not seem a high figure compared to other crimes covered in this book, but it's simply an indication of scale. As the NCA's Matt Sutton pointed out, much child sexual abuse material changes hands on a barter system, leaving no financial trace at all. At least in the Welcome To Video case, there was a money trail to follow. And, thankfully, the offenders' attempts at hiding and laundering their crypto were ham-fisted enough to give investigators a head start. In the classic three-stage laundering cycle – placement, layering, integration – Son had no problem with placement. His enterprise was digital-first and the payments were all in cryptocurrency, so he had no need to try and finagle the money into traditional finance. Instead, Son struggled with the layering stage; he did so little to obfuscate the money trail that it led police straight to his door. It's a vital stage in any effective laundering operation, throwing investigators off the scent. And as we'll see in the next chapter, even as the dust was settling on the horrific cases of Son, Falder and Graham, technology was already providing other crooks with a handy solution to just this part of the money-laundering problem.

5.

Dark Gold

Detroit has Motown. Vegas has casinos. Akron has rubber. The Ohio city of just under 200,000 inhabitants is nicknamed 'the rubber capital of the world', and has long been home to the famous Goodyear Tire company. But at the tail-end of the 2010s there was another, more white-collar industry taking off in the city: tech companies. A crop of digital start-ups had suddenly taken root in the area, bringing a bit of Silicon Valley stardust to the Midwest. Local media talked of lavish parties and extravagant bar tabs.[1]

Among the new arrivals was a tiny business called Coin Ninja. It was based in a converted period building conveniently situated right opposite one of the city's many indie breweries. Like any self-respecting tech firm it had an Instagram feed, with photos showing a buzzy, open-plan office populated by smiley young workers. They wore sponsored T-shirts and hoodies and enjoyed the odd pizza night. There was also the staple toy of many an IT start-up: Nerf guns.

'I got shot with a Nerf dart at least once,' remembers George Butiri. He'd started at the firm in April 2018, joining a team of about half a dozen, working as web developer. Butiri had a life-long passion for code, and enjoyed turning his hand to just about anything software-based, which made him the perfect employee for a scrappy start-up trying to get its ideas off the ground. He'd moved from California to Ohio for the job, and quickly fell in love with the buzz of the city and his new workplace. 'A lot of intelligent people, a lot of great minds to bounce ideas off,' he remembers. 'Everybody was friendly. One of the guys there, his wife even knitted me a sweater. The food was great, they always had snacks like protein bars that you could chew on, and the coffee was really good too. It was the perfect location because around us was just breweries and restaurants.'

A big part of Butiri's attraction to Coin Ninja was the company's boss, 35-year-old Larry Harmon. He was whip smart, technically skilled and managed to combine a laid-back attitude with a drive to succeed. Perhaps more importantly, he was loaded.

'He had a couple of Teslas,' remembers Butiri. The electric vehicles were a status symbol for any budding tech entrepreneur. 'One of them was the company's. He let employees borrow it over the weekend. I got to drive the Tesla for a bit, which was so cool.'

Tom Dodd started at Coin Ninja the same year as Butiri.[2] He also remembers the Tesla, a Model X, top of the range with its distinctively futuristic up-and-over Falcon Wing doors. Dodd too found Larry Harmon a gifted boss who was humble despite his apparent wealth.

Dodd and Butiri set to work on the company's big idea – an app called DropBit that would make sending cryptocurrency from one person to another as simple as sending a text message. Dodd also fell in love with the company and its team, describing them as 'visionaries'. 'It was one of the most collaborative environments I've ever been in. Everybody worked really well together. It was a fantastic place to work and I miss it every day,' he tells me. Adding to the family atmosphere was the fact that Larry's brother, Gary, was also working for the company and had taken up residence in part of the office complex.

But there was a niggling issue at the heart of Coin Ninja's chummy, easy-going world. No one seemed to know quite where Larry Harmon's money had come from.

'I kind of understood that he was an early investor in Bitcoin and maybe that paid off for him,' Dodd tells me. 'He'd retired, essentially, and then got bored and decided to start this company. It was clear that he probably didn't have to work. But he did. He showed up every day.'

Butiri wasn't sure about the origins of Larry's wealth either, despite regular chats with his boss. 'I didn't really ask too many questions,' he says. 'I was just really happy that I could do my own thing.' In fairness, it's hardly unusual to find an entrepreneur who's made a stack of money from some obscure tech venture. If you go to the right bars in San Francisco, Tel Aviv or Shanghai you'll find herds of them. But there were hints that Larry Harmon was suspiciously unwilling to discuss his earlier career.

'We talked about tech all the time,' says Butiri. 'He mentioned a search engine he had created, so I wanted to pick his brains about it. He told me it was just a cool search engine to be able to find things and just left it at that. He talked about it in general terms, he said it had some cool algorithms.'

In fact, Larry Harmon was hiding a very dark secret; one that he'd never share with the besotted employees of Coin Ninja, but one that would eventually massively impact on all their lives – Larry's especially. The easy-going tech bro had a sinister alter ego: he was the undisputed king of dark web money laundering, having made a revolutionary leap in the layering stage of the process. Once again, tech innovation had unlocked a key stage in the cycle, enabling crooks to wash their dirty funds with ease.

As the previous chapter detailed, the dark web was first created as a network of secretive sites only accessible using special anonymizing software. If anyone tries to visit these sites using a normal web browser like Chrome, they will get an error message. And that's why these sites don't show up on Google, Bing and other search engines, which work by scanning the web and indexing sites. The dark web sites don't exist on the normal web, so they don't get scanned.

So . . . how do you find your way around the dark web? When I first encountered it in 2011, there was no real search engine, no short cut, no index. I just had to dive in, follow some links and, most importantly, bookmark everything as I went along. (Dark web sites don't have catchy addresses like eBay.com or Facebook.com. They're long, randomly generated strings and you stand little chance of remembering them.)

It was only a matter of time before someone tried to bring this chaotic situation to an end and, sure enough, dark web search engines appeared. It can't have been easy for their developers. Unlike normal websites, a lot of dark web enterprises are cagey about being too high profile. While they're keen to get customers, they don't necessarily want to be scanned and indexed by a legitimate, mainstream search engine, for obvious reasons. But in April 2014, one of the most effective dark web search engines appeared on the scene.[3] Grams was a cheeky rip-off of Google, blatantly copying its colour scheme and layout. It even had GramsWords, an equivalent of Google's AdWords, which allowed advertisers to pay money so that their link would appear when someone searched a particular term.[4] Grams was a really handy tool for journalists like me trying to navigate the dark web, find data leaks and track hackers. But for others it had more quotidian uses: it allowed people to search for their favourite drug dealers' profiles on multiple dark web sites. Was Grams illegal? Probably not. After all, it wasn't creating the sites with their illicit content, it was just indexing them. But what its creators did next would prove a whole lot more controversial.

Grams had a problem: it wanted to charge money to the dark web sites that were keen to use features like GramsWords to increase their traffic. But of course, those sites' owners were mainly crooks, who needed assurances of anonymity before they would pay. Even using Bitcoin wasn't enough: by now, a lot of dark web site owners had figured out that Bitcoin was traceable via the publicly available online blockchain record and could end up revealing people's identities, as it did for the owner of Welcome To Video. What they'd learned was that, although Bitcoin solved the placement stage of the money-laundering process, it didn't necessarily help with the layering aspect that could obscure the trail from the money to the crime. If the dark web site owners paid Grams in cryptocurrency, they feared that the cops would have a money trail they could follow back to the people behind the sites.

So Grams's owners created a solution. It was a piece of software that would take in a customer's Bitcoins, shuffle them around with a whole bunch of other cryptocurrency, and then return Bitcoins to the customer that were unconnected to their original stash. In those days such tools were called 'tumblers', but now they're referred to as 'mixers'. There are some very reasonable arguments in favour of mixers: namely that they help to keep crypto transactions private. But, on the other hand, they're also a godsend when it comes to the layering stage of money laundering.

Grams's mixer technology started out as an internal capability, but in June 2014, its owners took the plunge and launched it publicly under the name Helix.[5] It wasn't the first or only mixer on offer, but its promotion on Grams made it very successful. The idea of such mixer software is that its owners remain wilfully blind as to the money trails going through it. Sure enough, Helix pledged to delete logs of all transactions after seven days, to erase any digital trace of the incoming and outgoing funds.[6] But if those behind Helix thought they could claim they didn't know what was being mixed and what trade they were enabling, their subsequent involvement in one of the biggest dark web crime sites ever created would go on to severely weaken that argument.

December 2014 saw the creation of AlphaBay, a site that would ultimately become a colossus of online wrongdoing. It followed in the footsteps of Silk Road, itself a site that had become iconic and introduced many people (myself included, in the capacity of interested journalist) to the dark web. Silk Road was a giant marketplace, mainly enabling trade in drugs, but had been shut down in a US law-enforcement operation in October 2013. AlphaBay appeared on the scene just over a year later, determined to inherit the legendary site's mantle.[7]

It carried over some of Silk Road's key innovations: buyers could leave star reviews and ratings for sellers, for example, to inspire the trust that might otherwise be lacking in an online criminal transaction. But as soon as I visited AlphaBay, I realized it had a key difference – it attracted more than just drug dealers. Hackers, fraudsters, data traders and more were all mixing freely. Adverts for high-quality cocaine could be found alongside those for stolen databases of personal information, fake passports and password-cracking tools. There'd been a bit of non-drug stuff on Silk Road, but not on this scale. AlphaBay was like the digital version of the Mos Eisley spaceport in *Star Wars* – a wretched hive of scum and villainy.

Perhaps as a result, within less than a year, AlphaBay was seeing traffic that put Silk Road in the shade, boasting almost double the number of drug listings and more than 200,000 users.[8] By 2016 it accounted for more than half of the entire dark web market,[9] and the following year was estimated to be handling revenues of $800,000 per day.[10] The drug dealers fuelling this trade were enjoying a bonanza: according to Chainalysis, one of them was spending $17,000 per year in crypto just on postal services to dispatch the drugs.[11]

All of this trade was conducted in crypto, mainly Bitcoin. With so much money sloshing about, perhaps it was inevitable that AlphaBay's buyers and sellers would be fishing for a service that could hide and launder their crypto, to achieve the all-important layering stage. The natural choice was Helix, the mixer launched by Grams. In November 2016, AlphaBay integrated Helix's software into its website, recommending it as their mixer of choice, and they weren't the only ones. Helix's owners were working to integrate with multiple dark web marketplaces, thirty-nine in all, tweaking Helix's software so that it could work with their different platforms.[12] There was a very good reason to do this customer outreach work: Helix charged a 2.5 per cent fee for every transaction sent via its service.[13] With AlphaBay handling millions of dollars of deals, even if Helix only handled a fraction of the trade, its owners would still be clearing hundreds of thousands of dollars a year.

But it wasn't just drugs dealers and hackers whose transactions Helix was enabling. Anyone could use the service on a no-questions-asked basis. Helix laundered at least seventy-three Bitcoins connected to Welcome To Video, for instance (so it seems that at least some of Welcome To Video's customers were taking precautions to hide their payments from law enforcement).

But it was AlphaBay that was Helix's biggest cash cow, providing an estimated two-thirds of its income.[14] Unfortunately for Helix, US investigators had their sights firmly set on this dark web leviathan, and their fates were to become intertwined.

As AlphaBay swelled in size, the US Drug Enforcement Administration (DEA) began to see it as the natural next target following the Silk Road bust. But AlphaBay seemed like it would be an even tougher nut to crack. The person running it, under the alias Alpha02, seemed exceptionally cautious, rarely making a mistake and boasting of his security prowess. He appeared to have learned many lessons from the downfall of Silk Road's founder, Ross Ulbricht, who was caught out after revealing his real email address in an Internet forum comment, posted in the very early days of the site. Yet, remarkably, it would be a similar email slip-up that would put law enforcement on the trail of the mastermind behind AlphaBay.

In November 2016, US police got a tip-off from someone who'd registered on AlphaBay and made a surprising discovery. He'd received a welcome email from the site, and hidden inside the email's background data was an address, pimp_alex_91@hotmail.com.[15] DEA agents started looking into the email address and found it had also been used on a French social media site, along with photos from a user named 'Alex'. It also appeared on another French website alongside the name 'Alexandre Cazes', who'd also used the username Alpha02.

Thanks to these online breadcrumbs, the DEA had a name for the mysterious owner of AlphaBay. With this information in hand, it didn't take US authorities long to trace their suspect to Bangkok, Thailand, where he was living a life of opulence. He had multiple properties worth millions of dollars, several mistresses and a garage full of fast cars (the latter was to prove a bit of a problem for investigators: when US cops asked if the Thai police could attach a tracking beacon to the underside of the suspect's $1m Lamborghini, they discovered it rode so low to the ground that the device wouldn't fit).[16]

Cazes was firmly in the sights of both Thai and US officials. As they studied his online habits, they found he had something else in common with Ulbricht. Like the Silk Road founder, Cazes used encryption software that would scramble the contents of his laptop if he so much as closed the lid. To catch him red-handed, they'd have to lure him away from his laptop, which wasn't going to be easy. And the pressure on the investigating team was about to go up a notch, thanks to a discovery by Dutch police that would move the case into high gear.

In 2016, Bas Doorn was a fresh-faced university graduate working for the Specialist High Tech Crime Unit at the Dutch National Prosecutor's Office. He'd watched the takedown of Silk Road, along with various subsequent dark web markets, with interest, but also with increasing dismay. Law enforcement, he concluded, faced a 'water bed problem'. If you jump on a water bed to try to burst it, the water just moves to another part. Similarly, each time a big dark web market got closed, its users would simply migrate to another site, swelling its numbers. To make a real impact, reckoned Doorn, police needed to dive on to multiple bits of the water bed at once. And because of the AlphaBay investigation, they would soon get their chance.

In autumn 2016, Dutch police had been tipped off that their country was home to one of the computer servers hosting Hansa, which at the time was the second biggest dark web market behind AlphaBay. They'd then found other Hansa servers in Germany, where police had identified the two people running the site and were ready to make an arrest. What's more, analysing the German servers had given Dutch police access to the two administrators' private encryption keys – effectively, the passwords to the entire site. They realized that with the site's administrators behind bars, they could use the encryption keys to log in as the admins, take over Hansa and run the whole thing, capturing reams of valuable criminal deals as they happened. It was a brilliant opportunity, but controversial: it would involve Dutch police running a criminal website, something they could only justify doing for a limited time, perhaps a couple of weeks at most. But as the Dutch worked out how to cuckoo their way into Hansa and deal with the ethical concerns, the investigation took another sudden lurch forward.

As part of their separate AlphaBay investigation, US police had discovered some Dutch aspects to the site's infrastructure. They went to the Netherlands to request help, letting the Dutch know about their work on AlphaBay. Suddenly, Bas Doorn and his colleagues saw a golden opportunity for a double dive on to the water bed. If US authorities could shut down AlphaBay, many of its users would simply head for the next best thing: Hansa. But if Dutch police were running Hansa at the time, they'd be able to hoover up all the new deals and data from this influx of crooks. Operation Bayonet was born.

To make the plan work, the Dutch Specialist High Tech Crime Unit would need to copy the entire architecture of the Hansa site, and rebuild it on their own computers at their HQ in Driebergen. Replicating someone else's code is tricky at the best of times. Every programmer has their own quirks. And in this case, Dutch cops could hardly ask the administrators for a helping hand. But, gradually, Doorn and his colleagues recreated Hansa. They even found a few tweaks they could make to improve the site. As if it wasn't weird enough for Dutch police to be getting ready to run a dark web criminal marketplace, they now found themselves actively improving it.

On 20 June 2017, German police arrested the Hansa administrators[17] and simultaneously the Dutch police went live with their version of the site. The switch-over had to be seamless; there could be no delay in payments or transactions, or users might be tipped off that something was amiss. The team sat glued to their machines, day and night, like parents of a newborn baby watching for any signs of trouble.

Meanwhile, as Greenberg details in *Tracers in the Dark*, an international delegation had arrived in Bangkok to oversee the arrest of Alexandre Cazes, who was of course oblivious to the secret police takeover of Hansa, and his own imminent capture. A veritable alphabet soup of law-enforcement agencies checked into the luxurious Athenee Hotel: the FBI, DEA, DoJ, IRS, DHS and even the Royal Canadian Mounted Police (as Cazes was a Canadian citizen) all joined the delegation.[18] A few of them were sitting in the lobby discussing their plot for the meticulously planned arrest of their target when, suddenly, Cazes walked right by them. The team froze: had they been rumbled? Had the canny dark web kingpin been counter-surveilling them? In fact, it was complete coincidence: Cazes happened to be going for a drink at the hotel bar. Luckily, he was entirely unaware of the identities of his pursuers, and the US agents slunk away to their rooms, furiously texting each other about their close shave.

On 5 July, Cazes was working at home in his luxury villa as usual, when there was a kerfuffle outside. A woman had been trying to reverse her car in the narrow lane leading to his house and had smashed into Cazes's front gate. She was now yelling at Cazes's wife. He went down to sort out the mess. But, in reality, the woman in the car wasn't an angry bad driver – she was a plain-clothes Thai police officer. The crash had been a stunt to lure Cazes out of his house, and he now found himself surrounded by US agents and Thai police.

Amazingly for a man who boasted on his site of his security prowess, Cazes had left his laptop inside, open and unlocked, and logged in as administrator of AlphaBay, allowing investigators to sweep in and take over the site. Handily, he'd also left files on his machine detailing his assets and net worth (Silk Road's founder, Ross Ulbricht, had in fact made the same mistake). The total was $23m.[19]

With AlphaBay under their control, US law enforcement were able to enact phase one of Operation Bayonet: they took down AlphaBay and replaced the site's front page with a notice in big letters stating 'This hidden site has been seized', along with the logos of the various law-enforcement agencies involved. Users were annoyed, but not deterred. They'd seen dark web sites go down before, after all. As Bas Doorn predicted, many of them simply migrated to the next-biggest option, Hansa, unaware that the site was now a honeypot being run by Dutch police.

Doorn and his colleagues worked furiously to handle the influx – Hansa witnessed an eightfold increase in traffic – and for a while they had to close the site to new registrations.[20] They also had to come up with a solution to the ethical problems of a police force running a criminal site and potentially enabling crimes. In the end, they meticulously tracked the transactions so that perpetrators could be arrested after the operation was over.

After three weeks, Dutch police felt they'd stretched the exercise as far as they could, and they shut down Hansa, slapping a 'seized' notice on the front page just as the US cops had done with AlphaBay. The reaction on dark web markets was swift: panic ensued, as users realized they'd been caught out in a carefully planned, two-punch sting operation. Dutch and US authorities parcelled up the intelligence they'd gathered and distributed it to relevant forces around the world so they could arrest AlphaBay and Hansa users.

Meanwhile, back in Thailand things were about to take a dark turn. AlphaBay's founder, Alexandre Cazes, had been in Thai Police custody since his arrest, as the US team tried to coax him into co-operating. But on 12 July 2017, his jailers found him pale and lifeless on the floor of his cell. The official explanation was that he committed suicide by hanging himself with his towel, although his lawyer and some in his family have never accepted this. Whatever the truth, Cazes would never face trial.

A few months later, a post appeared on the social media site Reddit from the administrator of Helix, stating that the crypto-mixing service was being halted. It made no mention of the demise of AlphaBay, its biggest customer. In fact, there was no mention of police activity at all. Instead, under the title 'So Long, and Thanks for All the Fish' (a reference to a Douglas Adams novel), someone with the username 'gramsadmin' wrote: 'It has become too difficult to get the listings from the markets and to keep up on even routine maintenance of the site. I have had a hard year personally and financially.'[21] What he almost certainly didn't realize was that, over the next few years, it would get a lot harder still. His hi-tech laundering empire was falling apart, piece by piece, as his careful efforts at layering his customers' illegal earnings (and his own profits) were unpicked by his pursuers.

★

It was less than three years after that Reddit post, on 6 February 2020, that Tom Dodd was getting ready for a normal day's work at Coin Ninja, the cryptocurrency start-up in Akron, Ohio, that he'd joined a couple of years previously. He was working from home that morning when one of his colleagues messaged him to say he was having trouble logging on to the company's network.

'So naturally I tried to log in, and I couldn't get in either,' recalls Dodd. 'I realized I couldn't access anything. We all thought "What's going on here?"'

Eventually somebody contacted Gary Harmon, who lived in the office building and was the brother of Coin Ninja's boss, Larry. 'That's when we found out the FBI had come in and raided the building,' says Dodd. 'They essentially took every electronic piece of equipment, which is why we couldn't log in. [. . .] We were all just in shock. Then it finally came out that they had taken Larry as well.'

Someone had discovered where Coin Ninja's well-loved boss got his money, and it wasn't going to work out well for Larry or his employees.

Investigators in the AlphaBay case had started digging into the site's crypto streams and had been looking deeply into Helix too. They discovered the mixer wasn't quite so effective as its owners made out. The specifics of how law enforcement undid the privacy-preserving tech and unscrambled Helix's layers of mixing haven't been made fully public, but Jonathan Levin, co-founder of crypto-currency chasing firm Chainalysis, gave a hint to journalist Andy Greenberg: 'Any decent mixer splits large sums of coins into smaller, less conspicuous payments when returning the money to its owner. But with transaction fees for every payment, there's a limit to how much big sums of money will be broken up.'[22]

To use an analogy: if a drug dealer gives you a $100 bill from cocaine profits, one way to wash it is to break it down into $1 bills, mix those with a whole bunch of other, untainted $1 bills, and then scoop up the equivalent $100 in change and hand it back to the drug dealer. That's because the more bills there are in the mix, the harder it is to link each dirty bill to a clean one. But if you have to pay a fee for every banknote you use, then that jacks up the cost. So instead of $1 bills, you might be tempted to break the $100 into $10 notes to save on fees. But if you do that, it makes the tracing a lot easier. When it comes to the layering stage of money laundering, the more layers, the better.

It seems Helix wasn't mixing as thoroughly as it should have been. The investigators were able to untangle some of its labyrinthine transactions, and as they did so, they noticed regular payments being made which looked suspiciously like the 2.5 per cent commission fee Helix was charging. If that was the case, wherever those regular payments went, it was likely to lead to whoever was behind Helix.

Sure enough, they tracked one of the 2.5 per cent commission crypto payments back to a company called BitPay, where it had been used to buy a gift card. The BitPay account in turn led police to a Google account, which they discovered belonged to none other than Larry Harmon. What's more, the account contained a photo he'd taken using Google Glass (it seems the tech-obsessed Larry was a keen user of the webcam-enabled specs). It showed him logged in to the administrator screen of Helix.[23] Harmon was bang to rights, caught on his own camera.

Investigators discovered that Helix had mixed more than $311m worth of crypto over its short lifetime.[24] At a fee of 2.5 per cent, that would have netted Harmon just over $7.8m. No wonder he could afford to rent a villa in Belize (which was also searched as part of the investigation). And he could bankroll the creation of Coin Ninja, the start-up where Tom Dodd and George Butiri worked, which seems to have been unconnected to Harmon's dark web escapades.[25]

Harmon's case provoked an intense debate – one that will percolate throughout this book – about money and privacy. One of the founding arguments for cryptocurrencies like Bitcoin is that they can enable anonymous transactions. In a world of near-ubiquitous online surveillance by private companies and public bodies alike, that debate is assuming increasing importance. Looked at through this lens, services like Helix take on a fresh hue.

As Tom Dodd, former Coin Ninja worker, observes: 'It was a tool that provided privacy. Granted, it was associated with less-than-ideal money transfers. I view it as Larry tiptoeing up to the line of legality, and perhaps he took a step over. In my opinion, they're using Larry to set the precedent that these sort of things are illegal. They were sort of questionably legal before, and now they're definitely illegal.' Harmon's partner, Margo, seems to agree. She told a journalist: 'He just wanted to help people have better privacy. It's a basic right we are guaranteed in the Constitution.'[26]

Ethics aside, Larry Harmon's case took a bizarre twist as it made its way through the courts. During his arrest, police seized an encrypted drive containing sixteen Bitcoin wallets, which they say held some of Helix's profits. The cops knew the wallet addresses, and thanks to the blockchain they could see their contents, though they couldn't get access to the money because Harmon refused to give up the password. Then suddenly, over five days in April 2020, the police could see on the blockchain that half of the wallets had been emptied out; $5.3m worth of crypto had vanished from under their noses. The encrypted device was locked safely away in their evidence room, unconnected to the Internet, and yet someone, somehow, had managed to get access to the wallets contained on it in order to steal millions. How?

It turned out the drive's encryption software had a backup feature, which allowed a user to recreate its contents by typing a unique sequence of words into a duplicate drive. Someone had used this ingenious backup procedure to steal the money – but who? The prosecutors' suspicions turned to Gary Harmon, who'd been in court for his brother's hearing when the wallets were mentioned. A string of tell-tale clues certainly put him in the frame. Prosecutors discovered that, during one week, Gary had received several emails from the company that made the encryption software for the drive the wallets were stored on. Then suddenly he bought an Audi S5 car, hired a private jet from a company that accepted Bitcoin payments and was photographed sitting in a bathtub apparently full of banknotes, surrounded by scantily-clad women. All this while he was unemployed and supposedly living on state benefits. He was arrested in July 2021, charged with money laundering, obstruction and removal of property to prevent seizure. In January 2023 he pleaded guilty and was sentenced to four years three months in prison.[27] Meanwhile, Larry also pleaded guilty in August 2021, agreeing to forfeit 4,440 Bitcoins, which were at the time worth $200m.[28]

Helix was meant to be the perfect laundry machine – a piece of software that could effortlessly handle the layering of vast quantities of crypto. But it had failed. In addition, Operation Bayonet damaged trust in dark web markets like AlphaBay and Hansa. Despite the takedowns and prosecutions, however, the dark web soon bounced back. AlphaBay was subsequently relaunched, apparently by one of its original administrators, and was joined by a slew of other sites keen to become top dog in a highly lucrative marketplace. Dark web drug dealers, hackers and fraudsters kept on dealing. But for some, the experience of Helix made them doubt whether crypto mixers were the best idea when it came to the layering stage of money laundering. They still needed some kind of solution, however, to mix their illicit profits and cover the tracks connecting the money to the crime. And there was no shortage of innovative financial criminals ready to supply them, as one enigmatic drug dealer's story illustrates.

Sam Bent is an instantly likeable character: he's short and rotund, with a wizardly beard, an infectious chuckle and a tendency towards long conversational meanders. He's also got an extensive criminal history as an inveterate drug dealer. He'd started selling cocaine and marijuana in his teenage years, but when he moved to Vermont, aged twenty, he hit a problem. 'In business you always have these bottlenecks,' he tells me. 'My bottleneck was distribution, because living in Vermont there are, you know, 600,000 people in the entire state. Finding buyers is a real challenge. I wanted to have a distribution network and I wanted it to be reliable.' It wasn't long before he discovered the solution: dark web markets. He soon rebranded himself (among other aliases) as 2happytimes2.

Like many dark web sellers, Bent dispatched his drugs via regular US post. To the uninitiated that may sound like a foolish tactic, but in fact it is a very popular approach. This is partly because national postal services handle so many parcels that they simply can't inspect every one. Bent liked those odds. 'How hard is it to find my one package out of 21.5 billion?' he reasoned. 'They also have more locations than anyone else, and they can get from "Tor to door" in three days, which is great,' he says, referencing the dark web browser software.

But there was a snag to using the service. 'You need to have a valid return address,' says Bent. It was no good simply making something up; Bent learned that the address had to be real, and had to have the real occupant's name to match. Of course, there was no way Bent was going to use his own details. And he knew that if he used someone else's, they could well get a knock at the door if the package was opened and drugs were found inside. Bent felt that incriminating unwitting, innocent people would be unfair. So, he started hunting round. 'I was sure that somewhere there existed a database of people that I considered personally to be people OK to screw over,'[29] he says. That's when Bent found the National Sex Offender Public Website, a US government-run register of convicted sex offenders, complete with their full names and addresses. 'If the parcel got sent back to them, or if they got raided, I didn't really have any qualms about that,' he says.

Understandably, Bent took his security very seriously. Rather than use his own Internet connection, he hijacked his neighbour's Wi-Fi. He then kept the neighbour's house under surveillance with a telescope, knowing that if law enforcement traced the Internet connection, they would go first to his neighbour, giving him some time to escape. 'If I saw a bunch of black SUVs rolling up, I could assume I had to . . . get rid of everything and clean the house, because my neighbour was getting raided,' he says.

All of this was part of Bent's 'opsec' – operational security. It even extended to hiding his linguistic tics when he communicated on the dark web, so as not to give away the slightest detail about himself. 'I'm from New England, and we tend to say the word "wicked" to describe something as very good,' he says. 'If I use that terminology in a forum and law enforcement picks that up, now they know, "OK, this guy's from New England".' So Bent learned to mind his language online.

With these counter-surveillance measures in place, Sam started making money from his dark web business; in cryptocurrency, of course. He then had to work out how to layer it, in order to wash it of any connection to crime. He was leery of using mixers or tumblers like Helix (rightfully, as it turned out). 'Personally, I hate Bitcoin tumblers,' he tells me. 'I never used them. I don't like sending my Bitcoin to someone I don't know.'

Then, one day, he found someone offering a great solution: a dark web user with the handle GOLD. People could send their Bitcoin to GOLD's wallets, and for a 10 per cent fee he would send them the equivalent amount of cash in the mail. For a homebody like Sam, it was handy. 'I don't have to go anywhere,' he enthused. But Bent's plan would backfire, punching a hole in his carefully nurtured opsec. Because, like many people on the Internet, GOLD wasn't quite who he appeared to be.

As an assistant special agent in the Cyber Division of Homeland Security Investigations' New York office, Ricky Patel was spending an increasing amount of time chasing dealers as the dark web took off. His team would often use fairly low-tech tactics, making small test purchases of drugs and looking for tell-tale clues on the packages, like fingerprints (exactly the kind of giveaways Sam Bent was keen to avoid with his obsessive opsec). But there was a frustrating sense that they were simply playing Whac-A-Mole at the downstream end of the business, and not doing enough to tackle the mechanisms supporting the trade.

And so in January 2016, he and his team, along with the US Postal Inspection Service, hit on a different idea. 'Let's figure out where all these drug dealers go to cash out. Let's target the money launderer,' he tells me.

And, handily, they didn't have to work too hard to find some likely candidates. Most dark web markets allowed users to leave star ratings for those offering their services. And that applied to money launderers as much as to drug dealers. 'It's all based on ratings, right?' says Patel. 'We were looking for the ones that have thousands upon thousands of reviews that are five star.'

And that's how they came across GOLD, who by this point was laundering millions by taking in Bitcoin from dark web traders like Sam Bent and posting out cash. Patel's team made some test purchases, sending crypto to GOLD, then trying to trace back the packages of cash that GOLD sent out to them. By October 2016 they'd tracked him down to an apartment in New York. Changing crypto into cash is not in itself illegal. But knowingly doing it for dark web drug dealers is. And besides, GOLD didn't have a licence to operate as a money transfer business. GOLD was eventually arrested and agreed to cooperate, meaning Homeland Security and Investigations could now use some of the same tactics the Dutch police had used on Hansa: taking over GOLD's account and interacting with his customers. Operation Dark Gold was born.

Ironically, as they posed as GOLD, Patel's team were very much alive to the same linguistic tics Sam Bent had been watching out for in his communications. The HSI team needed to impersonate GOLD perfectly. 'We were studying his text and writing. All of that was to try to keep the persona up,' says Patel.

As each laundering request came in, Patel's team had to connect it to the dark web ID of the person submitting it, substantiate that it came from some kind of illegal activity, dispatch the cash, and put in place local surveillance to track the package as it made its way back to the dealer. It created dozens of leads – one of which was Sam Bent.[30]

In June 2018, Bent was having his morning coffee when the doorbell rang. He should have been suspicious. After all, 'The only people in three or four years who had ever come to that house were

Jehovah's Witnesses,' he says. But he opened the door and was greeted by a Department of Homeland Security team in full tactical gear. 'I was like "All right, I guess you want to come in then?",' says Bent. 'He's like "Yeah, that'd be good."'

Bent pleaded guilty and in August 2019 was sentenced to five years in jail. He was among thirty-five people arrested as part of Operation Dark Gold, in which $23m was seized.[31]

But prison proved to be just another challenge for Bent's obsessive, febrile mind. He studied law, successfully applied for compassionate release on health grounds and was out in eighteen months. He now advocates on behalf of other prisoners.[32]

And what of GOLD, the Bitcoin launderer who sparked the whole sting operation in the first place? He'd clearly collaborated with the investigation, but that wouldn't have been enough to save him from prosecution. I imagined that the US Department of Justice would have no trouble fishing out the details of his case for me. But no. Despite several attempts, the DoJ was not forthcoming, which I found confusing. Then, several weeks after I'd finished researching the story, I received an anonymous email with a document attached. It was an Alabama District Court judgement from February 2019, in which a man had been sentenced to two years in prison with an additional two years' supervised release. This, the anonymous emailer claimed, was GOLD. The DoJ still refused to confirm it, but the details matched pretty closely: he was arrested at the right time and charged with the right offences – laundering and running an unlicensed money-transmitting business. And if the anonymous source was correct, GOLD had chosen a very appropriate pseudonym: in addition to the $10m the defendant had been forced to forfeit, he also gave up dozens of extremely rare and valuable gold coins, including a stash of South African Krugerrands worth more than $1,000 each.

GOLD's conviction may have been hush-hush, but the DoJ had no problem publicizing the dozens of others they'd nailed. The high-profile convictions of Sam Bent and others sent yet another shock wave through the dark web marketplaces. Between the

AlphaBay–Hansa double takedown, the Helix fiasco and now Operation Dark Gold, things were looking decidedly tough for dark web crooks looking to sell drugs and other illegal goods, and clean the resultant dirty money. It turned out that, while crypto was proving very useful for placing criminal cash into a financial system, achieving the layering stage of the laundering cycle wasn't as easy. One-person operations like GOLD's were clearly susceptible to infiltration, and relying on hi-tech crypto mixers would only work if they were of a big enough scale to fox the gifted analysts who'd broken open Helix. Thankfully for the dealers (and many other online crooks too), a site would soon emerge that would put the money-laundering skills of all its predecessors in the shade. It would become a true behemoth of financial crime facilitation, so big that for years it would artfully master the layering stage that had proved such a challenge for the likes of Larry Harmon and GOLD.

6.

The Hydra

Andrey Kaganskikh remembers the first time he saw them. It was late at night, and the Russian journalist was standing in the kitchen of his third-floor apartment in Moscow, smoking, when he looked down and saw three young men scrabbling around in the empty yard of a nearby apartment block.

'It was pitch black,' he remembers. 'They had their phone flash-lights on, they were digging up the ground, talking amongst each other, obviously failing at finding the thing they were looking for. They were there for half an hour.' Kaganskikh watched for a while, increasingly intrigued. Things got even weirder when the men finally found what it was they were hunting. 'They chewed a bit of it, trying to keep silent, and then they left.'

Kaganskikh wasn't the only one to notice this bizarre behaviour. All across Russia, in cities and towns, people were seeing mysterious for-agers, mostly young people, furtively arriving at parks, tower blocks and bits of wasteland, retrieving little parcels and then scurrying away.

In fact, what they were observing was the physical manifestation of a sprawling online phenomenon: a dark web site that had become a giant, overtaking Silk Road and AlphaBay by strides. And as it grew, money laundering would prove to be a pivotal part of its busi-ness model.

Hydra was launched on the dark web in 2015. For years it had lagged behind the likes of AlphaBay and, within Russia, the Russian Anonymous Marketplace (RAMP). But when both of these sites were closed down in 2017 (AlphaBay thanks to US government action, and RAMP due to a Russian law-enforcement takedown), the path was clear for Hydra to sweep in and dominate.[1]

As for many dark web markets, drug dealers formed a large part of Hydra's business. The site had reportedly forged links with chemical producers in China, especially those who made the precursors for the highly addictive and extremely powerful opiate fentanyl, something Kaganskikh himself had researched for an article on a Russian website.[2]

Fentanyl was a boom industry around this time, and for some of its consumers it proved to be a lethal addiction. There were multiple stories of accidental overdoses by users unable to safely judge their intake. Some dark web sites even banned its sale. It's possible Hydra's administrators were wise to this, because they proudly touted a host of 'safety features' for their users. Hydra introduced a 'certified producers' scheme in which 'Hydra would check the whole production cycle: the chemical reagents bought and used, the equipment, and the qualifications of the workers. The marketplace also claims to test the final product in its lab,' according to researchers who investigated the site. Amazingly, it also offered emergency medical help through the encrypted app Telegram, although as the researchers sagely pointed out: 'It is hard to evaluate the popularity or efficacy of Hydra's telemedicine services.' Whatever their effectiveness, it's clear there was a more cynical, profit-orientated motive to some of these measures too. To gain 'certified producer' status, for example, sellers had to pay an extra 3 per cent fee to Hydra on all sales. But these user-friendly offerings illustrate how seriously Hydra took its reputation.[3]

Hydra replicated AlphaBay's successful one-stop-shop model, with sellers offering personal data, fake IDs, hacking services and tools, as well as drugs. It also had a star-rating system for vendors. But Hydra added a few twists, and it was to be these that turned it into a dark web whale the likes of which had never been seen before.

From 2014, the Russian government cracked down on deliveries of drugs through postal services, the method employed by Sam Bent and many others around the world.[4] To get past this, Hydra's dealers came up with a remarkable and innovative solution. Buyers would pay for the drugs through the site as normal using cryptocurrency, and then the dealers' accomplices would hide the drugs in a location convenient to the customer, who'd then be sent the location for the pick-up. The package might be buried, hidden behind a loose house brick, or attached somewhere by a magnet. This hidden treasure was called 'klad', and the people who stashed it were the 'kladsmen'.[5]

This was the furtive activity Kaganskikh had witnessed outside his apartment, and soon he was seeing more and more drug diggers on the streets of Moscow. Everyone was. It became an open secret that narcotics were being squirrelled away all over the city. And after a significant mention in the Russian press, Hydra was exposed as the prime driving force behind it.

By 2021, klad was a thriving industry. Russian cybercrime forums were offering pay of up to 30,000 roubles a day (around $400) for kladsmen.[6] The recruitment wasn't just happening online. As discovered by a group of University of Pennsylvania researchers investigating the site, there were spray-painted ads in the street, blatantly hiring drug runners. Their analysis showed just how successful Hydra had become thanks to this burgeoning network: in April 2022 alone, they reckoned there were 417,000 drug drops across Russia, with services covering more than a thousand different towns and cities.[7]

Perhaps inevitably, this explosion of drug stashes created a shadow trade to the shadow trade. People began trying to intercept the goods to rip off the kladsmen and their customers. University of Pennsylvania researcher Alex Knorre told me: 'In the inner yard from the window of my apartment in St Petersburg, I once saw "shkurokhody" (literally translated as "skinner-goers"); opportunists who look for dead-drops from Hydra in random places but did not pay for it.'

Thanks partly to innovative trading practices like the klad system, Hydra's business boomed. It eventually accounted for 80 per cent of all dark web market-related cryptocurrency transactions.[8] In 2016, its annual revenue was estimated at under $10m. By 2020 it was $1.3bn; four times that of AlphaBay at its peak. A revenue growth rate of more than 600 per cent over four years is something many

Silicon Valley start-ups would kill for. But there were big questions about how Hydra was achieving it.

The site operated almost exclusively in Russia and former Soviet Union states such as Ukraine, Belarus and Moldova.⁹ For a long time, it was rumoured to be on the verge of going global, and in 2020 it went as far as seeking to raise $146m by selling a new crypto-currency to fund the launch of an international site, grandly named Eternos. But it never happened.¹⁰

Hydra was on my radar; alongside the Russian Anonymous Marketplace it was on my list of dark web bookmarks. But I never paid it much mind, as it seemed so very region-specific (unlike the more globally focused AlphaBay). How, then, did a Russian-language dark web market which specialized in highly localized drug delivery become a multi-billion-dollar enterprise, dominating the dark web and outperforming international rivals offering a much wider range of products? And how was it outlasting its competitors, surviving year after year? The answer was in the money. Hydra was gradually transforming itself into a dark web laundering machine of unprecedented scale.

To understand how this happened, it's important to keep in mind how the Hydra marketplace operated. Similar to eBay, it allowed sellers to post their wares, and potential customers to browse and purchase them. For basic users of Hydra – those who just wanted to buy some drugs for personal use – the process was quite simple. They could swap their pounds and dollars (or more likely roubles) for crypto, send that crypto to their Hydra account (Hydra gave each user a unique wallet address to which they could send their funds) and then use that money to buy drugs from Hydra's vendors, which could be delivered by the kladsmen. Drug purchasers could go direct to vendors to cut a deal, but that was risky: they might get ripped off. A safer route was to use Hydra's in-house escrow service – a sort of buyer-protection system under which, for a fee, Hydra would hang on to the buyer's money until both parties confirmed the deal was complete, and resolve any disputes, if they arose.

The only snag for buyers was that, once they'd deposited crypto into their Hydra wallet, they had limited options to withdraw it. They weren't able simply to transfer their Hydra-based funds back into their own crypto wallets. Instead, they had to use one of the exchange services listed on the site. As a result, in addition to Hydra's traditional offerings of drugs, hacking tools and leaked data, financial services started springing up. Many of these were so-called 'cash-out' services: a Hydra user could contact a cash-out provider, who would take the user's Hydra-based crypto and convert it into usable funds. That could mean sending it to a bank account, loading it on to a credit card, putting it on a prepaid card, or even turning it into cash and burying it in the ground (once again, there were kladsmen available for this).

In essence, this thriving industry was offering Hydra's customers the type of service that GOLD performed for Sam Bent and others, changing Bitcoin for fiat money, but on a vastly wider scale. Alongside the marketplace of drugs and illegal goods, Hydra's vendors were nurturing within it a parallel business. They had created a machine for the layering stage of the laundering process, taking people's crypto and swapping it into clean funds.

But while buyers faced restrictions on withdrawing their funds from Hydra, forcing them to use the cash-out merchants, such restrictions did not apply to those on the other side of the deal, the drug sellers. They were the lifeblood of Hydra, and placing any limits on their ability to control their money would have been perceived as an outrage. And so, unlike buyers, Hydra allowed sellers to withdraw directly to their cryptocurrency wallets outside Hydra, in addition to being able to send it to banks, top-up credit cards, and so on.

Buyers on Hydra gradually cottoned on to this. They realized that, if they could set up an account as a seller on Hydra, they could pull their money out more easily. So they started doing just that, registering as sellers and effectively paying themselves so they could extract their money from Hydra.

By 2019, Hydra had spotted this workaround and implemented a rule so that sellers could only withdraw if they had more than

$10,000 worth of funds in their wallet, or at least fifty successful transactions under their belt. Not only did this shut out the buyers who'd been posing as sellers, it also tipped the site in favour of the big vendors. If you were a smaller seller, you had to keep your money in Hydra's coffers. In the end, these premium seller accounts (which allowed extraction of funds from Hydra) were so valuable they started being bought and sold as a commodity in themselves, changing hands for as much as $10,000 a time.[11] Money and its movement in and out of Hydra was morphing and metastasizing, becoming an industry all of its own.

Perhaps Hydra's own administrators spotted this growth market, because they got in on the money-laundering act too. They started offering their own in-house crypto mixer, called Bitcoin Bank Mixer. It allowed anyone – buyers and sellers – to send Bitcoin which Hydra's mixer would wash around and deposit back into any address they specified.[12] Of course, as we've seen, mixers are not invulnerable. In the case of Helix, investigators were able to tease apart the web of transactions that were meant to mix up the crypto transfers, making it possible for the FBI to link incoming funds with outgoing. But the bigger and busier a mixer becomes, the harder it is to untangle its workings. Thanks to its booming trade, Hydra was moving way beyond the investigators' ability to keep up. It was becoming so big that it was transforming from a simple dark web marketplace and began to function like one giant mixer, layering millions of dollars of criminal cash. Money was flooding in from buyers seeking drugs and laundering services, but also from sellers who were reinvesting their proceeds back into Hydra.

Over time, people started using Hydra not to buy and sell narcotics, hacking services and stolen data, but purely for washing money. Chainalysis calculated that, of the $2bn flowing into Hydra in 2020 and 2021, half was tainted by crime before it even reached the site. In other words, half of Hydra's revenue came not from those swapping their roubles for Bitcoin and purchasing drugs or other illegal items, but from those who'd already committed crimes and needed to launder the resultant crypto proceeds.[13]

To keep track of all this, Hydra had its own internal ledger; a record of funds being sent from wallet to wallet. The incoming funds were being moved around on Hydra's internal ledger, mixed through its mixer, and then money was flowing out. Inside, Hydra's administrators could keep track of what was happening. But from the outside, it was an impenetrable vortex: a billion-dollar-a-year black box of laundering.

OK, so we know how money was going into Hydra: it was partly from people buying drugs, hacking services and so on, but also partly from people wanting to launder their dirty crypto. And we have an idea of what was happening to it inside Hydra, which was essentially operating as a giant washing machine, whizzing money from wallet to wallet, all tracked by Hydra's internal ledger. But what about the back end of the process, pulling the money out, the integration stage of the laundering cycle? Where was it all flowing to? Thanks to the publicly available blockchain, it's possible to track where at least some of it went.

An investigation by Reuters in June 2022 reported that between 2017 and 2022, buyers and sellers on Hydra made and received $780m worth of crypto payments using a mainstream, high-profile service called Binance.[14] You may well have come across the name: it's a giant of crypto, reportedly handling the biggest volume of trading on the planet. Probably no surprise, then, that Hydra users would try to use it to cash out their crypto, if they didn't fancy using Hydra's in-house services. 'This is the fastest and cheapest way I've tried,' a user reportedly wrote in March 2018. It seems that, at the time, some users were able to create accounts on Binance to achieve this. Reuters reported that the 'know your customer' (KYC) controls set up by Binance to police its users were weak. Reuters allege that, at one point, all the site asked for was an email address to sign up, with no supporting documentation (this has since changed and Binance's KYC is now more robust).

Binance said that Reuters' $780m figure was 'inaccurate and over-blown'. In a long blog post (which included its entire, fraught exchange with Reuters' journalists), Binance claimed that much of the money it received from Hydra had been washed through multiple addresses before reaching their company. As a result, Binance argued that there was little it could do to stop the arrival of dirty crypto at its doors, but countered that, once such inflows are spotted either by its internal teams or by law enforcement, Binance works hard to freeze the funds and investigate, and has assembled 'the most sophisticated cyber forensics team on the planet' to help do so.[15]

But even if the Reuters figure is accurate, it raises an interesting question. According to the US government, Hydra brought in $5.2bn of revenue over the five years prior to 2022. If $780m went to Binance, where did the rest of it go? Sure, some would have been left inside Hydra, from all those buyers who couldn't easily withdraw their money, and the low-level sellers who weren't allowed to cash out. But that still leaves billions of dollars' worth of crypto that must have flowed out of Hydra to . . . somewhere. But where?

The answer gives an astonishing glimpse into the scale of the Russian cybercrime economy, its money-laundering enablers, and how entrenched they both are within the country's financial system.

Analysts at tech security firm Flashpoint spent years dipping in and out of Hydra, trying to understand how the site worked and where its money flowed, and working with Chainalysis to do so. Their conclusion: the vast majority of cash-out and money-laundering services on offer were Russian or rouble-based. These services were focused on getting users' money into Russian banks, Russian credit and debit cards, Russian money changers, Russian gift cards and so on. In short, Hydra was injecting billions of dollars' worth of value into the economy of Russia and nearby states. And because many of these services don't play ball with foreign investigators, and aren't on any kind of publicly available blockchain, the money becomes incredibly difficult to trace. It effectively 'just disappears off the map', as Flashpoint's researchers told me. This is the ultimate goal of the layering stage of money laundering, of course, and Hydra was playing a pivotal role in making that happen.

As just one example, take a company called Bitzlato. It's a crypto-currency business headquartered in Hong Kong but run from Russia. It offers so-called 'peer to peer' exchange: the site simply connects people with Bitcoin to sell with people who want to buy. Users could put up an ad offering Bitcoin at a certain price, and then buyers would get in touch directly and send them money, some-times straight from their bank accounts. Bitzlato didn't intervene that much; it took a fee, but regarded this only as an introduction cost for putting the two partners in touch. It seems the business didn't feel it was its job to vet the incoming money to see where it was coming from, and when it was launched, the site had no 'anti-money laundering' or 'know your customer' section (this has subsequently changed). Bitzlato was apparently also a key conduit for those wanting to get their money in and out of Hydra. Figures from crypto-tracing firm Crystal Blockchain show that at least $173m worth of crypto went from Hydra to Bitzlato. And this hadn't come indirectly via a bunch of intermediary wallets, as Binance claimed its incoming Hydra money had. This was money sent direct from Hydra straight to Bitzlato.[16]

It seems Bitzlato was also a key service for getting crypto *into* Hydra too; about the same number of Bitcoins were spotted flow-ing into the site. In 2023, Bitzlato was designated a 'primary money laundering concern' by the US government; the first time such an accusation was levied towards a cryptocurrency exchange.[17] (One of the site's founders, Anton Shkurenko, defended the company. He told me that Bitzlato relied on a third-party firm to screen transac-tions, and that Bitzlato closed thousands of suspect accounts as a result. At the time of writing, Shkurenko is in Russia awaiting news on French criminal charges, which he denies. His colleague and fellow Russian, CEO Anatoly Legkodymov, had been arrested in Miami and was awaiting trial on money laundering and other finan-cial crime charges, which he also denies.)[18]

Bitzlato is just one example of a Russian service used by Hydra. There were many others. This use of Russian services is remarkable when you consider the scale of Hydra. We're talking about a giant underworld business, and it seems the vast majority of that money ended up cycling through the Russian Federation and former Soviet republics. (Bitzlato allowed users to run money through banks and payment providers in Russia, Belarus, Ukraine, Kazakhstan and more). To be clear, the fact that there are Russian criminals making money and pulling it back to Russia shouldn't surprise anyone, given the country's long association with the cyber underworld. But the Hydra story goes beyond that. If the estimates are correct and it was handling four-fifths of all dark web market money, then what we're talking about is a vast chunk of dark web activity given over to laundering via Hydra. This money was then pushed through Russian businesses – from the legitimate, like banks and card companies, to grey zones like Bitzlato – to the tune of up to a billion dollars a year. It represents nothing short of a giant onshoring of capital into the Russian economy.

Perhaps this explains why Hydra lasted so long. Given Russia's often-antagonistic relationship with many Western democracies, how much incentive was there to close down a site bringing money into Mother Russia that had been stolen largely from its adversaries? As one researcher put it to me: 'If I was a politician in Russia and I could see all this money coming in, would I want to shut it down? Probably not.'

Andrey Kaganskikh, the journalist who reported on Hydra and spotted its klad-collectors from his apartment block, takes a different view. He points out that the vast majority of Hydra money wouldn't have been taxed, so the government coffers wouldn't have benefited. Why, then, would the government incentivize behaviour that deprived them of income?

But Hydra's laundering and onshoring activity must be seen in the wider context of tech and organized crime within the Russian Federation. Time and again, we've seen examples that point to Russian hackers' belief that they may operate with impunity so long as they don't target their own. We've seen computer viruses that will only trigger on non-Russian computers. There are cartoons that show hackers with medals pinned on their chests, as though their work was a patriotic endeavour. In some cases, we've even seen direct collusion between Russian government agencies and organized crime, as when an FSB intelligence officer worked with a freelance hacker who was targeting Yahoo email inboxes.[19] As the UK's Joint Intelligence and Security Committee put it:

> Russia has sought to employ organized crime groups to supplement its cyber skills: GCHQ [the UK's signals intelligence agency] told the Committee that there is 'a quite considerable balance of intelligence now which shows the links between serious and organized crime groups and Russian state activity', something it described as a 'symbiotic relationship'.[20]

It's possible Russia's law-enforcement agencies simply saw Hydra as an economically beneficial arm of this relationship.

By 2022, Hydra's resilience and longevity helped it become the pre-eminent dark web money-laundering operation in the world – something that made it a natural target for law enforcement outside Russia. As the site grew into a giant of cybercrime and money laundering, Western agencies were circling. When they finally struck, it would reveal just how pivotal Hydra had become to the cybercrime industry – and reveal even more about the tangled money flows through Russia.

Lili Infante was in her freshman year studying Economics and Spanish at Columbia University when she found herself hunting around for a summer job. Bored with the usual, dry internship gigs on offer, she applied for an intriguing-looking post working as a language analyst. It wasn't quite clear who the ultimate employer would be – the role was via a contractor – but it was obviously something a bit unusual, as there were all sorts of officialdom to get through. It was only when she was finally offered the job that she learned why her new employer had taken such a cautious approach.

'That's when they told me what the job was about. I was going to be a language analyst on wiretaps at the US Drug Enforcement Administration,' says Infante.

Infante's family is from Russia, and her linguistic skills put her at the top of the heap. 'They liked me because I spoke Spanish and Russian,' she says. 'They put me on this huge Russian organized crime case. They had several wiretaps going at the same time. I was, like, nineteen years old. I fell in love with the entire job. And I fell in love with one of the agents also, who later ended up being my husband.'

No surprise, then, that after graduating with a masters in 2012, she was back at the Drug Enforcement Administration (DEA). This time it was her economics training that came to the fore, making her a natural fit for the agency's money-laundering unit, tracking the financial flows of the traditional, long-established drug cartels. But out of the corner of her eye, she could see the rise of dark web dealing, and how it was being fuelled by Bitcoin, a radical new form of money that she found fascinating. She watched with interest as the DEA took a pivotal role in the takedown of the giant marketplace Silk Road in 2013.

Infante instinctively felt dark web investigation had a natural advantage over the 'real-world', offline dealing she'd been concentrating on. 'In order to really infiltrate a criminal organization as an agent, you can't just be like, "Hey guys, I wanna know your secrets." Usually, you need a confidential source and confidential sources tend to be the biggest sources of problems, because these guys are usually former criminals, or guys trying to work off their charges [to negotiate a lesser sentence]. So often they're not the best people to really work with. They're our bread and butter for our cases, of course. But at the same time, they can be a pain. The dark web allows you to not have to go through a confidential source and to just go undercover right away. You can be anybody you want on the Internet.'

Realizing the potential for such covert work, Infante helped assemble the cross-agency Counternarcotic Cyber Investigations Task Force. Despite its drug-focused name, the task force was to investigate the full gamut of online badness, and to do so it brought together a compelling mix of skills: the DEA agents had vast experience running undercover operations, Homeland Security Investigations had a track record on child exploitation cases and the Internal Revenue Service had the financial chops from all their tax fraud work.

In the wake of Silk Road's takedown, the ever-growing darknet marketplace scene was a natural target for this new team. But among the plethora of sites springing up online, Hydra wasn't a big priority for Infante. 'I wasn't initially interested in it because at first glance it seemed so siloed to the Eastern bloc that it wasn't so much on my radar.' Unfortunately for Hydra, it wasn't going to stay off Infante's radar for long.

In 2018, she got a request from the MVD, Russia's Interior Ministry. They were looking for information on Americans they claimed were connected to Hydra (perhaps an indication that the Russian authorities weren't necessarily all turning a blind eye to the site's activities after all). Infante struggled to help them, as the Russians didn't provide quite enough detail to justify US cooperation. But the query revived her interest in Hydra.

By this time, more had started to come out about the site's money flows, and Infante grew increasingly fascinated – and concerned – by its role in money laundering. She saw the giant spider's web of crypto at the heart of Hydra, and innately understood how much crime it could be facilitating. If Hydra had remained simply a regional marketplace for locally delivered drugs, it might have escaped Infante's clutches. But the site had got itself deep into something much bigger. It was enabling a global cybercrime wave that was generating headlines around the world, and would now put it firmly in US investigators' sights. This crime spree was driven by a new generation of cyber crooks. Brash and brazen, they openly boasted of their activities, broadcasting their work online for all to see and thereby giving a fascinating insight into the tactics that were making them fabulously wealthy.

To the untrained eye, the website of the LockBit group doesn't look all that interesting. It's just a page full of boxes laid out in a grid, some red, some green, containing a seemingly random selection of company names, a brief bit of info on the company, a dollar amount, and next to each one a timer gradually counting down. If you stumbled across it by chance, you might think it was some kind of boring financial database; perhaps a tool for geeky share traders.

But for the companies listed on this page, their mere presence here is a terrifying experience. Their eyes will be glued to this screen. That's because the website is a live, rolling list of extortion victims. Every single one of the companies on this page is being held to ransom, sometimes for millions of dollars, and you can watch the whole thing unfold from your desk, in real time. And the timer counting down? If the victims don't pay the dollar amount specified by the time it hits zero, the consequences can be devastating, in some cases killing off the company for good, along with all its employees' jobs.

The LockBit site is on the dark web, and it's the homepage of what is currently one of the most prolific and dangerous ransomware gangs on the planet. Naming their victims on this site is part of the gang's strategy to intimidate them into paying up. LockBit is just one such group – there are many others, often with their own sites listing their victims.

Of all types of cybercrime, ransomware is perhaps the most direct and easy to understand: a hacker breaks into a computer, installs software that scrambles all the files, and then charges the owner a ransom to unscramble them. It's also among the oldest: often cited as the first example is a campaign targeting HIV and AIDS researchers in the late 1980s.[21]

From these humble beginnings, ransomware has been continuously honed over the years. As our lives have moved increasingly online, the cybercriminals have become more and more adept at finding new ways to trick users into unwittingly scrambling their data. But despite its relatively hi-tech nature, modern ransomware suffers the same problem as a lot of traditional extortion attempts. Making them work requires getting up close and personal with the victims. There's often an element of negotiation over the ransom, and ultimately a moment when the money's handed over – all of which provide police with valuable opportunities that occasionally allow them to identify the crooks and make an arrest. What the new generation of hi-tech extortionists really needed was some kind of financial tool that would allow victims to cough up easily and anonymously, minimizing the chances for banks and police to get involved. And in 2008 they got it, thanks to Bitcoin.

Suddenly, blackmailers could demand money from their victims via an anonymized cryptocurrency that could be sent across borders, outside the traditional financial system, and with no international fees. As we've seen, it's not a perfect solution, and with effort it can sometimes be traced. But the ransomware gangs embraced it with gusto, and from the mid-2000s it unleashed a tidal wave of digital blackmail. Over time, the ransomware industry has been honed to become possibly the most highly developed, industrialized and globalized crime campaign the world has ever seen.

At first, the defence against such attacks was simple: back up your data, so if it gets scrambled you can just wipe your machine, reinstall the software, restore your data and carry on. In response, hackers invented malware to hunt out the data backups and encrypt them too. Companies then started storing their data backups offline, sometimes in a completely separate building, meaning they couldn't be infected. This prompted the hackers to switch tactics again; in addition to scrambling their data, the hackers were now stealing companies' sensitive info and threatening to publish it unless they paid up (which is what LockBit does on its leaks site with the countdown clocks). Companies started taking out insurance to cover ransomware attacks, but hackers began scanning their victims' files to find the insurance certificate, then demanding a ransom equal to the maximum covered by the insurance. 'We know you can afford it, you're insured' ran the logic. Today, such gangs' software can even search a victim's network, find out how many computers it has, and set the ransom amount commensurately.[22]

This is the modern face of the ransomware industry: highly motivated groups of criminals with decades of experience and, consequently, reserves of money vast enough to engage in a veritable arms race with anyone who tries to stop them. And the industry is booming; in just ten years, we've gone from a handful of ransom-ware strains to over a hundred.[23] The average payment used to be just a few thousand dollars, but it's now $100,000. An attack on one victim netted the gang a whopping $40m.[24] Ransomware is seriously big business. And by the time Lili Infante started sniffing around Hydra, one gang had risen to rule them all.

It's May 2021, and a Russian computer programmer who goes by the nickname Sticks is nervously waiting for a job interview. Some time previously he had posted his CV to an online recruitment site, and now a prospective employer wants to talk. Better still for Sticks, they seem to be rolling in cash.

It's the middle of the coronavirus pandemic and so the whole interview process is going to be online. But there are some weird aspects. The recruiter Sticks is dealing with also uses only a nick-name, Salamandra. And he doesn't switch his webcam on. Neither does anyone else on the group interview call.

What Sticks doesn't know is quite how much pressure Salaman-dra is under to get these interviews done. He's getting a lot of heat from his boss, who's known inside the organization as Stern. His business is growing fast, but like many in tech, Stern just can't hire staff quickly enough. He sends a message lambasting his team: 'Where are the new coders?'

Salamandra's trying his best, but it's hard. Applicants keep drop-ping off the interview call, something seems to be putting them off. And he's having to pay more and more to the recruitment website to get access to potential employees' CVs. Meanwhile, Stern's keep-ing up the pressure.

'I gave you the direction I need 100 coders this summer,' insists Stern.

In private, Stern is restless. He's been running the organization for four years and wants to branch out into new projects, perhaps something involving crypto. But there's always so much work to do.

Meanwhile, there's good news for the job applicant, Sticks. He's got through the initial round of interviews and is now on to what they call 'newbie induction training', run by a guy known as Twin. A lot of it is fairly standard stuff, how to use the group's software, the internal chat system, and so on. There's one bit of the usual employee induction that's missing, however: they don't have to be shown around the building and told where the toilets are. There's no office, everyone will be working remotely and will probably never meet each other. But during the pandemic that was pretty standard practice too.

Finally, Sticks gets good news. He's passed the initial interviews, and it's time to meet his direct boss, the techie he'll be working under, nicknamed Revers. By this point, Sticks has figured out the job involves something to do with cryptocurrency. He thinks it may be some kind of mixing service, like the Helix system Larry Harmon invented. Finally, Revers is ready to come clean with Sticks. A message flashes up on the chat software from Revers: 'Have you heard of ransomware?'

Sticks has suddenly learned the truth about his prospective employer. He's just been recruited to the giant of online blackmail: Conti.[25] (It's unclear whether he decided to stay on after this revelation.)

There are companies that keep track of the ebb and flow of ransomware gangs as they vie for supremacy. Looking at their data for 2021, one gang gradually edges out all the others. Conti came to account for an astonishing 90 per cent of all ransomware revenue worldwide.[26] No wonder Stern was busy. His organization was spending something like $6m a year just on server space and other business expenses, including salaries for recruits like Sticks.[27]

If you're wondering how we know so much about Sticks, Stern and the internal recruitment processes of a secretive criminal cabal, it's thanks to Russia's re-invasion of Ukraine in February 2022 (one of the conflict's few happy outcomes). Conti is based in Russia, and when Putin's troops entered Ukraine, Conti was one of a slew of Russian organized cybercrime gangs to declare their support for his so-called 'special operation'.[28] In response, it's believed that a

Ukrainian who had access to the gang's communications leaked the group's internal chat logs, thousands upon thousands of messages that had been sent back and forth between every level of Conti's organization as it went about extorting its way across the world.[29]

Among them are glimpses of the ethical dilemmas the group occasionally faced. At one point, they vowed not to target hospitals, perhaps as a way to avoid greater scrutiny from governments during the pandemic. There then ensued a heated debate between two members about whether one particular health facility counted as a hospital or not. But aside from the occasional moral quandary, much of the chat was the kind of snarky, stressed gossip and backbiting that goes on every day in offices around the world.

As a journalist, I'd often been told that cybercrime gangs had effectively become businesses like any other, with bosses, bureaucracies and staff clocking in and out. But to be presented with this kind of fly-on-the-wall evidence of it was incredible. Partly as a result of its tightly controlled organizational structure, Conti managed to out-perform every other ransomware gang in the world, making commensurately giant levels of profit. They took at least $180m in 2021;[30] that's $20,000 an hour. A big chunk of that money was, unsurprisingly, heading into Russia. Cryptocurrency-tracing firm Chainalysis estimated almost three-quarters of ransomware revenue they tracked in 2021 went to strains of the virus released by Russian-affiliated groups.[31]

But the explosion in ransomware left its operators with a problem: scale. To create a continuous revenue stream, you need to be constantly hunting out new victims and sending them virus-laden spam, or otherwise infiltrating their computer networks to infect and scramble the data so you can begin the extortion. Ransomware gangs may be good at designing the viruses, but they don't necessarily have the resources to spread them around. Many of the gangs took a forward-looking approach to this problem, by outsourcing it to affiliate networks. The ransomware bosses would give them the virus, and the affiliates would infect the victims. When the target paid up, the money was split between the virus writers and the affiliates. It was a neat business model, and helped further rocket-fuel the ransomware boom. But it would also create an unintended fallout that would rebound on the ransomware gangs – and eventually on the Russian Hydra site too – with catastrophic effects. Russia's cybercrime underworld was about to go head to head with the US government.

Cybersecurity experts sometimes talk about attacks having 'kinetic effects'. It's a way of saying that a particular outbreak has gone beyond computer networks and is starting to cause major problems in 'meatspace', as some hackers call the physical world.

In May 2021 in parts of the eastern US, one particular hack was causing very, very significant kinetic effects. From Florida to Virginia, there were long queues of cars at petrol stations lining up for gas. Worried drivers were panic-buying, topping up containers and hoarding in case supplies ran out.[32]

It was news of a cyberattack on a company called Colonial Pipeline that caused anxious motorists to head to the pumps in droves. Colonial Pipeline is 'the largest refined products pipeline in the United States' as its website proudly states, pumping more than 100m gallons of fuel per day through a network stretching from Houston to New York Harbor.[33] In other words, it's a major artery in a country for which the black gold is lifeblood. But the hack had turned off the taps. A Russian-based cybercrime group called Dark-Side had penetrated Colonial's computer networks, scrambled their files, crippled the oil supply system and was now demanding a ransom. The gang was highly professional and well resourced: DarkSide ranked number two behind Conti for the amount of ransoms extorted. For six nightmarish days Colonial's pipeline ran entirely dry. Some flights had to be re-routed so planes could still stock up on fuel.[34] In the end, the company paid out $4.4m in Bitcoin to its blackmailers and managed to restore supply.[35]

Suddenly, ransomware was headline news. Hitting critical national infrastructure like fuel supplies was always bound to get the attention of politicians, and an under-pressure US government swung into action. The hunt to trace the ransom money began, and the US authorities were eventually able to recover $2.3m of it.[36] How they did so has never been made public. After the seizure, the US Department of Justice put out a press release and supporting information about the operation, which on first glance appeared to offer a lot of tantalizing detail about the recovery of the money. But all it really said was 'we got the password to the Bitcoin wallet where the ransom ended up'. They never revealed how they got it.

However the money was recovered, two things stand out about the Colonial Pipeline case. Firstly, despite the US seizure, DarkSide and their accomplices still ended up $2.1m richer. That's a big payday. Secondly, the effort to trace the money revealed that the Colonial hack was an affiliate-led job. After the ransom was paid, blockchain tracing showed that 85 per cent went in one direction (presumably towards the affiliate who chose to hit Colonial), the rest in another (towards the virus creators).[37] But it seems the DarkSide gang didn't always know who their affiliates were targeting. In the wake of the incident the gang appeared to distance itself from the Colonial attack, writing on its website: 'our goal is to make money and not creating problems for society [sic].' There's a grain of truth in that: cybercrime gangs in general would rather work in the shadows, undisturbed by law enforcement.[38] When their affiliate chose to hit such a prominent victim, it suddenly put a big target on DarkSide's back.

The attacks on critical American services continued. A month later, ransomware hit JBS, the world's largest meat-processing company. All of its beef facilities in the US were shut down – suddenly the company that put the meat into meatspace was at a standstill.[39] The firm eventually paid $11m to the extortionists – more than double the Colonial ransom – and, this time, none of it was recovered.[40]

You can do many things to Americans, but targeting their oil and beef supplies is a surefire way to provoke a reaction. By the middle of 2021, ransomware attacks were surging up the news agenda and many politicians and commentators were demanding that the government hit back. Anyone connected to the shadowy industry was ripe for investigation, and that included those laundering its profits.

The US Treasury had been looking into Hydra and discovered what DEA agent Lili Infante and others already knew: of the millions of dollars of ransomware money being paid, much of it was being washed through Hydra's accounts. As a result, the Russian darknet market became a target.[41] Suddenly, Infante had the green light to go after it.

In 2021, she and her colleagues began hunting for ways into Hydra, and they made a breakthrough thanks to a top-secret technique that can sometimes be used to expose the IP address of a dark web site. Infante wouldn't tell me the details as she doesn't want to tip off the criminals. All she would say was that it's hit and miss as to whether it works. In this case, it was a hit. The DEA team had a potential server location for Hydra: a German data centre. Infante's team reached out to the German authorities and the query ended up on the desk of Carsten Meywirth, head of the cybercrime division for the Federal Criminal Police Office, the BKA – Germany's answer to the FBI. Armed with the Americans' lead, Meywirth and his team started pulling the threads. They were stunned at what they found.

'Based on findings from the US authorities, we started with one or two servers in Germany – and then we started digging,' Meywirth tells me. 'You start with one server and you try to find out which other servers are connected. Over time you find more and more connections. And after a while you realize, it's not just the one server, not just two, not ten or twenty. We ended up with more than sixty servers. The infrastructure was so big that it was four times larger than other marketplace infrastructures we've seen before.'

In the end, they found a total of sixty-two servers. They held within them the entire Hydra site, its listings, records of transactions, backups, chat logs and more. All of this had been hidden behind the onion layers of the dark web, but now the Germans were inside the loop. The temptation was to lurk there for a while, secretly surveilling the site as the Dutch had done with Hansa, and gathering as much intel as possible. But world events were soon to force the investigators' hands.

On 24 February 2022, Russian Federation troops surged into Ukraine, unaware at that stage that their lightning attack would turn into years of grinding war. The re-invasion of the country had ramifications for almost everyone, and Hydra's owners and users were no exception. Hydra was paying for its servers at the German data centre using Russian credit cards, and as the international financial community moved against Russia, that was causing problems for Hydra's payments. And from their vantage point inside Hydra's network, German police could see that the site's sales were declining. They feared its owners would pull an 'exit scam', disappearing with customers' money and depriving law enforcement of the chance to move in. The decision was made to get in first and close the site down. For Meywirth's team at the BKA, that meant a trip to the data centre itself, because the only way to be sure of killing off the Hydra was to disable its physical manifestations.

The location was incongruous: the buzzing, hi-tech Internet nerve centre of the world's biggest darknet market was to be found in a quiet rural area surrounded by farmland. As the BKA team entered the building, the scale of the challenge hit them immediately. In front of them were several giant halls, stacked floor to ceiling with racks full of identical computer servers, hundreds of thousands of them. It's sometimes odd to think that the shiny, attention-sucking services we use so often, the Facebooks, Amazons and eBays with their whizzy text, photos and videos, are all just ones and zeros stored on rectangular boxes no bigger than a DVD player, piled up in halls like these.

Yet somewhere among the mass of these boxes in the German data centre were the sixty-two servers that composed one of the most successful online criminal enterprises in the world. 'It is a strange feeling when you realize there are thousands of servers around you and you don't know what's on them,' says Meywirth. 'One server may be a completely legal server for the bakery next door. And the other server is the biggest darknet marketplace in the world. Of course, there isn't a separate section for criminal marketplaces and a section for bakery websites in a data centre.'

According to Infante, the data centre was owned by a big German company called Hetzner (there's no suggestion that the company was aware of Hydra's presence among their thousands of other customers), which helped German police track down the right boxes. It took the officers days to find them all, working two shifts, twenty-four hours a day, among the howl of the fans that keep the servers from overheating.

On 2 April 2022, when they were sure they'd found all the right boxes, the Germans pulled the plug, and the world's most successful dark web marketplace suddenly went offline. And just a few days later, the Americans went public with an exciting piece of news. Lili Infante's DEA team had been trying to get to the bottom of who actually ran Hydra. Its servers were inside the Hetzner data centre, but they had been leased out by another company called Promservice Ltd. It looked like a classic 'bulletproof hosting' set-up, in which a shadowy player rents out a bunch of servers and sublets them to allow criminal dark web sites to be hosted on them, in the same way Freedom Hosting served the child sexual abuse sites covered in Chapter Four. But there was something odd about Promservice: it didn't seem to be servicing any other clients apart from Hydra. And when US investigators looked back at the sites that Promservice had hosted in the past, they found two other Russian drug forums that had merged back in 2015 to create Hydra. It looked very much like Promservice and Hydra were one and the same.

Helpfully, according to the US Department of Justice, the man who'd rented the servers in Germany for Promservice had left his name on the account: Dmitry Olegovich Pavlov. The US didn't waste time going public with its allegations against Pavlov. The 30-year-old Russian has denied the accusations, claiming he only operated a licensed hosting company, and had no knowledge of what was on the servers.[42] The US allegations remain unproven.

At the same time as accusing Pavlov, the US authorities also revealed they'd seized $25m of cryptocurrency as part of the take-down of Hydra. A lot of money, to be sure, but a fraction of the $5bn the site generated over five years. The rest of the money had vanished into the hands of crooks, drug dealers, data thieves and ransomware gangs, many of whom had used Hydra to launder their criminal proceeds before slipping away to commit more crime. The laundry had done its job, layering the money and putting it beyond the reach of investigators.

For these criminals, the next stage of the process was integration. With the money successfully washed through Hydra and cleaned of its connection to crime, it was time to pull it out of the financial system and put it to use. Moving it through services like Bitzlato was a helpful step, but the ultimate goal was to turn the funds into ready, disposable income. And this is where things get decidedly physical, because it may surprise you to learn that the final stage in the laundering cycle sometimes comes down to networks of human beings, who physically go to the ATMs and withdraw the money in old-fashioned, untraceable cash that can then be spent on something fun and, ideally, lucrative in the long-term.

But even here, in meatspace, technology is driving profound changes in the way this aspect of money laundering is run. Over the past couple of decades, a toxic alliance of highly evolved fraudsters and real-world money launderers has spawned a sprawling, global network of crime dedicated to the integration stage of the industry. It has brought about devastating consequences not only for its victims, but also for those who find themselves caught up in the launderers' web. And the intriguing story of this giant crime wave starts decades before the invention of things like Bitcoin and online banking, in the febrile political landscape of 1970s Nigeria.

7.

Black Axe

It was nearing midnight when John Omoruan sneaked out of his dorm room at the University of Benin in Western Nigeria. As he made his way through the dark towards the university's sports complex, he could hear drums in full flow, pounding out a steady rhythm into the night. Apprehension built in his chest. Just to get this far, he'd already endured a lot of physical pain. But now the moment of truth was approaching. He'd heard troubling tales about what was going to happen to him on this night. There were rumours he'd be forced to drink blood and eat raw human flesh. Now, at least, he'd get to know for sure.

As he neared the complex, other figures emerged from the gloom; some he recognized, others were strangers. Gradually, they all converged on the sports field where a crowd stood in a circle, singing and dancing to the drums. Omoruan was told, like the others, to line up on his knees in front of an older man seated on a stool. One by one they approached the man, still on their knees. When it was Omoruan's turn, he was ordered to present his right thumb, which the older man sliced with a surgical blade. He was told to open his mouth. A piece of meat was used to wipe Omoruan's blood, then he was commanded to chew and swallow it. Next came a cup of strong-smelling drink, a punch called Kokoma made from home-brewed gin, hemp, coffee and other ingredients. It smelled powerful but Omoruan drank it down, and then returned to join the group.

'We danced around, carrying a coffin,' he recalls. 'Round and round we danced in a circle, with the drummers stationary at the center of the dancing formation, until I was almost dizzy and drunk with their Kokoma. And by 5.30 a.m. we were done with the initiation ceremony.'[1]

This night in January 1982 was to be a turning point in Omoruan's life. The group into which he had just been inducted would obsess him for decades to come. For others, it would be the source of immense damage, ruining lives economically and emotionally. It was called the Black Axe.

The group had been founded at Benin University several years before Omoruan's initiation. It was created as a black emancipation movement and its aims were forward-looking and progressive. Apartheid was in full flow in South Africa, and Omoruan was told that fighting against its inequities was a key focus, as was campaigning against racial injustice in the US. The eponymous axe, the logo of the movement, was a symbol of breaking the chains of oppression.

Omoruan had studied medicine at the university and was one of only a few dozen Black Axe members at this point. A few days prior to their initiation ritual, he and the other would-be recruits had endured another harsh night at the sports complex, during which they were subjected to what Omoruan describes as 'drilling'. They were forced to do a series of gruelling physical exercises – at one point, jumping while an axe was swung at their feet. He says anyone who tried to bail out was beaten until they relented, on the basis that they had seen the faces of existing Black Axe members and could not be allowed to leave until they had agreed to join up. While its presence on campus was known, the organization was highly secretive.

Omoruan had endured it all. He'd got through the initiation, known as 'bamming', and was now a fully fledged Axe-man. He was given a small black axe and was issued with his 'strong name'; recruits to the movement were given these names (sometimes those of prestigious Black freedom fighters) by which they could refer to each other at meetings – again, to maintain secrecy. And so Omoruan received his alias: 'Koleagbo the Second'.

Aside from being part of a movement fighting for Black people's rights, membership of the Black Axe gave Omoruan a lot of cachet within the university. 'I was a big man on campus,' he tells me. 'People started dreading you. They'd be scared of you.' In the ensuing years, it would be this side of the Black Axe – its intimidating aspect – that would throw the organization into infamy.

The Black Axe was just one of a number of campus confraternities in Nigeria. Others included the Pyrates, the Buccaneers and a string of other, smaller, splinter groups. There was infighting between them, and soon enough they were dragged into the fevered political life of Nigeria. College campuses were part of the ideological (and sometimes physical) battleground, and the confraternities became combatants in the fight. This, in turn, forced them deeper underground. 'The groups were outlawed, and much of their ritualistic element – night-time ceremonies, code words – seemed to evolve to avoid detection,' a student at the time recalls.[2]

Gradually, the Black Axe moved away from its origins as a racial justice movement, and towards its future as a criminal enterprise. But even then, few could have predicted its eventual destiny. As it evolved, the group would become pivotal in laundering billions for a wave of cybercrime, spreading from its Nigerian homeland to become a global underworld financial phenomenon.

Nigeria is a country famously rich in oil, but the 1980s were a grim time for its economy, with inevitable knock-on effects on wider society. As a Chatham House report summarizes:

> After the mini-booms in world oil prices in the 1970s and early 1980s, Nigerian administrations, in collaboration with Western governments and companies, began a disastrous programme of investment in industrial projects. Once the oil price tumbled in the 1980s, Nigeria was tipped into a debt crisis ... According to one estimate, Nigerians' incomes fell by three-quarters between 1981 and 2000.[3]

Two Nigerian sociology researchers analysed the impact of this economic turmoil and found it affected one group in particular: 'A substantial number of bankers lost their jobs during the economic recession in the country,' they wrote. 'The fact that those sacked never collected disengagement fees increases the vulnerability of those within the banking sector (mostly youths), with opportunities to explore other means to sustain their lives.'[4]

In other words, young, financially savvy Nigerians found themselves suddenly out of work and uncompensated. For a small minority of these people struggling to survive, the 'other means' they found involved fraud. And the particular type of fraud they turned to had been honed by Europeans centuries earlier.

Eugène François Vidocq was a celebrated criminal-turned-policeman born in eighteenth-century France. He wrote books in which he mapped out the innumerable different types of crimes, cons and scams he'd witnessed in his colourful career on both sides of the game. One was known as the Spanish Prisoner trick. In it, a wealthy person receives a plaintive letter requesting help. The letter's author claims to have been travelling with a rich companion when they were attacked, and he was forced to hide their gold and diamonds in a ditch. The letter's writer now claims to be in prison, but if the recipient can loan some money to secure the prisoner's release, they will be repaid many times over. The letter's author is keen to stress their bona fides as a gentleman, and to impress upon the recipient how trustworthy they are. It's a scam, of course. There is no prisoner. There is no fortune to be shared. If the recipient of the letter is foolish enough to send funds, the money will simply disappear into the pockets of the letter's author, accompanied by a series of increasingly vague and infrequent excuses until the scammer vanishes for good.[5]

During the 1990s, it was this Western-originated scam that some Nigerians began to deploy. In the early part of the decade, thousands of companies around the world began receiving letters apparently sent from a director of the state-owned Nigerian National Petroleum Corporation. As *The New York Times* reported:

The writer says he wants to transfer $20 million to your bank account. The money, he writes, was budgeted but never spent, and your help is needed to spirit the questionable funds out of Nigeria. The letter hints strongly that such official shenanigans are a routine part of government and business life in Nigeria. Your company gets to keep 30 per cent of the total – a cool $6 million – for playing along.[6]

But in order to pocket the money, the recipient must first put up some cash – say, a few hundred thousand – to cover expenses. It worked, generating an estimated $200m profit worldwide. Schemes like this are a numbers game: you only need a few people to fall for the con, and the more messages you send, the higher your chances of profit. Handily for the scammers, the Internet boom of the 1990s was about to deliver a quantum leap in mass communication that could be used for these cons: email.

Meanwhile, back in Nigeria, the economic prospects for young-sters weren't getting any better as the new millennium dawned. Overall unemployment started at just over 13 per cent in 2000 and gradually climbed to 21 per cent over the following decade. It was even worse for those with a bachelor's degree, at almost 25 per cent.[7]

Faced with such a grim outlook, a small minority of this young, tech-savvy generation realized they could combine newly emerging email technology with Vidocq's age-old advance-fee scam. They became known as 'Yahoo boys', because they tended to send their dodgy messages using the free email accounts provided by the US tech firm.

In 2011, researchers Oludayo Tade and Ibrahim Aliyu surveyed this new cadre of crooks, interviewing twenty Internet fraudsters at their college, Ibadan University. They found a wide-scale, highly developed criminal underworld that cut across all social groups. The motivation seemed to be as much about prestige as money. As one 23-year-old student told them: 'If you are a Yahoo boy . . . you will have a self-esteem and also be respected among girls and even among the lecturers.' While such motivations may be common to youngsters in many countries, Tade and Aliyu also found some factors more specific to Nigeria, with its economic strug-gles and political instability. 'Yahoo-boyism is a glaring reflection of institutional anomie in Nigerian society,' they wrote ('anomie' being defined as 'social instability caused by erosion of standards and values' – a word that should probably get a lot more use than it does). One young scammer summed it up, stating (*sic*):

I will not even like people calling it Internet fraudster . . . Those senators embezzling money, are they not committing fraud? Those governors and ministers siphoning the benefit of the youths, are they not fraudsters? If you can't accept those people as fraudsters, then those involved in cyber crime are not fraudsters. They are smart guys.[8]

The Yahoo boys and other Internet scammers working in Nigeria's universities had a big advantage: compared to some other crimes, fraud is cheap. As one police officer noted:

If you were going to distribute cocaine, for example, you have to buy that cocaine from another smuggler somewhere, and you have to put up money for that. In fraud, what is your put-up? Your commodity that you're selling is BS. BS is cheap, it's abundant, it's infinite. It can be replicated again and again and again and again. And that's why it's a better business.[9]

Thanks to these factors, by the early 2000s the advance-fee fraud had become rife. It seemed like everyone with an email account had a story about getting a message, often from a 'Nigerian prince' desperate for help disposing of some outlandish sum of money in exchange for a small payment from the recipient. Some people started baiting these scammers. Users on one infamous website would string them along before finally insisting that, before sending any money, they required that the scammer take a photo of themselves holding a fish and a loaf of bread, claiming this was a local custom to demonstrate good faith. The photos were then posted online. The site's owner was keen to disavow any racist intent, arguing that the scam-baiters simply engaged with whichever fraudsters came their way, a large proportion of whom happened to be Nigerian.[10] But looking at the website today, it's hard not to see the racial undertones. Some believe that prejudice may actually have accounted for the success of the scams. A 2006 Chatham House report on Nigerian financial crime notes:

> At their worst, the argument goes, scam victims are led by a conscious or subconscious white Western sense of racial superiority . . . a European who believes in this might find it unremarkable that a Nigerian holding tens of millions of dollars would be clueless about what to do with it.[11]

To be clear: the vast majority of Nigerians have absolutely nothing to do with such scams, and feel the same abhorrence about them as anyone else. Moreover, many are dismayed by the damage the fraudsters have done to the country's reputation abroad. As Nigeria became increasingly associated with scam activity, the country's authorities made efforts to combat the crime wave, arresting some who used Internet cafés for their nefarious work. However, growth in home Internet provision made this tactic increasingly ineffective, and thanks to the work of a tiny criminal minority in the country, by the mid 2000s Nigeria had become a powerhouse of computer-enabled fraud. In 2008 it ranked third (behind the US and UK) for Internet crime perpetrators according to America's Internet Crime Complaint Center.[12]

But while the advance-fee 'Nigerian prince' scams were a near-ubiquitous presence in people's email inboxes at this time, I suspect many regarded them as a low-level annoyance. After all, surely the only people to fall foul of such obvious con tricks are the gullible and the money-grabbing? In which case, why should we care? As one interviewee told a journalist: 'The people who would bite on this are greedy.'[13]

If this was the attitude, it was deeply unfortunate, because our failure to tackle the growing trend of email scams laid the groundwork for a much bigger problem to come. Think about those Ibadan University students interviewed by Tade and Aliyu: they may have started out as college Yahoo boys pulling basic cons, but at the time I'm writing this, they are grown men in their thirties. Assuming they kept going with fraud, they now have more than a decade of criminal experience and income, and some of them have expanded their frauds to an industrial scale. As it turns out, those dumb email scams were simply creating the seed capital for a much bigger crime wave – one that would ensnare many, many more victims, and foster a global laundering network to wash the profits.

John Omoruan quit the Black Axe in 1982, after an incident on campus made him realize that their 'one for all' ethos had surprisingly rigid limits. He then watched as, over the next two decades, the group descended into corruption and, occasionally, violence. During one incident at Obafemi Awolowo University, forty Black Axe members arrived one Saturday morning, seemingly seeking revenge for attempts by the university's student leaders to crack down on the group's activities on campus. As one article reported:

> Pouring into the residency, the killers then indiscriminately annihilated every student in their path. Local newspaper reports described the horror of the crime scene: mattresses saturated with blood dripping through floors into rooms below, walls splashed with brains. Five died on the scene; three more expired in the following days and eight more remain in critical condition.[14]

The Black Axe was completing its transformation from political pressure group to violent organized criminal enterprise. Along the way, its members ended up forming an ad hoc alliance with the Yahoo boys carrying out the email fraud campaigns. It's unclear quite when and how this happened, but in hindsight, it seems inevitable that the two eventually collided. As a campus movement, the Black Axe was moving in the same circles as the student scammers. For some, the boundary between the two was almost invisible. One youngster, 'John', recounted to a journalist his experience of being initiated, or 'bammed', into the Black Axe in 2008, and then almost immediately put to work on Internet crime:

> John's scheme was to pose as the owner of a lottery, offering lucrative prizes in return for a few bank details. He camped out at the Internet café of a seminary near his home, spending long afternoons sending thousands of messages to potential marks. He was good at it. By the end of his sophomore year, John owned a large sneaker collection and a Mercedes that he drove home between semesters.[15]

As the crime and violence escalated, Nigerian authorities moved to outlaw the Black Axe, which is now often described as a 'campus cult' rather than a confraternity. Membership was deemed illegal in several states. But it all came too late. The university students who swelled its numbers had grown up and some had assumed positions of power, meaning there were Black Axe members (or at least sympathizers) in high office. The group was too entrenched and, partly thanks to its Internet scam campaigns, too rich to be simply cut out of Nigerian society. And besides, the problem was no longer just Nigerian. The Black Axe had spread overseas, and it was there that it would carry out its most damaging criminal work, as one researcher was to discover.

Gary Warner leads a double life. On the one hand, he's a professor teaching cybercrime at the University of Alabama, grading papers, giving lectures and teaching students. On the other hand, he's a financial crime investigator with years of experience tracking hackers. He once helped the FBI crack a $70m payroll theft case.[16] And back in 2015, he discovered a handy way of keeping tabs on the crooks' latest movements: Facebook. Despite the social network's prohibitions, Warner found members-only groups on the site in which white-collar crime was openly discussed. Without giving their true identities, he and his colleagues would join the groups to see what they could learn.

But then something weird happened. Facebook has algorithmic software that looks at its users' behaviour and suggests other groups and accounts that the algorithm thinks they might like. In Warner's case, it was recommending that he join various African political groups. Warner was confused. 'I'm in financial crime groups. Why does it keep showing me these African groups?' he remembers thinking.

Following his investigator's nose, Warner joined up, and quickly discovered why Facebook had suggested he do so – the groups had a dual purpose. 'They're talking about political movements, African politics and African economics. But they're also offering credit card fraud and telling people how they can do it,' he says.

As he dug deeper into this murky online community, one name popped up repeatedly: the Black Axe. Warner compared the Black Axe Facebook groups' membership with that of the financial crime groups he'd been tracking, and found a massive crossover between the two. As he followed the links from account to account, he found groups and members spanning the globe, from Japan to Brazil. What Warner was witnessing was the Black Axe's next evolutionary step: from its roots in Nigeria, the group had gone global, creating a tightly organized diaspora network that would become a giant criminal franchise.

The trend had started decades before. Around his time in the Black Axe in the 1980s, John Omoruan had watched as the political instability in Nigeria had triggered an emigration of intelligent youngsters. 'That was the initial exodus,' he tells me. 'A lot of graduates ran out of this country. They ran away because they were just locking people up. And amongst people running away were the cult members.'

This was what Gary Warner was seeing in his Facebook groups at the University of Alabama: the Black Axe crime branches that had popped up in other countries around the world, following the exodus. And he soon discovered that, like any successful franchise, it ran on a strict organizational structure.

The Black Axe has divided the world into 'Zones', each of which is controlled by a Zone Head. Underneath him (according to Gary there are no known female Zone Heads) are various deputies, including a Chief Priest who operates as a second-in-command and an 'Ihaza', who functions a little like a Chief Financial Officer, according to Warner. 'There's a very formal structure to this,' he tells me. Warner began to map this network, taking careful note of who was communicating with whom, and trying to plot out the organizational hierarchy.

By the 2010s, the Black Axe had become a widely distributed, highly evolved global network. As one police officer put it to me: 'It's a worldwide organization that has a company structure to rival Coca-Cola.' Unlike Coca-Cola, however, the Black Axe was neck deep in financial crime. It would go on to facilitate one of the most damaging and lucrative cybercrime campaigns in history, further refining its money-laundering tactics, leaving victims scattered all over the world – one of whom would find himself face to face with some of the gang's most senior members.

Compared to the gritty, high-octane criminal cases covered elsewhere in this book, Michigan native Tom Cronkright's chosen legal career path might seem quite sedate. In 2005, he co-founded a firm called Sun Title with a fellow lawyer. A title company's job is to facilitate property transactions, working with the buyer and seller to make sure all the paperwork is in place and offering 'escrow' services, holding on to money until deals go through (similar to conveyancing in the UK). It's conscientious, important work, though it's unlikely to be the next hit drama on Netflix. But in 2015, Cronkright was suddenly dragged into a roller coaster of crime involving fraud, fakery and even murder-for-hire. It all started with an innocuous-looking email.

In March of that year, his firm received a message asking for help with the sale of a small petrol station, just a few miles from his company's HQ in Grand Rapids, Michigan. The buyer and seller had agreed the price at $670,000, but they wanted Cronkright's firm to dot the i's and cross the t's. Keen to secure the sale, the buyer was offering a $180,000 deposit of 'earnest money' to seal the deal. This deposit was to be paid to Cronkright's company, which was then to transfer it on to the seller. 'No red flags, nothing uncommon to speak of,' says Cronkright.

Sure enough, the buyer sent Cronkright's firm a cashier's cheque for the deposit, which Cronkright paid into his company's bank account. He waited for it to clear, then sent the money onwards to the seller's account in New York. As far as he was concerned, that was that.

But then, six days later, Cronkright's executive assistant contacted him with some awful news. The incoming cashier's cheque had bounced. Yes, it had cleared at Cronkright's local bank, but full clearance across all the necessary financial institutions in the US can take up to ten days. Cronkright didn't know this, it had never come up before, and the revelation was a sledgehammer blow. His firm had sent the money before the cheque had been fully processed. They'd just been scammed for $180,000.

'I remember I stepped out of the office and time slowed down,' he tells me. 'It's almost like if you've been in an accident, time actually moves into frames rather than real-time. I was gripped with fear and shame and blame. It was, like, "How could this ever have happened?"'

The loss wasn't fatal to Cronkright's business, but it stung. He was determined to show that the scammers had targeted the wrong victim. 'You picked the pocket of two lawyers in Michigan. We went on the offensive to grab that money back,' says Cronkright.

He approached his local bank branch, but they were of no help ('It was like I was speaking some other language,' he says). Like-wise, he struggled to get the police interested in his relatively small loss. So Cronkright went on the hunt himself.

The first stop on the trail was the New York bank to which his firm had sent the money, allegedly to the seller of the petrol station. CCTV showed a smartly dressed, middle-aged couple arriving at the bank just after midday on 10 April 2015 to pick up the money. The woman then arranged for it to be wired to two accounts in

Texas belonging to a real estate and insurance broker. Cronkright began following the money, chasing it down as it was used to pay deposits on property, invested into stocks and shares, and funnelled through solicitors' accounts. He was witnessing steps one and two in the money-laundering process: the crooks had used Cronkright's firm to place criminal money into the banking system, and were now using every trick in the book to layer it. Cronkright had to fight hard to keep up.

It was eye-straining, time-consuming work, but speaking to Cronkright you get the feeling part of him enjoyed it – something about the satisfaction of painstakingly righting a wrong. In the end, he did have some success. 'We were able to recover about $140,000 of the $180,000,' he says. 'We spent, I think, all of that in legal fees. But the lessons learned were fascinating.'

In March 2017, almost exactly two years after the original fraud, Cronkright settled the final legal action, against a chap called Mark Hopkins, and breathed a sigh of relief: 'We're done,' he remembers thinking. 'We had two years of our life that was exhausted into this insane event.' But he was wrong. It was far from over.

In August of that year, Cronkright got a call out of the blue from Patrick Scruggs, an assistant US attorney from Tampa in Florida. Scruggs began quizzing Cronkright about his civil case against the folks who laundered his stolen money. One of the cast of characters was of particular interest.

'He was specifically asking questions around Mark Hopkins,' remembers Cronkright. ' "Have you met him? Have you emailed him? Any text messages? Any direct communication?" And I said, "No, but just several months ago, he had been the last defendant to settle."

'And finally it comes out that there is no Mark Hopkins. Mark Hopkins does not exist.'

This is quite a revelation. While Cronkright never physically met Hopkins, he did receive and cash a cheque from the man's lawyers. And yet, according to Scruggs, Hopkins was a phantom. How could a phantom come up with a payment to settle a court case?

But Scruggs had got an even bigger shocker for Cronkright. US law enforcement had been on the trail of the mysterious Mark Hopkins and, after much painstaking work, they had discovered his true identity. And it was going to put Cronkright at the centre of a sprawling international investigation. 'He tells me Mark Hopkins is actually Ikechukwu "Ike" Amadi,' says Cronkright. Amadi was part of a fraud and money-laundering operation run by one of the most senior Black Axe members in North America. It was the first Cronkright had heard of the group – but as the story progressed, he would end up knowing far more about them than he ever wanted.

After revealing Mark Hopkins's true identity, Scruggs told Cronkright they'd also been investigating Ike's brother Okechukwu Desmond Amadi, and discovered he was also very high up in the gang's North American operation. The US authorities had been carefully working to expose the Black Axe's network as it infiltrated the country. And it turned out the Amadis had been on US law-enforcement's radar for quite some time.

The US investigation into the brothers started when a 23-year-old woman called Anjuli Gupta began dating a 32-year-old man called Muhammad Naji. By all accounts, it was a whirlwind romance. They started the relationship in August 2013 and within a month she'd moved into his home in Tampa, Florida.[17] In hindsight, that was probably her biggest mistake. Naji was soon pestering Gupta to set up a business bank account for him, so he could do property deals. He told her he couldn't do it himself as he had a prior felony conviction (among the many lies he would go on to tell her, that bit at least was true).[18] As she rang the bank he stood beside her, coaching her on what answers to give. There was a reason he was so clued-up on bank account creation: unbeknown to Gupta, Naji was a professional money launderer who by this point had set up and rinsed his way through so many accounts that he'd been barred by many institutions. Gupta was his ticket back into the financial system, his gateway to the placement stage of the laundering process.

Next, Naji created a company called A&M Enterprises. He told Gupta he'd chosen the title because it incorporated the first initial of both of their names, implying it was created for both of them. But this seemingly romantic gesture was merely another part of the web of deceit into which Gupta was gradually being drawn.

Under Naji's supervision, Gupta set up three business accounts at Bank of America under the A&M Enterprises business name. She made a minimum deposit, handed over the bank cards to Naji and, it seems, thought nothing more of it. But as soon as the accounts were set up, Naji sprang into action. Hundreds of thousands of dollars began flooding through the accounts Gupta had created, whizzing their way to other accounts around the world.

Banks often use automated anti-money-laundering software that triggers an alert if it spots suspicious behaviour. With so much cash washing through such recently created accounts, Gupta's profile would have lit up like a Christmas tree.

By November 2014 she'd been pulled in for interview by the FBI, and agreed to have one of her phone calls with Naji taped. The transcript is heartbreaking. Gupta (having at last learned of the abuse taking place on her account) desperately tries to get answers while Naji gaslights her with vague non-answers.[19]

The truth was that Gupta's duplicitous boyfriend had been engaging in exactly the kind of fraud perpetrated on Tom Cronkright's company. But rather than title companies, Naji's specialism was conning law firms. Working with a gang of accomplices, they would pose as clients who needed help resolving a contract dispute. Other members of the gang would then pose as the people on the other side of the dispute, offer to settle, and send a cheque as payment. Like Cronkright, the law firm would wait a few days for the cheque to clear, before paying out the settlement money to what they thought was the injured party, but was in fact Naji and his gang. Like Cronkright, the law firm would then discover too late that the initial cheque had in fact bounced, leaving them hundreds of thousands of dollars out of pocket. Naji's scam caused losses estimated at more than $2.5m.[20]

Of course, what Naji needed to make the scheme work was bank accounts into which his victims could transfer their money. At first, he did this himself, but when the banks cottoned on and shut him out, he took to conning women into helping him. Gupta wasn't the only one he'd co-opted. Naji would often recruit escorts he met on websites such as Craigslist or Backpage (the two classified advertising sites covered in Chapter Three). He'd get them to set up businesses in their names, then use those businesses to set up bank accounts to launder his stolen money. In all, he'd opened about eighty bank accounts in the Tampa area alone.[21]

With the police circling him, in February 2015 Naji agreed to cooperate with US law enforcement, who eventually learned that Naji was working with the Amadi brothers, Ike and Desmond. Canadian police had also been tracking the brothers' activities for years: Ike had dual Nigerian/Canadian citizenship and was living in Toronto. Desmond had Canadian citizenship too and was living in Texas. Between them, US and Canadian police started putting together the jigsaw puzzle pieces of their spiralling money-laundering empire, which was part of a criminal operation that had tried to scam victims out of at least $5bn.[22]

The Amadis, US investigators now believed, played a pivotal role in the scam on Cronkright's business (among many other frauds), and had overseen the operation to launder the stolen money, with Ike posing as Mark Hopkins to get his cut. Ike had been arrested in Toronto in October 2015, but extradition from Canada would take a while. Being on US soil, Desmond was an easier prospect. He was in custody and due to stand trial in October 2018. So Assistant US Attorney Patrick Scruggs went back to Tom Cronkright with a request: 'He told me: "I need you to testify in Tampa,"' says Cronkright.

This was a troubling ask for Cronkright. Prior to Scruggs's call, he'd been reading about one of the lower-level launderers in his case, a woman called Priscilla Ann Ellis. She'd been tried and sent to prison for her role. But in a remarkable postscript, despite her conviction, Ellis had tried to get another inmate to hire a hitman to murder several witnesses in her case. An undercover FBI agent posed as the hitman, showed up to the jail and met with Ellis in person to obtain the specific details of the plot. They'd even got as far as talking about possible methods of killing.

'One of them was a Colombian necktie, specifically,' says Cronkright.

I was unfamiliar with the term, so I asked him to explain.

'Yeah, I mean, I wish I didn't know this,' he replied. 'It's where they actually slice the middle of your throat, they grab the tongue and they pull it through. It's a message that you just simply don't talk.'

For this incredibly foolhardy act, Ellis got another sixty-five years' jail time, on top of the forty she was already down for.[23]

With this in mind, Cronkright was understandably reluctant to testify in the trial. Eventually, it was agreed that he'd have an armed escort to the court, where he finally came face to face with Desmond Amadi.

'Very well dressed, incredibly clean-cut and you could just tell by his reaction and his mannerism and the way he was interacting with his lawyer that he was probably a well-educated, intelligent person,' remembers Cronkright. 'You'd cross him on the street or in a meeting and you'd think he was a very successful, professional business person.'

Which he was: the only difference being, his business was laundering millions of dollars.

Cronkright's description reminded me of something former Black Axe member John Omoruan told me: 'Most of the criminals captured by the police and arrested abroad are more educated than your policemen,' he asserted. 'They have masters [degrees].' As a result, they can often argue their way out of prosecution. The tragedy, of course, is that they don't put their considerable financial acumen to legitimate use.

In April 2019, Okechukwu Desmond Amadi was sentenced to eleven years three months in prison for his laundering offences. Six months later, his brother Ikechukwu went down for fifteen years eight months. He was ordered to pay back $4.3m to his victims and held accountable for at least $16.4m of fraud losses. Meanwhile, Muhammad Naji was eventually sentenced to two years nine months.

The whole experience was time-consuming and occasionally traumatic for Cronkright, stretching over several years. But on the plus side, it's given him a whole new line of business. He created a company called CertifID which helps other firms avoid falling foul of the same scams by assisting them in checking people's identities before transferring money – something that might have helped Cronkright's title company avoid the clutches of Amadi's fraud gang. 'If we don't have technology to help verify identity before financial information is exchanged, we're going to end up in the same spot over and over again,' says Cronkright. I ask him how many victims he's seeing. 'It's gone up exponentially and I think it will continue to,' he says. 'I hate to say it, but it's just so easy [for the criminals].'

The kind of fraud Cronkright's firm was subjected to – and which is hitting countless other organizations around the world day in, day out – was simply the next evolutionary step for the gangs who cut their teeth doing the advance-fee, 'Nigerian prince' email cons. As the Yahoo boys grew into men, from among their ranks came a new cadre who called themselves 'next-level' cybercriminals. The tactics are very similar: scope out your victim, come up with a reason they have to send money, craft a convincing message and wait for the cash to roll in. The difference for the next-level players is the scale of the targets: rather than hitting individuals for a few hundred bucks, the gangs are now going after organizations with hundreds of thousands in their accounts. Pulling off such work requires patience and planning. It's a switch from short-con to long-con, from pickpocket to bank heist.

Tom Cronkright is seeing exactly this trend of growing skill and foresight in the cases on which his firm is now helping. A couple of years ago, he says, the fraudsters would just send a single email, hoping to quickly trick the target into mistakenly wiring money to the crooks' account. Now, they spend a lot of time grooming their victim, gaining their trust, and making sure all the pieces are in place for when they finally transfer the money.

As these types of fraud have exploded in popularity, the gangs behind them have diversified and refined their tactics. Some will concentrate on invoice redirection, in which the victim company is contacted by someone who claims to work for one of the firm's existing suppliers (say, the office cleaning firm), and informed that the supplier's bank account has changed. The victim changes the payment details and unwittingly ends up sending money to the crooks.

There's payroll scamming too: the victim's HR department is contacted by what seems to be an employee, who tells the HR team that their bank details have changed. Come payday, the company pays their worker's salary into the criminals' account. By the time the real employee complains about not being paid, the money is long gone.

Then there's mortgage redirection fraud, in which a solicitor receives an email shortly before they're due to transfer a big sum of money for a property deal. The email appears to come from the seller or their mortgage company, informing the solicitor that their bank details have changed. Once again, by the time the fraud is spotted, the money's been spirited away.

They're all twists on the same trick, a so-called 'business email compromise' or BEC attack. But it's now been honed into an artform – and a hugely profitable one. For example, earlier chapters mentioned ransomware, the cyber extortion tactic that often grabs the headlines. In 2022, the FBI logged 2,385 ransomware attacks, generating $34.3m of losses. By contrast, they saw 21,832 BEC attacks, with losses of $2.74bn. And those figures will be a vast underestimate of the true picture, because they only cover the US, and only include the attacks the FBI is seeing.[24] The total global figures will be much, much bigger. All of these frauds require bank accounts through which to wash the money, and the launderers providing those accounts play a pivotal role in the industry. It's how the Amadi brothers got rich.

But it's not all plain sailing for the crooks. Some people are fighting back against the BEC scammers. The crooks are harnessing the latest technology to steal and wash their money, but now the defenders are tooling up too.

*

It's May 2019, and a finance department employee called Lexy at a
US shipping company has just received an email from a regular supplier. The email comes from a woman named Louise, who tells
Lexy that a payment of $87,440 is due, and asks Lexy to make the
transfer to a bank account in Malaysia. Lexy is helpful and tries to
send the money, but hits a roadblock because her company isn't able
to make direct transfers to foreign bank accounts.

No problem, says Louise. She sends Lexy the details of a different
account for the supplier, this time based in Chicago. That's more
like it. Lexy tries to make the transfer again, but to no avail: it seems
the account doesn't exist. Confused, Lexy emails Louise, who
quickly provides another option – an account for the supplier at a
bank in Trussville, Alabama. Lexy tries again, and this time it seems
to work, the payment is going through . . . But then the bank contacts Lexy and tells her there is some kind of problem, and the
transfer's been put on hold. Lexy goes back to Louise with the bad
news, at which point Louise confers with a colleague called Garry,
who gives her the details of yet another bank account, this time in
Davie, Florida. Armed with this info, Louise goes back to Lexy and
asks her to give it another try. Between them they're gradually
grinding their way through the kind of arduous admin hassle that
back-office folks deal with all the time.

And as the emails fly back and forth, Lexy is getting pretty friendly
with Louise. She invites her to the leaving party of a colleague called
Eric. Louise can't come, but suggests they meet up for a drink some
other time. Lexy says she'd like that. Meantime, she's getting ready
for the weekend, having her nails done. It's the kind of chummy
chit-chat that greases the wheels of everyday bureaucracy.

But the payment still isn't going through. Lexy's trying her
darnedest to help, but no matter what they try there always seems
to be some kind of problem. Meanwhile, Louise is looping in more
and more of her team, and keeps suggesting new bank accounts,
but to no avail.

In reality, 'Louise' does not exist. Nor does her colleague 'Garry'.
Nor do any of the other colleagues she claims to be consulting. The

whole thing is a scam. 'Louise' is the alias being used by a scammer, who's created a fake persona pretending to work for a supplier of Lexy's company. The goal is to trick Lexy into making a payment. The bank accounts 'Louise' is providing are there only to launder the money, which will then be spirited away by her accomplices. It's a classic business email compromise attack.

But there's something 'Louise' doesn't know. 'Lexy' doesn't exist either. All this time, 'Louise' has been corresponding not with a helpful-but-flustered finance department worker, but with a piece of chatbot software that's been automatically generating responses to string 'Louise' along and extract information.

The person behind the 'Lexy' persona has little interest in getting his nails done. Crane Hassold is a 40-year-old researcher working for a US tech security company. He originally graduated in psychology, but then went on to join the FBI, where he worked for eleven years.

'Most of the time I spent in the behavioural analysis units in Quantico, Virginia. I did six years of the sort of traditional serial killer profiling, violent crime and behavioural analysis stuff,' says Hassold matter-of-factly, as though profiling serial killers is an everyday occupation.

After leaving the Bureau, Hassold decided to put his skills to use in private industry. His current company, Abnormal Security, has come up with a neat way of dealing with the explosion in email fraud. Their software automatically intercepts the dodgy emails trying to trick the target into transferring money to the crook's bank account. Hassold's software then sends out an automatic reply offering to help with the payment. The software then strings the scammer along, generating auto-replies about an imminent payment that somehow never quite comes off, just as Louise received from Lexy. 'We have dozens and dozens of excuses about why payments don't work,' says Hassold. Not that it deters the crooks. 'As long as there is a sliver of hope that they're going to make something at the end of the day they'll continue.'

Meanwhile, Hassold is able to gather vital intelligence on how these scammers work, filling in the psychological hinterland that's been of interest to him since his college days. Eventually, however, even the most tenacious scam artist runs out of patience and stops playing the game. At which point, Hassold makes a bold move.

'Once an engagement seems to sputter out, we would de-cloak ourselves. We would say, "Hey, do you want to have a conversation?" ' he says. Remarkably, some of the scammers say yes (perhaps attracted by the $50 in Bitcoin that Hassold sometimes offers as a sweetener).

'We'd be able to set up a Skype call, and have a recorded interview with them,' he says. Through this, Hassold has gained unprecedented insight into the inner workings of these BEC fraud groups. Perhaps unsurprisingly given its decades-long history of fraud, most of those he's talked to are in Nigeria. 'It's essentially like a business in Nigeria,' he says. 'You have all these guys. They may be working with some guys one week, next week they're working with some other guys. It's very fluid. It's not very centralized or structured.'

However, Hassold has divined a rough separation of roles. There are researchers, who scope out potential victims, working out which companies might be worth targeting. Then there are the spammers, who send out the initial emails (like the ones from Louise that Hassold's software is intercepting). Then there are the loaders, who gather together the bank accounts that can be used to receive and launder the money. Finally there are the pickers, who pick the money up from those collector bank accounts and move it onwards, eventually paying back the researcher, the spammer, the loader and anyone else who's earned a cut from the criminal proceeds.

Because Hassold's software is intercepting the scam emails, it's the spammers whose contact details he's gathering, and therefore those are the people he's talking to. He's done about a dozen of these interviews, so it's not an exhaustive survey, but it is very illuminating.

'Whether they're being truthful or not, probably half the folks that I've talked to are like, "I don't want to be doing this, but this is what I have to do," ' he says. 'That's the only way they can make a living . . . They're trying to provide for themselves and for their families. They're not making millions of dollars and flashing on Instagram and stuff like that. If they get one good hit, that's like a year or two's salary.'

This is where Hassold's psychology training butts up against his working life in law enforcement and security. 'I understand why you would want to figure out any way you can to make money. But on the other side of it, seeing how it impacts victims . . . that empathy sort of goes away.'

As well as the psychological insights, Hassold's work auto-baiting the scammers produces a highly valuable side-product: lots and lots of bank accounts that are being used to launder money. Often, when told that a payment hasn't gone through to one of their laundering accounts, the scammer will simply provide another bank account for the payment. And then another. And another. Just as 'Louise' did with 'Lexy'. Hassold's software strung her along for an incredible fourteen days, during which 'Louise' sent no less than twenty-two different bank accounts – every one of them set up to potentially launder that promised $87,440 payment. Hassold's company hands these accounts over to the banks and law enforcement, who can then start monitoring them for suspicious behaviour, potentially closing them down.

As a result, Hassold's software is burning through the scammers' stock of bank accounts. Every time his fake personas claim to have a problem with an account, the fraudsters have to come up with another. They need a constant supply of fresh accounts. And they need them in countries around the world. Think about the Louise/ Lexy example: when Lexy (quite reasonably) pointed out that her company wouldn't transfer money to an account in Malaysia, Louise immediately came back with accounts in Chicago and Florida (and went on to provide more in Maryland, California, Washington DC, Virginia, New York state, and on, and on).

Not only do the launderers need accounts all over the place, they also need people on the ground to administer them. Think back to Tom Cronkright's example: the money he was tricked into sending arrived in New York, where the mysterious middle-aged couple was there to intercept it and send it on. Someone has to manage all these people.

This is why the Black Axe has become such a pivotal and powerful operation: thanks to its worldwide distribution, it provides the Nigerian fraudsters with the global money-laundering network without which they simply could not function. It performs a vital role in the final, integration element in the classic three-stage laundering process – pulling the stolen money out of the financial system in whichever country it's in and distributing it back to the criminal network, who can then spend it as they see fit. Black Axe's diaspora network has got it down to a fine art.

But there's more to it. Simply having an international presence is not enough, because as the scale of the fraud and money laundering expands, it presents a problem. Mike Kelly of Toronto Police spent years tracking the Black Axe, and sums it up: 'The further you are away from your other fellow criminal who's doing your money laundering for you, the more it gives them the opportunity to steal from you. There is no honour among thieves.'

This is part of what the Black Axe provides: trust among a federated, globally distributed crime and laundering network. As observed by John Omoruan (who's now an academic at Ibadan University and writes books about his time in the cults), the Black Axe is a 'brotherhood of man, where Kokoma is thicker than blood, and where everyone is everyone's brother'.

But to make a globally distributed laundering network function, you need more than just cultural bonds. You have to have some way of exerting control, and that often comes down to something very basic: violence. As an illustration: in the Tom Cronkright case, Priscilla Ann Ellis had no qualms about ordering the murder of witnesses in the most gruesome way possible. The financial and cyber crimes of the Black Axe and its associates may seem very cold and clinical, but with no courts or governments to enforce order, physical consequences are a grim necessity. At a certain point, white-collar crime turns very red indeed.

In addition to threats, there's one other thing that the Black Axe's criminal enterprise is totally reliant upon: bank accounts. Going back to Tom Cronkright's case again, without the New York bank account to shuffle his money into (and the subsequent network of accounts in Texas) the fraud couldn't have worked. Without accounts through which the funds can be moved and eventually extracted, this whole scheme, and every other one like it, grinds to a halt. Added to which, the Black Axe's accomplices are now faced with people like Crane Hassold, whose software is chewing through these laundry accounts dozens at a time, reporting them to law enforcement who then shut them down. Replacements are in constant demand. Where do you get them? How do you procure a bank account for washing dirty cash? And how do you eventually withdraw the money? It's not as hard as you might think. Once again, modern technology is transforming the integration part of the money-laundering process. And for fraud and laundering gangs like the Black Axe, it would turn one country in particular into a bountiful supply of accomplices.

8.

Smurfing on Snapchat

It's a big day for Kenoly Ugbodu. He gets up early and puts on some understatedly smart clothes – sharply pressed trousers, a grey shirt and stylish loafers – and journeys into the centre of his home town of Cork, in the Republic of Ireland. It's a harbour city of just over 200,000 people, clustered on the edge of the Loch Mahon inlet that leads, eventually, to the Atlantic Ocean. Ugbodu heads for Anglesea Street, to the criminal courthouse, and makes his way inside. At 2.30 p.m. on 15 May 2023, he's waiting in Court 4, as the Judge Helen Boyle arrives and takes her seat. Ugbodu shifts nervously. This moment will decide his future. From here, there are two paths: one leads to prison, and the bewildering, occasionally frightening daily regime of custodial living. The other leads back to his old life, his family home and his new fiancée. He's about to be judged for a series of catastrophic decisions he made years earlier; decisions which brought him face to face with the underworld of organized crime, and which, from his family's home in Cork, pulled him into the fringes of a global money-laundering scheme of dizzying proportions.

Ugbodu's story doesn't start in a courtroom in Cork, however. It begins 150 miles north, at a four-star hotel called the Carlton in Blanchardstown, a suburb of the Irish capital, Dublin. It's the kind of hotel you find lurking on the edges of freeways the world over. From the outside it looks a bit like it was assembled from mismatched Lego sets. Inside it's clean and colourful, with smartly uniformed receptionists lined up to assist. But in February 2020, there was whispering among some of the staff. In the past few days several men had checked in who'd raised concerns. At one point they'd arrived with a girl who looked decidedly young, and took her to their room. It would later transpire that the girl wasn't underage, but the hotel workers didn't know that, and to be on the safe side they called in the local police, the Garda, who agreed to visit the men and check it out.

So at about 2 p.m. on 21 February, a team of uniformed officers arrived outside room 419, accompanied by hotel staff. They knocked on the door. No answer. They knocked again. Still no answer. But there was clearly someone inside, because they could hear the toilet being flushed – several times, in fact. In the end, the hotel staff opened up the door and let the police in. Inside, everything looked fairly normal, until they got to the toilet, which was crammed full of printed paper. One of the officers took the plunge and ferreted out the sheets, which had survived despite the frantic efforts to flush them away. They were torn-up receipts, dozens of them, for cash withdrawals made all around Ireland. Meanwhile, the man in the hotel room remained unsettlingly calm.

The documents weren't the only fishy thing the police found. They also discovered thousands of euros of cash around the hotel suite. At this point, the man who'd booked the room showed up, and began filming the police on his phone, clearly very unhappy about their presence – so much so that he had to be restrained by some of the officers. He identified himself as Damian Stander, and told police that the money was his and came from a used car deal he'd done. But that didn't explain the receipts, or the hurried efforts to destroy them. Stander's phone was seized by the police, but he wouldn't give them the PIN, and they couldn't force him to.

The local police realized there was clearly some kind of financial oddness going on, so they referred the case to the Garda's National Economic Crime Bureau, where it ended up on the desk of a detective named Sean Sheehan. Nattily dressed and softly spoken – so softly, in fact, that it's sometimes hard to make out what he's saying – Sheehan seems like a born investigator: once he finds a loose thread, he'll keep pulling until there's no jumper left.

Investigators at the Bureau's money-laundering unit carefully laid out the receipts and dried them off, reassembled them and started trying to work out where they all came from. One was for a cash withdrawal from a nearby post office in Blanchardstown, so Sheehan and the investigating team paid them a visit, pulled the CCTV and watched as Damian Stander walked in and withdrew 5,000 euros, filling out a form and providing a French driving licence as his ID. But there was something amiss. The bank card he used was in a different name. The post office should have spotted this discrepancy, but didn't. They gave Stander the cash and he walked out.

First there was his behaviour outside the hotel room, then the wads of cash, then the receipts in the toilet, and now this. There was something deeply suspicious about Damian Stander. And it was all about to get weirder.

In April 2020, a couple of months after the incident at the Carlton Hotel, two men walked into a bank in Lucan, twelve miles away, with a remarkable story. They claimed to be a pair of high-rolling music producers. They said they were staging a series of concerts around the world, and had secured a major coup: a performance by an African act they described as 'the next Drake' (a reference to the multi-million-selling hip-hop star and entrepreneur). But they'd hit a problem. The bank had frozen the money they were going to use to stage the concert in Ireland. They'd sent several emails to try and sort the whole thing out, but to no avail. That's why they were at the bank, to explain the matter and get their funds released.

The bank had good reason to freeze the cash. The money which was supposedly for the concert had come from a Spanish company called Imprex. They're a big distributor of consumer goods, handling everything from razors to WD-40. The two music promoters claimed that Imprex was sponsoring the concert. Sure enough, around 294,000 euro had been sent from Imprex to a business account at the Irish bank in the name of Your Highness Records, which had been set up by one of the promoters. But then the bank had become suspicious. For a start, it was a large amount of money. And when it hit the account, the concert promoter immediately sent a chunk of it to his own personal account and a chunk to an account in Lagos, which seemed unconnected with the music business. Alarmed by the account holder's behaviour, the bank tipped off the police, who requested CCTV of the two men. And this is when the music impresarios' luck took yet another downward turn. It just so happened that the team of officers looking into the bank's concerns was the same unit running the Carlton Hotel investigation. Sean Sheehan and his colleagues took one look at the footage from the bank and immediately recognized one of the music promoters: it was Damian Stander, the man from the hotel.

Except, it wasn't. Police had been doing some digging into Stander and realized it was a fake ID. In reality, the man's name was Junior Boboye, a Nigerian in his twenties who lived in Ashbourne, a small town a few miles outside Dublin. As if his fake identity wasn't suspicious enough, here was Boboye turning up at a bank with a colleague, trying to get his hands on some money and giving a fishy story about a concert they were organizing for a big rap star.

Meanwhile, things were not going well at the bank for the two music producers. Their attempt to explain themselves wasn't cutting any ice. The bank still wasn't convinced and wouldn't let them have the funds. In the end, they left, only to be intercepted in the car park by a police team from the Garda National Economic Crime Bureau who'd come to question them. They found a phone belonging to Boboye in the car and seized it. Just as he'd done at the Carlton Hotel, he refused to surrender his PIN. But this time, the police managed to use digital forensics to extract the code. It turned out to be 3194 – Boboye's date of birth. Sheehan had a brainwave: 'I wondered would 3194 open the phone from the Carlton Hotel?' he says. 'And it did.'

The phone seized at the hotel turned out to be the kind of goldmine most police investigators can only dream of. 'There was a multitude of evidence in relation to thousands upon thousands of text messages, screenshots, banking details, money mule details, account details, which all showed the level that Junior Boboye operated on,' says Sheehan. As they scrolled through the phone, the police realized they'd landed a key middleman in a giant financial operation. They were uncovering a sprawling criminal conspiracy to wash tens of millions of pounds of stolen money through Ireland's banking system, via a network of thousands of money mules recruited across the country to withdraw the money. It was industrialized money laundering and running it was a web of organized crime gangs, with the Black Axe at their heart.

As a former British colony, Nigeria has strong, historic links with both the UK and Ireland. Emigration from the country has been going on for years, and during the economic slump of the 1980s and 1990s the British Isles were a natural destination for Nigerians in search of better outcomes. Thousands still arrive in Ireland every year, and there's been a bit of a boom in recent times. From 2016, rates doubled over the next four years to 14,000 annually. For some, it's become a permanent home; at one point, Nigerians were the largest single group to gain citizenship of the country.[1] To be clear: the vast majority of these Nigerian diaspora members have nothing whatsoever to do with the Black Axe or any other organized crime groups, and abhor their activities as much as anyone else. But as the Nigerian community took root in countries like Ireland, there was always the risk that Black Axe elements would be imported too. According to Gary Warner, the University of Alabama academic who's tracked the movement's global spread, the UK and Ireland was one of the first Black Axe Zones to be created outside Nigeria, dating back to 1996. Warner says that a leaked message from inside the Black Axe reveals that the first summit meeting of the UK and Ireland region was on 12 August 2009. That's several years before it got started in North America and Europe. By this stage, the Black Axe was deep into business email compromise and other highly lucrative frauds. Ireland has a well-developed banking system, so it was no surprise that when searching for opportunities to launder the money stolen by its criminal network, Black Axe organizers saw the country's potential and began setting up operations there.

The first hint Irish law enforcement got about what was happening was an anonymous letter sent to the government in December

2016. The letter writer wanted to tip the government off to some strange goings-on at a big fruit farm north of Dublin, which hired a lot of seasonal workers, including many from Nigeria. Someone close to the farm was approaching these Nigerian workers and asking for their bank details so that money could be moved through their accounts, with the promise that they would get 10 per cent of the cash. At least nine people took part and were subsequently prosecuted. As the Irish police's financial intelligence unit dug deeper into this group of money mules, they discovered that the enterprise went far wider than the fruit farm. They uncovered more and more of this kind of activity, all linked to West African organized crime gangs working in the country. Some of it was traceable to specific Black Axe members, but as more laundering was carried out, the lines between the different operators started to blur.

'We're seeing crossover between the Black Axe and these sort of less formal groups that are operating,' says Detective Inspector Steven Meighan. He was once Sean Sheehan's boss in the Economic Crime Bureau and has spent years tracing the wider footprint of laundering gangs working in the country. 'We are seeing the Black Axe operating in Ireland on a very formal basis, and if the need arises, they will utilize these less structured groups. It's almost like you have a money-laundering hierarchy ready and the Black Axe will come in and exploit that.'

Irish police believe that, some time around 2017 or 2018, the Black Axe became unhappy with Ireland's performance in the organization's illicit money-making, and sent across a big player to ramp up its laundering activity. It worked. The underground financial trade has exploded in the country in recent years. Driving it all is a desperate need by the crime gangs for one commodity: bank accounts through which stolen money can be moved and withdrawn. And that's where the world of international fraud and cybercrime hits the streets of Ireland. Getting hold of bank accounts means getting hold of money mules – and lots of them.

'They're recruiting mules and they're not fussy about the mules that they're recruiting,' says Meighan.

This was the job of Junior Boboye, the man who pretended to be Damian Stander and posed as a music promoter, and whose phone Sean Sheehan was busily scrutinizing after it was seized in the car park outside the bank in Lucan in 2020.

'It took months to go through it,' he tells me. Boboye had sent and received thousands of messages, and through analysing them, Sheehan gradually built a picture of his suspect. Boboye was a link-man, essentially. He would receive messages from higher-ups in the gang, alerting him to frauds that were about to happen (like the one perpetrated on Tom Cronkright's company in the last chapter), and tasking him with providing a bank account through which the fraudulently obtained money could be moved. Boboye would then go out and recruit money mules whose accounts could be used for the purpose, and send their details back to the higher-ups.

As Sheehan sits in a Dublin police office explaining all this to me, he's leafing through a sheaf of hundreds of A4 pages of evidence: screenshots of the contents of Boboye's phone, with messages he's sent and received, photos of receipts, money mules' bank cards, bank statements and so on. And that's not all. Also on Boboye's phone, Sheehan found a video he'd secretly filmed in the bank on an earlier visit, as he and his 'music promoter' colleague had tried to convince the staff to unfreeze their money for the mythical concert. Altogether, Boboye's phone was like the secret diary of a money-laundering middleman. Which makes you wonder, why on earth didn't he delete it all?

'You might think it's silly, but it's actually self-protection,' says Meighan. Boboye is working on behalf of higher-ups, and he has to convince them he's doing his job, Meighan explains: 'He can say, "I tried really hard. This is what the bank said. If you don't believe me, here's a video of that." And that's why the phones are a treasure trove of information, because people are taking lodgement slips, they're taking copies of emails. It's saved and it's sent to the next level up in the chain.'

Piecing together this evidence, Sheehan can now see that over the preceding few years, Boboye had been the link-man in at least half-a-dozen frauds on businesses, in which the victim was tricked into sending money to a mule account which Boboye had prepared. This was the truth behind his visit to the bank in May, during which he argued for the release of the money from the Spanish distribution business, Imprex. He'd claimed the company was an eager investor in his hip-hop concert plan. But of course they weren't; they were the victim of a scam, and had been tricked into sending the 294,000 euro into Boboye's accomplice's account, which Boboye was then going to launder.

Imprex wasn't the only victim. As Sheehan dissected Boboye's phone, he came across another target: a company in Carrickmacross, a town sixty miles north of Dublin, called Excel Plastics. It's part of a big multinational manufacturing conglomerate, and in September 2017, they'd been hit with a classic business email compromise attack. They received an email claiming that one of their suppliers' bank accounts had recently changed. They paid 91,000 euro into what they thought was the supplier's new account, not realizing it was a scam. As Sheehan checked the details of this fraud, he discovered the name on the account through which the plastics company's stolen money was washed: Kenoly Ugbodu. For Boboye, he'd been just another money mule whose bank account could be used to wash yet more stolen money. But for Ugbodu, it was a journey into global financial crime that he'd never forget.

You don't have to look very hard to find Kenoly Ugbodu online. He's on YouTube, Instagram and Snapchat, and if you're into men's fashion, he's a mine of advice. His slickly produced videos cover different looks and trends, often accompanied by a commercially savvy hat-tip to whichever company he bought the clothes from. Like many youngsters on social media, Ugbodu's pushing hard to get influencer status. But the problem with the febrile world of online celebrity is that there's always someone further ahead than you: they have better clothes, cooler shoes, glitzier locations – and consequently, bigger followings. It's hard not to feel left behind. A bit of extra cash might just give you the boost you need to join the big players.

So in 2017, when Ugbodu's friend mentioned a way to make some quick money, he was interested. All the 19-year-old psychology student had to do, his friend explained, was to connect with a certain few accounts on Snapchat, and they'd take it from there. Snapchat started as a video-sharing social media app, but for many young people it's now the messaging tool of choice, and Ugbodu was soon contacted by his friend's associates. He says he never found out their real names, but they were very convincing.

'They really try and draw you in and try and make you feel comfortable,' Ugbodu tells me. 'They don't do it in one day, it's over time. They just become your friend and then once they see that they have your trust and that you will listen to what they say, that's where it begins.'

Ugbodu was told that if he gave them his bank account details, he'd get 10 per cent of whatever money was put through the account. He says he was never told an exact sum – something he thinks was a ploy not to put him off: 'They don't mention a specific amount, because they know that young people will obviously panic when they hear such a large amount,' he says.

'I kind of caved in to the idea and I said OK because they make it sound like it's going to be a ten-minute process. That's how they love to make it sound, like you give your details, and then they give you the money, and then you're off.

'As a young boy trying to impress your friends, trying to have what your friends have, the newest this or the newest that, you don't really think of the consequences until after.'

With that, Ugbodu handed over his info, including the PIN for his online bank account.

And then . . . nothing happened. For several months, Ugbodu's account sat untouched by his Snapchat contacts, and according to him there was no further contact from them. But in the meanwhile, the gravity of his predicament was gradually starting to dawn on Ugbodu. As the months ticked by, he realized this wasn't going to be a ten-minute deal for some easy money, but something much longer and potentially far more serious. It ate away at him.

'Sometimes I'd just wake up and I'd be like, how did I really allow that to happen?' He says he feared what his Snapchat bosses would do. 'It was actually that bad where I would have dreams of these guys coming to the house and they felt so real I'd wake up in the middle of the night and I would think that they're outside my house.'

Ugbodu says he had second thoughts, but didn't want to go to the police because he was fearful of what the gang would do. He even claims that at one stage he threatened to block his card, putting a stop to the scheme. But at that point, he says the gang told him they would 'come after' his family.

'You're imagining, [what if] they hurt my mum, my dad, my brother or my sister because of me, because of something I did?' he tells me.

It wasn't an unreasonable fear. 'Junior Boboye is not afraid to administer threats in order to achieve a desired outcome,' says Garda Detective Sean Sheehan. In a message on Boboye's phone about another money mule, Boboye asked, 'Can that bitch not be patterned?' – slang for beaten up.

'It might be a threat against yourself, it might be a threat against your family,' says Sheehan's former boss Steven Meighan. 'Or even in one extreme case we saw threats made against a relative who lives in Lagos.'

However, the police insist most mules are operating without threat of violence, and that if it does happen it's only later on, if the mule threatens to back out. And in Ugbodu's case, Irish police firmly dispute that there were any threats at all. They say they found no such messages on Boboye's phone, and that, by contrast, Ugbodu's interactions with his handler were enthusiastic and fully complicit, with something like five hundred messages being sent back and forth. It's possible that both sides are true: that Ugbodu was outwardly keen to cooperate and get his cut, but privately worried about the consequences if he didn't. Whatever the truth, Ugbodu didn't tell his family what was going on, and hoped it would all just go away. 'It's kind of like denial,' he tells me. 'You want to keep them out of it and just try and face it by yourself.'

Then, one day, a message finally appears on his phone. Ugbodu is being summoned. It's time to make good on his deal with the devil. And contrary to the reassurances he's been given, this isn't going to be a quick, online job. He's going to have to go and meet the gang in person.

By September 2017, the fraud on Excel Plastics was ready to go. Ugbodu's bank account had been picked by the fraudsters to be the recipient for the stolen money, having been provided to them by their middleman Boboye. Excel Plastics received the scam email and was tricked into sending 91,000 euro. The money headed into Ugbodu's account. Now the gang had to extricate it before the victim raised the alarm and potentially clawed back the funds. And this is where Ugbodu's testimony again clashes with the police evidence against him. In our conversation Ugbodu says he merely watched online from Cork as the money washed in and out of his bank account. But the police record of his messages to Boboye tell a very different story. Ugbodu was told to get on a train to Dublin and, when he arrived, Junior Boboye was waiting for him. Once there, Ugbodu stayed with Boboye for two days while the pair toured the city, withdrawing wads of cash from different locations. ATMs were no good – the cap on daily withdrawals is only a few hundred euro and it would take months to extricate the whole 91,000. Instead, they went for post offices and money exchanges, where the limits are higher. All the while, Boboye was messaging his superior, whom he refers to as 'sir', to fill him in on progress. In the end they pulled out around 75,000 of the stolen 91,000 euro in around thirty different transactions.

Then Ugbodu was released, free to go back to Cork. But he says he remained fearful for months afterward: 'I would still be thinking, "Are they gonna come back? Have they left me alone?" But after a while when nothing happened and nothing was brought to my attention, then naturally you forget about it.' He says he blocked their numbers and broke off contact. Meanwhile, his promised 10 per cent cut of the money never materialized.

More than three years later, on 15 April 2021, there was a knock on the door of the family house at 7 a.m. It wasn't the Snapchat gangsters – but in some ways, it was worse. 'I looked out the window and I saw three squad cars and two police vans,' says Ugbodu.

By this point in time, the police had carried out the raid at the Carlton Hotel, identified Junior Boboye, analysed his phone, discovered the fraud on Excel Plastics, and of course found Ugbodu's name on the account through which the money was laundered. His past had finally caught up with him, and he immediately thought about the impact of a possible criminal conviction on his future. Having recently graduated in psychology, he'd set his sights on becoming a counsellor. He worried that his attempts to gain professional qualifications, registrations and jobs would be severely hampered by any previous criminal convictions, which he'd have to declare. He also had concerns closer to home: 'I didn't want my parents to be ashamed of the kid they rose,' he says. His father is a pastor in a local church, where Ugbodu says he sometimes plays keyboards. He feared the impact on his family's reputation in the community.

After initially denying it, Ugbodu eventually admitted taking part in the Excel Plastics fraud. By this time, of course, the money stolen from the company was long gone. It was withdrawn in cash in 2017, way before the police arrested Boboye, and they've never recovered it. Boboye almost certainly sent most of it back to his accomplices, who initiated the scam on Excel Plastics. Ugbodu had played a key part in the crime. Using him had allowed the fraudsters to fulfil the integration stage in the laundering process, by withdrawing it in cash and thereby pulling it out of the financial system in readily usable funds. They hadn't done very much to layer it – they hadn't mixed it around among a bunch of accounts, for example – but they probably didn't feel the need to do so. After all, if anyone tracked the money it would lead straight to Ugbodu, and they were happy for him to take the fall, which is exactly what happened.

Meanwhile, Ugbodu had learned that he'd helped launder money stolen from a local business, which made him feel even more guilty.

'When they told me that, I was even more distraught because I basically cheated my own. I've been here twenty-two years with my family. This country is amazing compared to other countries. It's a great country to live in. So when I found out that it was one of our own it was like "ouch".'

Ugbodu's family moved to Ireland from Nigeria when he was four. When I asked him whether he felt this had some bearing on him being drawn into West African organized crime, he said no, he didn't think so. The evidence bears him out: Ugbodu is very far from alone in being swept up in this crime wave, and the demographics of the money mules pulled into it seem to span the whole range of Irish society. Police believe there are as many as 4,000 mules active in the country at this time, the vast majority working for the Black Axe and related gangs. They're currently looking at around 800 suspects and have made hundreds of arrests. Of those whose prosecutions are reported in the media, there's a slight predominance of young white men, but there are also men and women with different backgrounds, ethnicities and ages. It feels like an epidemic; a constant stream of people appearing before judges and telling the same sorry tale: they wanted some quick money and while they knew the offer was a little dodgy, they really didn't think it was anything too wrong. Most end up with short or suspended sentences, but that's still a criminal record, with all the attendant consequences. Some defence solicitors have concerns about how the cases are being dealt with. Many end up in Ireland's Circuit Court, where a conviction (albeit often suspended) is almost inescapable – something one defence barrister told me he felt was heavy-handed prosecution. Irish police say it's up to the country's Director of Public Prosecution to decide which court the case goes to. But it's clear what they think of the idea that these money mules are poor, vulnerable innocents being duped into criminality: 'bullshit', as one officer put it to me. They also point out that the effect on victims – like Excel Plastics – can be devastating.

But Irish police also know they can't arrest all the mules; just like the army of little blue Smurfs, they're seemingly infinite and easily replaceable. Their only chance is to work their way up the chain to more significant players, and that's why the arrest of Junior Boboye was so significant – he's one of the first senior members of the money-laundering gangs to be caught. In December 2022 Boboye was sentenced to five years in prison for a string of money-laundering offences – a major prosecution under Ireland's organized crime legislation. The person pretending to be his fellow music producer, Emmanuel Olanyian, got three years.[2]

And then there was Kenoly Ugbodu. After graduating, he got a job as a supervisor at a children's play company, eventually getting promoted to manager. But he's still working on his dream to become a counsellor, doing a higher diploma. His online videos are taking off too – his TikTok account has half a million likes, and of course there's the wedding to plan. He's working out if he can afford a mortgage. His future is full of promise. But as he waits in the Cork courtroom on a May afternoon in 2023, that could all change. Soon he may have to leave his job to serve months or even years in prison – with unknown and troubling consequences for his future.

Back inside Court 4, Judge Boyle is ready with her sentence.

Ugbodu makes his way to the dock. The courtroom is cold, metaphorically as well as physically. Instead of the dark wood of older buildings, this one is all bleached panelling and natural light. It's justice by IKEA. The judge asks her clerk the maximum sentence for Ugbodu's offence. Fourteen years, she's told. I can almost see Ugbodu's jawline tighten. As she reads out the mitigating circumstances, it's clear Ugbodu's will be nowhere near that. But then she starts the sentencing, and suddenly she's talking about a two-year stint. In his mind's eye Ugbodu can see his immediate future slipping away. No counselling career. No house purchase. And then there's the prospect of having to tell his fiancée to delay the wedding plans while he goes to jail. But then, just as quickly, the judge says the sentence will be suspended, providing Ugbodu commits to good behaviour. He's spared jail. The wave of relief is palpable. After they make their way outside, Ugbodu's mother hugs the defence barrister. 'Relief,' Ugbodu tells me when I ask how he feels. 'Experiences like this happen to teach you a lesson, and I've learned it.'

Garda detective Sean Sheehan is there too. In court he testified to Ugbodu's good behaviour, telling the judge he'd been in no trouble since the run-in with Boboye. It almost certainly helped in getting Ugbodu's sentence suspended.

Engrossing as the twists and turns of Ugbodu and Boboye's story are, it merely serves to illuminate one tiny strand of a much, much larger network of organized money laundering that seems to be washing over Ireland like a tidal wave. Senior police estimate that more than 50m euro has been washed through the country by the Black Axe and its related networks. To stress again: without organized money-muling operations like these, the frauds cannot happen. Without mules like Ugbodu whose accounts can be used to receive and extract the cash, companies like Excel Plastics simply cannot be robbed in this way. The scam would fail because there'd be nowhere to send the money and no way to pull it out.

It may appear that Ireland is deluged with this criminality, but there's another explanation: maybe they're just paying more attention to it. The business email compromise and other frauds run by the Black Axe and their accomplices are international and rake in billions of dollars every year – it stands to reason they must be washing vast amounts of it through multiple jurisdictions besides Ireland. If other countries had more officers like Sheehan and his colleagues pulling at the threads, perhaps we'd see thousands more convictions worldwide, like Kenoly Ugbodu's and Junior Boboye's.

Beyond the cyber-enabled nature of these business email compromise attacks, Ugbodu's experience also highlights another pivotal aspect of technology's impact on the money-laundering industry: social media. Without it, it's likely he might never have ended up in that courtroom in Cork. Snapchat was a key conduit for his laundering recruiters. They could use it to stay anonymous while also convincing and cajoling him to take part, and other social media apps are just as useful. And as well as being handy communication methods, social media's currency of conspicuous consumerism and narcissistic one-upmanship is a powerful grooming ground for mule herders.

While many people might use their Instagram profile for restaurant plate boasts and holiday selfies, the man behind the 'Money Plugs' account uses the app to show off a different obsession: cash. Wads and wads of it. His account consists of photo upon photo of bundles of notes – £10s, £20s, £50s – unwieldy, tottering stacks held together with rubber bands. Scrolling through his profile, he seems to be drowning in the stuff. It's piled up against the skirting boards, stashed in cupboards, spilling out of carrier bags. Aware that social media is awash with fakers, he's keen to convince his followers that he hasn't just downloaded these photos from the Internet, so he'll often attach a Post-it note to the bundles of cash with the day's date and his account name written on it. When he's not posting photos of banknotes, he's uploading images of mobile phone screens showing banking app balances, which seem to show huge amounts flooding into the accounts of his satisfied 'customers'. The overall impression he gives is one of torrential, bountiful riches.

The man behind the Instagram account, called Moneyplugukkashh, describes himself as a 'financial advisor', and his offer to his 21,000 followers is delightfully direct: 'Want to make £500 a week doing nothing?' reads a typical post, over a photo of yet another stack of cash. Who wouldn't?

It didn't take me long to find him. I set up a fresh Instagram account with a few random photos, then searched some obvious hashtags: 'quickmoney', 'fastmoney', and so on. I followed any accounts that looked interesting, and was soon directed towards more, thanks to Instagram's recommendation algorithms (the same type of software that helped Gary Warner stumble upon the Black Axe's Facebook groups). I found dozens and dozens of Instagram users making the same pitch as Money Plugs.

If you're short on cash and long on gullibility, these accounts offer a vision of paradise. Young men (it's almost always men) are pictured living a life of unimaginable wealth and luxury, much of which seems to take place inside obscenely expensive cars. The photos are carefully framed – partly to trim out the men's faces, but also to exhibit the bling to the max. It's vitally important that the brands are front and centre. A Rolex watch sits on the wrist of a hand gripping a Mercedes steering wheel, on the pedals are £500-a-pair Yeezy trainers, the dashboard is heaving with more piles of banknotes and maybe a few iPhone 14 Pros dotted around for good measure. Sometimes, a pair of lithe female legs appears in shot. According to Sean Sheehan at the Garda, Junior Boboye was adept at this kind of online image-building too, filming videos while carefully rotating his phone to show off his Merc, Yeezys and Balenciaga T-shirt. To appeal to their targets, these meticulously constructed images have to hit every note perfectly, promising money, power and sex in abundance. What's more, they have to promise that the lifestyle is tantalizingly within reach for anyone who wants it. To get a piece, all you have to do is drop the account holder a line. It's not hard – they're on Instagram, Snapchat, WhatsApp and more. So, having set up my fake account on Instagram, that's exactly what I did.

Within a few hours, the phone number I'd set up for my new Instagram account started ringing. One of the callers turned out to be the man behind the Money Plugs Instagram account. When I picked up, he answered with a heavy West Midlands accent, and was keen to get going as soon as possible. 'No time-wasters,' he said. The first thing he wanted to check was which bank I was with. Satisfied that it was a major high street name, he then outlined what was required from me. All he needed, he said, was my name, address and date of birth. With that, he would set up a UK company, and then create a bank account in that company's name. I was quite surprised, as I was expecting him to request my bank login details, as Kenoly Ugbodu's recruiters had. But it seems Money Plugs had a different technique in mind. He was going to use the company he created with my details to set up a business bank account, and use that to move money through because, he explained, with a business bank account you can change the name on the account.[3] His behaviour – the flashy, banknote-laden Instagram account, the get-rich-quick lure, the urgent request to move money through an account set up in my name – bore all the hallmarks of a money-laundering operation.

If he or those connected to him were trying to convince a potential fraud victim to pay money into a new account (like the trick that had been played on Excel Plastics) it would be very useful if they could alter the recipient account name to suit the fraud. For example, if they were trying to fool a building company into paying into a new account for their brick supplier, they could change the business account name to 'Brick Supply Ltd', which looks a lot more convincing than asking them to pay into a personal account in the name of some guy called Geoff White.

I asked the man behind the Money Plugs Instagram account if I might get into trouble by doing this. He reassured me that he would close the account down as soon as the money was moved. 'There's no comebacks at all,' he told me. Needless to say, I declined to give him my details. However, I did hand his social media details to Meta, the company that owns Instagram and WhatsApp, who shut down his accounts and told me, 'We don't allow money laundering or the recruitment of money mules on our platform.'

I may have declined the offer of involvement in Money Plug's laundering plans, but tens of thousands of others are quite happy to play ball with him and others like him. Figures from CIFAS, the privately funded UK body that monitors and takes action on fraud, is currently holding the details of more than 40,000 people whose accounts bear the 'hallmarks of money muling'. This may well be the first time you've heard of CIFAS – they're not exactly a household name. Yet if you end up on their list, it can have a massively detrimental impact on your life. Money Plug's reassurances to me that there would be 'no comebacks' from taking part in his scheme were a lie, as those tens of thousands of people on the CIFAS list are currently finding out to their cost.

CIFAS's membership is made up of, among others, hundreds of financial institutions including insurers, investment firms and pretty much every UK bank you've ever heard of (and plenty you haven't). If, for example, one of those banks spots suspicious behaviour – like a student account suddenly receiving £10,000 and immediately sending on £9,500 of it to someone else – they can investigate and ultimately close the account. But they can then also file a case to the CIFAS database of suspected money laundering which could result in what's called a Category E marker. In plain English, that means the individual is flagged and can be effectively locked out of the mainstream banking system for up to six years. If they go to another high street bank and try to get an account, the bank can check the CIFAS records, find the marker and will almost certainly turn them down. Gradually, they will find the doors of UK finance closing on them.

It may not sound like the harshest of penalties, but it's hugely disruptive. In an increasingly cashless society, not having a bank account causes you constant trouble. From Netflix subscriptions to mortgages: almost everything financial relies on a bank account. If you don't have one, what do you do? How do you pay and get paid? A quarter of those on CIFAS's list of suspected mules are under twenty-one. That shouldn't come as a surprise: they're more likely to be short of cash, and often hanging out on social media where the mule recruiters lurk. But these youngsters who've got involved in muling face serious consequences. They've lost access to banking just at the time they're applying for their first jobs. How do you tell your new employer that they can't pay your salary into your bank account because it was closed for suspected criminal behaviour? Not exactly a great start to your new career.

In the UK, police don't appear to be taking the same approach as their Irish colleagues – there doesn't seem to be a campaign to pursue and prosecute mules, let alone the recruiters who pull them in (I could only find two cases of recruiters being convicted, despite multiple requests to various bodies). Instead, most UK mules are being caught up in the extra-judicial process via CIFAS described above – something they may not even realize is happening. The Category E markers don't show up on a credit report. The only way to proactively check if you have one is to make a request to CIFAS –

which, of course, you'd only do if you already knew about the process and suspected you'd been hit by it. As a result, often the first people learn about it is when their account is closed down and they realize they're potentially locked out for six years. Some manage to get a very basic account with one of the new start-up banks, but online forums for students and those with financial problems are teeming with posts from people who've suddenly found that their get-rich-quick plan has backfired catastrophically and they're now frozen out of the banking system.

The coronavirus pandemic put boosters under the industry of online mule recruitment. The stark rise in unemployment meant there were many more people searching for a quick source of income, and therefore willing to answer the herders' tempting calls. Suddenly it wasn't just hard-up students and youngsters responding. CIFAS noted a 33 per cent rise in the over-forties whose accounts were being flagged by banks. It makes sense from the mule herders' point of view: unlike for younger customers, moving large amounts through older folks' accounts might raise fewer alarms at the bank.

Once again, the tech industry has inadvertently created powerful tools for the money launderers to use. Social media has undoubtedly fuelled the trade, helping the mule herders expand their operations. The non-stop feed of conspicuous consumerism and ease of communication on apps like Instagram and Snapchat is a compelling recruitment method. But there's a problem with hiring helpers in such an overt way. For a start, it's very public: it didn't take me long to find Money Plugs on Instagram, figure out his scheme and get his accounts closed down. In addition, while many mules might claim to be ignorant of the wider criminality they're involved with, it's inevitable that some of them will realize that something dodgy is going on – just as Kenoly Ugbodu did. And at that point they might try to back out, like Ugbodu claims to have done. Or they may even try to rip their mule herders off, keeping the money rather than playing ball. Or they may go to the police.

In order to counter all of these risks, the herders must set up an enforcement operation to keep the whole thing on track, cajoling or sometimes even threatening their mules to continue cooperating and stay away from the authorities. All of that entails logistical overheads – teams of people like Boboye to manage the mules. It would be far more convenient for the herders if they could somehow recruit accomplices who are unwitting – people who are oblivious to any wrongdoing and who don't need any strong-arming to keep them on track. Luckily for the fraud gangs, they have a ready supply of such helpers thanks to another development in the global collaboration between cybercriminals and the laundering networks that support them. It has pulled some of society's most vulnerable people into the hi-tech laundering industry. And the consequences for these unsuspecting mules has been even more devastating.

In the early 2000s, as the advance-fee, 'Nigerian prince' email gangs were cutting their teeth, a splinter group of Internet fraudsters emerged with a cunning and highly profitable new strategy. At heart, the psychological tricks were the same as the classic advance-fee scams: they would reach out to an unsuspecting victim, spin them a tale and convince them to send money. But in this case, the tactics were even more venal and ruthless: they targeted those looking for love.

As Internet dating took off, this splinter group of scammers began creating fake accounts on dating sites. They would scour the web for photos of real people, use them to set up convincing-looking profiles on the dating sites and then message those seeking a relationship. Thus would begin a careful and often lengthy process of grooming the victim. The scammer would 'love bomb' their unsuspecting target, flattering and fawning on them, convincing them that a genuine, loving companionship was in the offing. They would often target the elderly, perhaps those who'd divorced or been bereaved. Those of more advanced years tended to have more money and were also less distrustful of online interactions, being less familiar with modern technology. As a result, they were ripe for the scam that became known as 'romance fraud'.

Posing as their suitor, the scammer would often pretend to be a wealthy person, living in a different country or working abroad (being employed on an oil rig was a frequently used ruse). This gave a convenient excuse for the scammer to continue the grooming online, and not to have to meet up in person. It also set things up for the next stage of the scam. The admirer would begin to talk of visiting their potential paramour, making arrangements to finally meet. The relationship-building would reach an exciting, feverish pitch. But then would come a problem. The suitor would message to say there'd been some kind of financial issue. Their account had been inexplicably frozen or their credit card lost, for example.

The victim would be asked to help – just temporarily, of course – by sending some money to fund the trip. By this stage, they'd been the target of a carefully managed grooming process potentially lasting for months, with the exchange of perhaps hundreds of seemingly heartfelt, intimate messages. As far as they were concerned, their admirer was earnest, committed and certainly wealthy enough to reimburse them. So they'd transfer the money, sometimes tens of thousands of pounds. The suitor would reply enthusiastically, maybe mentioning that they were about to get on the plane and their mobile phone would be switched off for some time. And so the victim would wait patiently for the long-awaited moment of meeting. But it would never happen.

Over the next few days as they heard nothing more, they would gradually realize that the relationship that had captured their heart and kept them hopeful was nothing but a lie. And to add to their pain, they'd been robbed of the money they'd spent their life saving.

Given that romance fraud has vast potential for profit that relies on duping victims and spiriting away their hard-earned money, it's perhaps no surprise to find that the Black Axe is a big player in the space. When Tom Cronkright went to testify in Tampa against Okechukwu 'Desmond' Amadi, he met eight other witnesses who'd also been scammed by the Amadi brothers. One was from a company in California, but the other six were 'all female, aged from their late fifties to their late sixties, most of them recently divorced or widowed,' remembers Cronkright. They were all victims of romance frauds connived in by the Amadis. As he heard their stories, Cronkright was horrified: 'What they did to these people emotionally and financially, it was just absolutely heinous,' he says.

Thankfully, media coverage of the issue has alerted more and more potential victims, who are increasingly wise to the game. But the criminals are constantly evolving. The skilled gangs who run these frauds have not gone away, and thanks to the Black Axe's international crime network, they've even discovered a new use for their victims, one which combines their old deception tactics with the globalized world of money laundering.

The scam gangs have realized that the romance fraudsters' elderly targets can also be a source of fresh bank accounts and have exploited this with gusto. They are utilizing them in the same way they wash money through the accounts of people like Kenoly Ugbodu, but with one big difference – they don't need to be ready to threaten or intimidate the romance mules into cooperating, just sweet-talk them into unwittingly complying.

The initial playbook is often the same as in a traditional romance fraud: an elderly person on a dating site will receive a message from an attractive would-be partner who, for some reason, can't meet them in person just yet. They're wooed over time. Then comes the tantalizing offer of a visit – then some kind of financial snag that threatens to prevent it. But this time, the solution isn't for the victim to send emergency money to their overseas suitor to pay for their visit. Instead, the admirer offers to send the victim money, requesting that they transfer it to a 'friend' who can sort the whole thing out.

At this point, the victim becomes even more convinced that their suitor is a person of great wealth – after all, they seem to have tens of thousands of pounds at their disposal. In fact, the money arriving in their account has come from another fraud victim like Tom Cronkright's company or Excel Plastics in Ireland, who've been tricked into sending it. The would-be suitor's 'friend' is in fact their criminal accomplice, who spirits the money away.

The net result for the victim is the same: they face the heart-wrenching realization that their entire online relationship was a fake. But now they have the added knowledge that their account was used to launder money from yet another victim of the same gang.

Like the traditional model, this new twist on romance fraud – tricking victims into becoming money mules – is only possible thanks to the Internet dating boom. Tech has inadvertently opened yet another avenue for the launderers to exploit.

At the heart of this grim trade, once again, are the crime gangs who coordinate the business email compromise attacks, and then line up the accounts to clean and vanish the stolen money. They have slick operations running in countries all around the world and their reputation as money-laundering experts is formidable, largely because they have access to huge numbers of accounts that can be used for washing money, whether from social media accomplices like Kenoly Ugbodu, keen to make a quick buck, or from victims of romance fraud unwittingly making their accounts available. Groups like the Black Axe have become the Interflora of money laundering. If you have a massive amount of dirty money and you want it cleaned across multiple continents, no questions asked, you know who to call.

Over the preceding chapters, you've learned the key steps involved in any successful money-laundering operation, and witnessed how constantly evolving technological innovation has – often unintentionally – transformed these steps to create myriad opportunities for the hi-tech money movers to do their work. Now it's time to look at an example that brings many of these strands together. An illustration of how cutting-edge laundering can enable crimes that threaten not just individual victims, but each and every one of us.

It starts with the story of one Nigerian money launderer and his incredible journey from the streets of Lagos to one of the finest hotels in the world, living a life of luxury, before it all came crashing down. His story is perhaps the greatest illustration of how hi-tech crime and street-level money laundering are merging together. It's also one of the most jaw-dropping. That's because the money he was washing wasn't just the takings of some skilled scam artists. It was the profits from crimes allegedly conducted by one of the most dangerous and repressive regimes on earth – profits which researchers claim are funding weapons that now threaten the entire world.

9

Hushpuppi and Big Boss

A giant, gleaming palace of luxury overlooking the glittering waters of the Dubai Creek, the Palazzo Versace is fighting hard for a spot as one of the world's most glamorous hotels. It's a place where every meal is snapped for Instagram, where the rubbernecking for celebrity guests never stops, and where the rooms feature 'a canvas of elaborate white and cream boiseries' (otherwise known as wood panelling).

If you book far enough in advance, you can bag a room here for a few hundred pounds a night. Not cheap by any standard, but affordable enough to be a blow-out treat for many middle-class folks. Those in a higher income bracket, however, might look upon such entry-level options with disdain, and opt instead for the Grand Suites, which come with private balconies and commanding views of the city. For these, you're looking at up to a thousand pounds a night.

But for those even *further* up the economic ladder, there is the option to take not just a room, but an entire apartment. For this, the Palazzo provides the 'residences' – private, self-contained zones of opulence, complete with powder rooms, kitchens full of Miele appliances, and of course, space for the maid. For these, the nightly bill can run to several thousand pounds, and for the vast majority of guests fawning over the Palazzo, that's as outrageous as it gets. A stay in a residence puts you at the very top of the tree.

And yet, there is another, higher level of service available only to those with stratospheric budgets. For these guests, it is possible to take out a year-long tenancy. They can make the Palazzo their home. Imagine that: no need to make the bed ever again. Fresh sheets just a housekeeping call away.

Such is the tormenting spiral of wealth: just when you think you've reached the highest level, you turn a corner and there's someone ahead of you.

But in June 2020, Ramon Olorunwa Abbas could have been forgiven for thinking he was truly approaching the zenith of this gilded chase. The 37-year-old Nigerian had not only taken out a year-long contract at the Palazzo, he'd shelled out for a Versace residence too. What this meant in practice was that, in his suite of rooms, the brand was ubiquitous. The famous Medusa's head logo appeared everywhere from the bedsheets and towels to the cups and plates. Not everyone would find this a compelling reason to pay extra on top of an already astronomical bill, but for Abbas, such fripperies mattered immensely. He was an Instagram influencer with millions of followers, and for many of them, the Versace logo was the ultimate stamp of achievement.

And so, as he sat back on his Versace sofa and gazed at his wardrobes full of Fendi clothes and his shelves full of Gucci shoes, Abbas probably felt the warm glow of a man who'd climbed the mountain of money and now sat at its peak, gazing down. Life was good. Or #blessed, as he told his millions of online followers.

Then came the knock at the door.

Within minutes, a SWAT team of armed Dubai police officers wearing ski masks and body armour had burst inside. They swarmed through the residence, grabbing laptops and phones, photographing and bagging everything they found. Abbas stood, perplexed, in the middle of it all, his arms held behind his back by a black-clad police officer. On his face was the look of a man suddenly remembering all the bodies he'd climbed over to get to the top.

This modern-day Icarus had indeed reached the zenith of his meteoric journey. He was now as close to the sun as he'd ever get. His wings were on fire, and below him was only the long, long drop. It was the stunning denouement of a rags-to-riches tale that had taken Abbas on a wild journey, from the depths of poverty to the heights of power. His is the story of an endlessly fascinating double life. In public, he was a ludicrously wealthy entrepreneur living in the lap of luxury. In private, he was a venal crook, one half of a crime duo who ended up laundering money for some of the most dangerous people on the planet. It was a path Abbas had set out on decades earlier from the most unlikely starting point.

Abbas was born on 11 October 1982 in Bariga, a poor area of the Nigerian capital Lagos. His father was a civil servant, his mother a businesswoman. Life was hard and housing was tenuous; the family received their fair share of eviction notices. But they still managed to pay for private after-school tuition for the bright young Ramon. He studied business at the University of Nigeria and dreamed of success. At this time in his life, that meant perhaps owning a few buses and motorbikes that he could rent out as part of Lagos's public transport system. Abbas had no idea just how far he would exceed those humble aspirations.[1]

But, like many smart youngsters in 1980s Nigeria, Abbas struggled to gain steady employment. So he hustled; he began selling clothes out of the boot of his car. By this time he'd moved to nearby Oworonshoki, another poor area, where he lived in a one-storey house fronting on to a busy, unpaved road. Abbas was slowly but surely getting ahead, apparently fuelled by honest, entrepreneurial ambition. But those who knew him at this time were under no illusions as to how Abbas was really making his money. According to them, he'd joined the 'Yahoo boys' – the small but increasingly powerful minority of Nigerians who'd turned to online scamming to make ends meet.[2] Unlike his fellow fraudsters, however, Abbas would not linger long in Lagos. His future lay far outside the country, and his fate would be intertwined with that of a man thousands of miles away, who would also become a globally successful crook and would ultimately take the pair to dizzying heights of criminal success – before bringing them both crashing back down.

Ghaleb Alaumary was born two years after Abbas into a world which could not have been more different to the Nigerian's. Alaumary was born in Oxford, Mississippi in the US – a town of 25,000 people with tidy streets, a neat, well-groomed square and a smattering of art galleries, concert halls and bookshops. Alaumary's mother ran a restaurant and his father had several clothing businesses.[3] After high school in the US, Alaumary moved with the family to Montreal, Canada, where they owned Château Olivier, an eight-bedroom property in the Saint-Laurent area of the city. It's a stunning house. Guests who've stayed there have compared it to the world of Bruce Wayne, Batman's multi-millionaire alter ego. There's a heated pool and a hot tub for six people out the back. There's also a private gate that leads directly into a large, lush public park, with views over the Rivière des Prairies waterway. It was in these well-to-do surroundings that Ghaleb Alaumary grew up with his brother and sister. As Abbas was dodging the grinding traffic in Lagos's inner city, Alaumary could simply open his back gate and disappear into the greenery.[4]

After finishing high school, Alaumary dropped out of college and took a few private university courses, ending up working in similar retail businesses to his father, selling clothes and jewellery. And then things started to go off the rails. By 2009, Alaumary was a regular attendee at Quebec's criminal courts. His offences were relatively low-level: fraud and credit-card crimes which mostly resulted in short, probationary sentences.[5] But it was a troublingly frequent occurrence. He was arrested nine times and convicted on five occasions. For anyone watching, it was obvious Alaumary was on a dangerous slide into career criminality.[6]

But then, after a short spree of offending, his criminal record in Canada came to a halt. Alaumary dropped off the courts' radar. Did he see the error of his ways and give up crime? Not a bit of it. Alaumary had evolved. He'd discovered that, away from the meatspace world of clothing shops and retail outlets, there was a whole new realm where he could run his fraudulent schemes. Alaumary discovered the dark web. To operate in this murky, anonymous space, he needed to assume an identity, and the name he chose gives a strong clue as to his level of hubris and self-belief: Alaumary became 'Big Boss'.

According to research by tech security firm Intel471, from around

2012, Big Boss pops up on fraud and crime sites across the dark web, in addition to various other monikers also used by Alaumary (including G and Backwood). In these underground forums, Alaumary was touting for business, offering to use the credit-card fraud skills he'd honed on behalf of other crooks.[7]

He wasn't the only one reinventing himself. At exactly the same time, on the other side of the world, Ramon Abbas was also evolving. Like Alaumary's, his criminal career was taking shape. And also like Alaumary, he was forging an online persona. In Abbas's case, however, his emergence into a new identity would not take place in the gloom of the underworld, but under the full glare of social media. His alter ego would be a giant presence, so loud and so extravagant that it would drown out his private misdeeds – or, at least, that was the plan. In 2012 Abbas created an Instagram account. From then onwards, millions would come to know him – like Madonna or Prince – by just one name: Hushpuppi.

As well as a new handle, Abbas had a new playground. By 2014 he'd moved to Malaysia, where he continued to study business and worked as a club promoter, plugging African musicians into the nightlife of the capital, Kuala Lumpur.[8] He'd also begun making serious amounts of money in a short space of time. His Instagram account illuminates the bewildering speed of this transformation. In his first post from October 2012, he's photographed in Nigeria. The buildings around him are dilapidated and his clothes creased and unflattering. He looks uncertainly into the camera. By the time he hits Malaysia, however, his transition into the larger-than-life persona of Hushpuppi is complete. Abbas is videoed in Kuala Lumpur where he boasts that the Versace store has voted him customer of the year – something he celebrates by spending $20,000 in the shop.[9] But his stay in Malaysia was relatively short-lived. By 2017, Abbas had moved again, this time to the location that would become not only the perfect canvas for the ever-increasing promotion of his wealth, but also the scene of his greatest crimes: Dubai.

Abbas ensconced himself in the glitz of the Palazzo Versace and at this point was presenting himself as a real-estate developer, although there's no indication of which real estate he was developing. Instead, the endlessly updated feed of attention-grabbing photos continued unabated. Abbas was pictured attending fashion shows, sitting on private jets and posing next to flash cars. There's something odd about many of the shots: Abbas seems to be standing strangely, with one of his feet turned at an awkward angle. I found this confusing until I realized it was so he could show off the side view of his expensive designer shoes. When you're trying to build a career as a fashion influencer, such details matter.

Abbas was gaining hundreds of thousands of online followers. Those who were invited into his inner circle during this time were astonished by the grandeur of his surroundings. One of them was Olukoya Abisoye. Also an influencer, online he goes by the name Oyemykke, using apps like Instagram to promote his range of style and grooming products. He was nowhere near Abbas's level, but nonetheless, the two fellow Nigerians started chatting online and fast became friends. 'I knew he was from trenches like I am, from the ghetto,' he tells me.[10] Eventually, Oyemykke got an invite to visit Abbas in Dubai. The more experienced man took him under his wing, and offered him a vision of what his future life as an influencer could be like.

'I had never been in that sort of environment,' Oyemykke says of the Palazzo Versace. 'It was beautiful. Stunning. I was amazed.' Abbas showed Oyemykke his wardrobes full of designer clothes and shoes, and invited him to sleep over. 'I had a great dream. I never dreamed like that,' he remembers. 'And then I woke up on a Versace bed.' The pair chatted about their lives as influencers; how to get more followers and more success. Oyemykke remembers Abbas as patient, quiet and generous.

To people like Oyemykke, it looked like Abbas had finally made it, leaving behind his roots in Nigeria and carving out an immensely lucrative legitimate career as a social media influencer: a strange, through-the-looking-glass world in which meritless narcissism could generate a seemingly limitless income stream. Influencers provide publicity for companies on social media by posting photos wearing their clothes, visiting their restaurants and so on. In return, the companies offer freebies and sometimes even direct sponsorship. From the outside, influencers like Abbas seem to have discovered the keys to a perpetual motion money machine: the more followers they get, the more luxury perks they're given; and the more they post about the perks, the more followers they acquire. But, of course, the problem with a perpetual motion machine is how to start it off. How do you buy those first pairs of expensive trainers or designer suits that boost your follower count? This is where Abbas was being less forthcoming with his legions of social media followers. Increasingly, his extravagant lifestyle was funded by crime. In truth, he'd never left behind his roots as a scam artist. But he kept this hidden from people like Oyemykke, who had no reason to suspect that Abbas's wealth might have been acquired by nefarious means.

'I didn't know exactly what he did. I knew he had money. The lifestyle was a lot – but it's Dubai. Everybody there is rich!' says Oyemykke. And as he points out, how often do we probe the provenance of successful people's bank balances? 'Human beings, we are all actors,' he says. 'I could tell you that I have a clothing business, and after I leave here, I go to rob a bank. The truth is, you wouldn't know.' As far as Oyemykke was concerned, Abbas was just 'a guy who liked what I did and showed me love'.

Staff at the Palazzo Versace hotel also seemed to have had no suspicions about Abbas. Those I've spoken to saw him as just another fabulously wealthy guest. They told me he was quiet and shy, but friendly. Apparently he wasn't a particularly extravagant tipper, but his generosity manifested itself in other ways. According to one staff member, when honeymooning couples arrived at the hotel, he'd sometimes lend them one of his luxury cars for a nuptial joyride.

But Abbas's charm and his very public displays of wealth were simply a smokescreen. The truth was that the money for the flash vehicles, the designer clothes and the Palazzo residence was largely coming not from Abbas's high-profile influencer career, but from his secret alter ego as an international fraudster and money launderer handling millions of dollars of stolen money. By the time Oyemykke visited him at the Palazzo and enjoyed his night in the Versace bed, Abbas was at that very moment in the midst of a jaw-dropping crime spree. In the preceding years he and Ghaleb Alaumary had become partners in crime and, unknown to Abbas, they were locked in a death spiral that had only one possible outcome. Their victims spanned the world, including in Alaumary's native Canada.

In 2017, MacEwan University in Edmonton was undergoing a major refurbishment. A new building, at a cost of 143m Canadian dollars, was to house dance studios, lecture theatres and classrooms.[11] It was a major piece of work, and a lot of bills and invoices were coming into the university's finance department. On 27 June an email arrived from one of the contractors, requesting that payment be made to a new account. Readers who've paid attention to the previous two chapters will know what happens next. The email was a fake, sent not from the building contractor but from a business email compromise (BEC) fraudster. The bank account belonged to Ghaleb Alaumary. In August, the university sent 1.9m Canadian dollars to the account, which Alaumary duly laundered, partly via a bank in Dubai. The fraudsters kept trying, and a week later the university sent another payment of 10m Canadian dollars. Then the following week, the university got an email from the real building contractor, asking where their money was. Realizing their mistake, the university frantically chased the funds they'd been tricked into sending. In the end, they got back 10.9m Canadian dollars.[12] But that still left a million that had slipped into the fraudsters' hands, never to be recovered. Not a bad payday for Alaumary and his accomplices. Schemes like these were helping turn Alaumary – under his dark web identity as Big Boss – into a big-time crook. He was making a lot of very useful underworld connections along the way, but his growing network of contacts and their ever-expanding criminal aspirations would prove to be Alaumary's undoing. At the very time he was rejoicing at receiving his cut of the stolen university money, a plot was being hatched that would lead police straight to him. And it all came about because of a seemingly random encounter between two old school friends.

In Spring 2017, as Alaumary's crew were gearing up to hit Mac-Ewan University, a woman called Jennal Aziz was catching up with an old friend called Kelvin Desangles. The pair had met in high school in the early 2000s but had lost touch. Aziz was now living in Orlando, Florida, while Desangles told her he was in Savannah, Georgia, where he ran an investment firm. A 'tight ship', as he described it. When he found out Aziz worked at SunTrust Bank, Desangles suggested Aziz give him the details of some of her customers so he could pitch his business to them. In exchange, Aziz would be paid a fee. It was a breach of the bank's rules, but Aziz agreed to do it anyway. Perhaps she regarded it as a little off-the-books favour for an old friend. 'Are u doing anything shady?' she asked at one point. 'Come on juju seriously,' Desangles responded, using a nickname, 'I would never.' But that was a lie. Desangles was not an investment manager but a career criminal who at that very moment was on supervised release having been convicted of fraud. He took the data Aziz gave him and worked with accomplices to commit more such crimes. Meanwhile, her promised fee never materialized.[13]

Aziz wasn't the only one. Desangles was handsome, and used his good looks to strike up conversations with women in clubs, targeting those who worked at banks, flirting with them and convincing them to part with sensitive data on customers.[14]

Desangles and his gang used the data they gained from people like Aziz to carry out a very basic but highly lucrative con. Using the personal information they'd acquired about their victims, they would go into the person's bank, impersonate them and take out loans in their names. It was all going well until one of the gang got caught trying to scam a loan from a bank in Dallas, Texas, in November 2017. He ended up being questioned by a US Secret Service agent named Glen Kessler, based in Savannah (prior to its role in protecting the US President, the Secret Service was originally set up to tackle counterfeiting, and it still handles a lot of financial crime cases today). The arrested man told Kessler his story: he'd been recruited by the fraud gang to impersonate their victims. The gang would give him a packet of personal information about the target of the fraud. He'd have one night to memorize all the details, and then the next day would go into the bank and try to fool the staff into authorizing the loan. As he talked, the suspect's story got wilder. He told Kessler that the gang involved a global conspiracy of players, including a nation state. Kessler was sceptical. 'It just seemed very far-fetched,' he says.

Nonetheless, the suspect agreed to cooperate with the US Secret Service, which meant Kessler could put the gang under surveillance, tapping their phone calls and tailing them. Some turned out to be highly adept at evading surveillance. On one occasion, Kessler's colleagues tracked one of the suspects to a bar, where they planned to grab his glass to try to pull fingerprints and identify him. But when he left the bar, they discovered he'd taken his glass with him. Clearly, this crew knew the tricks of the trade.

But as they continued to monitor the group, the Secret Service gradually unpicked their inner workings. They discovered that much of the work was being controlled by someone who went by the nickname Ockie, among others. The gang members described him as the 'logistics guy' – the man who organized travel and accommodation for the identity thieves, and checked up on them to make sure everything was running to plan. His messages were impatient and brusque: he clearly had his eye on the bottom line. 'We need to get paid this time,' he told them as they prepared for a forthcoming fraud. ''Cause, you know I'm already six grand in the hole from hotels and flights.'[15]

A key task for the Georgia Secret Service office was now to identify the mysterious Ockie, the man seemingly running the identity theft gang. They had phone numbers, email addresses and so on, but to make headway and eventually launch a prosecution, they needed to definitively link all this to a real person – and that wasn't going to be easy. Ockie had been extremely careful to disguise his identity, almost always using online communications, never giving his real name, and using burner email addresses and phone numbers. His opsec was clearly top-notch. Then finally, after almost a year of working, the Secret Service got a breakthrough. Kessler's team discovered a single photo, a shot of a credit card taken by Ockie and sent to one of his accomplices. Ockie had made a slip-up: one of his fingers was visible in the shot.

'On the big screen, when you zoomed in, you could actually make out the ridges on his finger,' recalls Kessler. They sent it to the forensics lab. Incredibly, the lab managed to pull a fingerprint from the photo. They compared it to the US national database and came back with a match – a single record, of someone who'd been arrested as a juvenile for a minor offence in Mississippi years before. The name on the file was Ghaleb Alaumary. It turned out the 'big boss' behind Desangles's identity theft gang was . . . Big Boss, Alaumary's alter ego.

It didn't take the Secret Service long to trace Alaumary to his base in Canada. The Georgia agents realized this was a crime that went far beyond state lines and across international borders, so they called in the help of the Service's newly formed Global Investigative Operations Center, which was under the leadership of Deputy Special Agent Matthew O'Neill.

As O'Neill and Kessler dug into Alaumary's past, they realized this wasn't the first time he'd appeared on the Secret Service's radar. Way back in 2013, he'd come up in its investigation into a hack on the Bank of Muscat, which cost the target $39m.[16] But at that time, he was a relatively low-level player in the crime, and the investigators hadn't pursued him. Once you're on law-enforcement's radar, however, it's hard to escape. 'We keep a Rolodex on who the bad guys are,' says O'Neill. Alaumary had been placed on the Rolodex and, thanks to a single fingerprint, he was back in the picture and linked to a series of the Desangles gang's frauds. It was a great breakthrough for the investigators, but it presented a problem.

Alaumary was in Canada. Applying to extradite him to the US was an option, but O'Neill was worried that would kibosh the chances of gaining valuable intelligence by keeping him under surveillance.

'We were thwarting a lot of crimes, because we had a whole network of people that were getting the information as to where the targets or the targeted banks were. Alaumary was a significant player,' says O'Neill. 'If we did the extradition route, he'd be taken offline. If you started taking people off the chess board, so to speak, you would lose the ability to stop those attacks.'

In other words, O'Neill faced a similar dilemma to that of Inspector Roger Smethurst, the Greater Manchester Police officer who investigated the Din family in Bury: take action to shut things down, or let the suspect keep going in the hope of future wins? Ultimately, O'Neill and his team took the latter option. For now, they would sit and watch Alaumary, waiting for their chance. Never in their wildest dreams could they have predicted what was going to happen next, though. Big Boss had become a key money-laundering accomplice in a giant, global cybercrime campaign, emanating from one of the most dangerous countries in the world.

On Saturday, 11 August 2018, hundreds of people across the globe, from the US to the UK, to Turkey and Japan, set out on a secret mission. In their pockets they carried stacks of ATM cards. Their task was simple: they were to take the cards to a cashpoint, pull out as much money as they could, walk to another cashpoint, repeat the exercise, and keep going. At the end of the day, these money mules would hand over whatever cash they'd gained to their handlers, who would pay them a fee for their work. The ATM cards they carried did not belong to them, but had been issued to them by those running the scheme. The money they were extracting was the proceeds of crime – the mules were helping to launder the profits from a carefully orchestrated hacking attack that had been months in the planning.

Using these tactics, in just over two hours the thieves made the ATMs spew out millions of dollars in stolen funds. In the tech security world it's known as 'jackpotting' – because pulling out cash from ATM after ATM feels a lot like winning big at a casino. Meanwhile, urgent messages had been arriving at a bank in India called Cosmos Co-Operative Bank. It's one of the oldest and largest co-op banks in the country. Such institutions were originally set up to serve India's agricultural sector and were envisioned as 'credit unions' for localized finance. But, over time, banks like Cosmos became mainstream entities, sitting on billions of dollars of customer deposits – a juicy target for hackers.

The urgent messages Cosmos was receiving were from Visa, the global payments company, and they were deeply worrying. Visa was seeing a flood of ATM withdrawals being made simultaneously around the world, all using Cosmos Co-Op Bank cards. It was far in excess of normal levels. Even though Cosmos could find no record of suspicious transactions, it finally opted to shut down its ATM systems. As the dust settled and Visa did more digging, the true scale of the incident came to light. A network of money mules in twenty-eight different countries had stolen $16.3m in 12,000 withdrawals. It was all done in 2 hours 13 minutes. Because the withdrawals were made using Cosmos cards, Cosmos had to reimburse the ATMs for the transactions. The bank was left reeling.[17]

'They were all shattered. They didn't exactly know how to respond,' says Inspector General Brijesh Singh, who headed up the cybercrime unit in Maharashtra state, in which Cosmos is headquartered. Singh was pulled in to investigate and soon discovered how the hackers had initially penetrated the bank. They'd sent phishing emails to employees claiming they'd won a prize, but when they clicked on the link or opened the attachment, their 'reward' was a virus which secretly implanted itself on the employee's machine, giving the hackers access. From there, the attackers had squirrelled their way through the bank's networks until they reached the software that controlled ATM withdrawals. They worked out how to seize control of the software, and so had the power to authorize any cashpoint withdrawal made using a Cosmos Bank card, anywhere in the world, regardless of how much money was in the account attached to the card. But before they could use this extraordinary power to steal money, they needed two things: a stash of Cosmos Bank ATM cards and a network of people to take them to cashpoints. And that's what led them to Ghaleb Alaumary.

By this point, under his pseudonym Big Boss, Alaumary had become a significant player in the underworld of financial crime. Thanks to his work with the Desangles gang and the BEC attack on MacEwan University, word of his abilities was spreading fast through dark web channels. When the hackers who'd penetrated Cosmos Bank needed assistance with cards and money mules to launder the profits from their imminent heist, they turned to Big Boss for help with the North American end of the operation. In the lead-up, Alaumary started getting messages on WhatsApp and Telegram from someone who went by the pseudonym Sweet, asking for assistance. Sweet had first contacted Ghaleb several years earlier, in 2013, and they'd pulled off a few jobs together. Sweet was now working with the Cosmos Bank hackers, and would be Alaumary's contact as they formed a plan to exploit their access and hit the ATMs.

The first task for the hackers was to get hold of a stack of functioning Cosmos Bank cards with which to make the withdrawals. For this, Sweet and his colleagues worked with accomplices like Alaumary to create 'cloned' cards. They took a bunch of loyalty cards (the kind you get from shops and businesses; they're the same size as credit cards and have a black magnetic stripe on the back). They used a special machine to wipe the loyalty data off the card (the same kind of machine hotels use to encode your room key card; you can buy one online for a few hundred pounds). They then took the account details of 450 genuine Cosmos Bank customers (which Sweet and his team had gained as a result of their hack on the bank) and encoded that account information on to the blank loyalty cards, using the machine. Hey presto, they had a stack of hundreds of duplicate ATM cards, linked to real accounts.

It may sound terrifying that, with just a store loyalty card and a cheap machine, someone could create a clone of your bank card.

However, you can be reassured by considering the problems any criminal would have when they try to use such a clone. There's no computer chip inside, so it can't be used for contactless payments. And under normal circumstances, they can't use it in an ATM because they don't have your PIN. But remember: in this case, the hackers had direct access to Cosmos Bank's internal ATM authorization system. Therefore they didn't need the PINs. Instead, they could simply watch for any incoming withdrawal made using any one of their 450 cloned cards, and immediately authorize it without even checking the PIN.

The next task for Sweet was to find the money mules to take these cloned cards to the cashpoints and fulfil the final part of the laundering process, extricating the money. Again, Alaumary was able to help. He had a network of 'runners' he could deploy to cover the US end of the operation.[18] Similar operations were being set up in more than two dozen other countries around the world. Finding the collaborators and arranging the logistics must have taken weeks, if not months, but by Saturday 11 August they were ready to go, and at a given signal, mules all around the world went into action. To pull off such a job would have required hundreds of mules hitting ATMs under strict supervision. For the police, tracking down these operatives was key to the subsequent investigation.

As he looked into the case, Singh focused on the Indian end of the jackpotting operation, concentrating particularly on the city of Kolhapur, where most of the withdrawals had been made. Working with Cosmos Bank, he was able to plot the locations of the ATMs the mules had hit. He then requested CCTV from the cashpoints and watched the recordings, which showed a succession of small groups of Indian men pulling out wads of money before wandering away. But the men were canny and had worn hoodies and caps to hide their faces from the cameras. Identifying them wasn't going to be easy. Singh requested data from the mobile phone masts in the area around each ATM, and painstakingly compared them to work out which phones belonged to the money mules. He then plotted the movements of those phones around the city, finally linking them to CCTV footage showing the cars the gang had used to drive the money mules around.

Arrests quickly followed. The mules turned out to be a rag-tag bunch: a pharmacist, a taxi driver, a caterer, among others; 'gentle people', as Singh describes them. Like Kenoly Ugbodu, the young man in the previous chapter who was recruited by money launderers in Ireland, they'd all been pulled in on the promise of a fee, almost certainly without knowing the full scale of the crime in which they were caught up. Some had even been tricked into thinking they were playing a role as extras in a movie, for a scene in which a withdrawal is made from an ATM.

As he questioned the suspects, Singh also learned how the handlers prevented the mules from simply walking away with the cash themselves once they'd withdrawn it. It seems the money mule herders were being fed live ATM information directly from the hackers. 'The local chap who was handling operations in Maharashtra was given a laptop to monitor what kind of money was being withdrawn,' Singh says. 'One of the [money mules] tried to hoodwink this local handler. He withdrew a particular amount of money. He came back to the car and he showed him less money. The handler gave him a tight slap because he is monitoring the transactions on his laptop.'[19] According to Singh, the laptop in question was tossed from the criminals' car as they made their getaway with the mules and the cash. Despite much searching, it was never found, and is presumably still somewhere on a hillside near Kolhapur; a treasure trove of evidence gathering dust.

As Singh's investigation expanded, more and more suspects were pulled in. But the wheels of Indian justice turn slowly. It was only as I was writing this book that it was reported in April 2023 that eleven people had been convicted, with sentences of several years each. 'One of the accused had died before the pronouncement of the judgment,' the reports stated.[20] And there are still at least half-a-dozen people awaiting trial with no clear idea when their day in court will come. Some are languishing in squalid, overcrowded jails. And Indian police admit that most of those caught were low-level offenders. The criminal bosses are outside the country and there-fore much harder to pursue.

Chasing down even the low-level money mules in countries out-side India proved difficult. Indian police put out requests for assistance, but they went largely unanswered. Some of the ATM withdrawals took place in the UK, so I asked Britain's National Crime Agency (NCA) if they'd received a request from Indian police, and if so, what they'd done. They weren't able to find any information on it. The sad reality is that many police forces have quite enough on their plates without having to help out another country's officers too. It's very possible the hackers knew this when they plotted their jackpotting spree. It's a type of 'jurisdic-tional arbitrage' – spreading your crime across borders to make it harder for law enforcement to keep up. In this way, it's a method of achieving the layering stage of the laundering process: the ATM cash ends up in so many hands, in so many countries, in so many currencies, that it's very difficult to link it back to the original crime. Indeed, Cosmos Co-Operative Bank never got back any of its stolen money.

In North America it was Alaumary, under his pseudonym Big Boss, who'd played the key role in extracting and laundering the loot. And he'd clearly impressed Sweet, the hacker who'd got in touch via WhatsApp and Telegram to request his help. Within a couple of months, Sweet and his gang got back in contact to loop Alaumary in on another job: the same MO, but a different target. This time it was BankIslami, a Pakistan-based institution. On 27 October, they hit it with a similar ATM hack, pulling out $6.1m worldwide. By this point, the exchanges between Alaumary and Sweet had moved beyond mere texts. Occasionally they would talk directly via WhatsApp or Telegram, albeit with their webcams switched off. Alaumary noticed Sweet's strange accent, but couldn't place it. One thing was for sure, though: from the hints Sweet gave away in his chats, he was in a country considered hostile by the US.

In fact, Sweet's homeland was not just an adversary of the US, but its sworn enemy: North Korea. Sweet's real name is believed to be Kim Il, and according to the US government, he's a key member of a state-led computer-hacking team known as the Lazarus Group. The fact that North Korea has government hackers shouldn't come as a surprise to anyone; most nations now employ cyber teams. The difference, according to investigators, is that as well as hacking for informational advantage and espionage, North Korea's teams hack for cash.

Thanks to its belligerent pursuit of nuclear weapons and missile technology, North Korea is now subject to rigid sanctions which effectively isolate it from international trade and finance. According to researchers in the US, the United Nations and various tech security firms, part of North Korea's solution to this economic straitjacket has been to use its government hackers to simply steal money. (The North Korean regime has consistently denied any connection to cyberattacks, calling them a 'smear campaign' by its enemies, notably the US.)

According to the American authorities, Kim Il and his Lazarus Group accomplices were responsible for – among many other cyberattacks – the hack on BankIslami and 'another incident in 2018' when ATMs were jackpotted in two dozen different countries, which is widely believed to be a reference to the raid on Cosmos Co-Op Bank in India. The work of North Korea's hackers occupies a fascinating and febrile crossover space where nation-state cyber activity meets organized financial crime. That's why I've spent years covering it. It's an opportunity to analyse each of those worlds through the prism of the other; an irresistible two-for-one offer for an investigative journalist interested in organized crime and technology.

North Korea's money-orientated hacking has led it into some intriguing alliances with groups and individuals within the global crime community, whose help it needs to wrangle the cash it's accused of stealing. After all, as we have seen, hackers might know a lot about how to penetrate a bank's computer systems, but they don't necessarily understand how to launder the money thereafter. For that, they often need help from the experts. And if that laundering requires deploying a network of street-level money mules in countries around the world, then North Korea's hackers are definitely going to need on-the-ground assistance from local accomplices, because many countries are cagey about allowing North Korean passport holders in.

All of this is exactly why Kim Il reached out to Ghaleb Alaumary, using his hacker nickname Sweet to disguise his North Korean identity. The Canadian launderer had done good work for his mysterious hacker buddies so far, and now they needed his help for another job. This time, however, it would be something quite different. The North Koreans were being forced to switch tactics. US law enforcement had been watching their ATM hacking games, and started applying subtle pressure to derail them. That pressure would force the North Koreans to adopt new technological methods for stealing and washing the funds, which in turn would bring Ramon Abbas, aka Hushpuppi, into the game.

Ever since they cracked the Desangles gang in 2017, the US Secret Service had been keeping tabs on Ghaleb Alaumary from south of the border, watching closely as he and other launderers deployed their money-mule networks for the jackpot operations that stole millions from Cosmos and BankIslami in ATM raids. It was a superb intelligence position for US law enforcement: they could find out about the heists before they happened, and alert the card companies and financial institutions to avert disaster. As a result, the Lazarus Group and others were finding it harder and harder to make the ATM jobs work. In the wake of the Cosmos heist, at least nine other similar attacks were organized by Sweet and his colleagues, most of which were never publicly reported, but many of which were disrupted thanks to US intervention.

'They had to switch tactics because we were doing a really good job at squashing all their attempts,' says Secret Service financial forensic analyst Christine Pellerin, a colleague of Matt O'Neill's in the Service's Global Investigative Operations Center.

In early 2019, the Lazarus Group broke into yet another target:

the Bank of Valletta, one of the key financial institutions on the Mediterranean islands of Malta. Again, they used phishing emails to get inside, making them look like important messages from the French financial markets authority. Once inside the bank's networks, one option was to try the same trick they'd attempted at Cosmos and BankIslami: hijack its ATM systems and make cashpoints spit out money. But with ATM attacks increasingly being foiled by the work of agencies like the Secret Service, the hackers decided to switch tack.

They went back to an approach they'd used before, when they broke into the national bank of Bangladesh in 2016. In that attack, the Lazarus Group targeted the bank's SWIFT system, the software used to make transfers between financial institutions. In some ways, it's much neater than a cashpoint attack, because you don't have to marshal gangs of accomplices around the world, who in turn have to control groups of money mules withdrawing stacks of cash hundreds at a time. Instead, using SWIFT, the hackers can steal money by simply transferring it digitally, millions at a time, to a recipient account. But therein lies the rub: to whose account are you going to transfer it? The crooks can't exactly wire it directly to any North Korea-linked accounts, as that will give the game away as to who's behind the hack. Instead, they need to wash it through multiple accounts before extracting their profits, just like the business email compromise launderers. But whereas the BEC gangs are often stealing tens of thousands, the Lazarus Group bank hackers are targeting banks holding many millions. Stealing large amounts via SWIFT is a serious challenge, because there's far more potential scrutiny around such giant transfers. Any movement of money between accounts leaves a trail, and that can potentially be used to stop or reverse transactions. Getting the layering stage right is a real headache. Famously, in the Bangladesh heist, the Lazarus Group are suspected of trying to steal almost $1bn, but in fact only gained $81m, partly because they struggled to line up recipient accounts through which to launder the SWIFT transfers.

In the Bank of Valletta job, they naturally wanted to guard against such slip-ups. They needed help and so, once again, Sweet dialled up Alaumary. He told the Canadian that a big job was in the offing. Millions of dollars were going to be stolen from a bank and Sweet needed accounts through which to wash it. Did Alaumary know anyone who could help? Alaumary, ever helpful, knew exactly who to call. And that was partly because he'd found himself living slap-bang in the middle of a place that was fast becoming an unlikely hang-out for some of North America's biggest money launderers: Mississauga.

A city of 700,000 people, Mississauga generally bumbles along peacefully in the shadow of its larger and more famous neighbour, Toronto, and I'm sure most of its residents would be shocked to hear that it was a hub for financial criminals. But the truth is that, during Alaumary's time there, Mississauga and its surrounding areas were home to a disproportionate number of very senior launderers, as well as their wider network. Ikechukwu Amadi – the man we met in Chapter Seven, who helped move the money stolen from Tom Cronkright's title company – owned a house just a few minutes' drive from Alaumary's. Some of Amadi's family lived on the same street as Alaumary, and Amadi's wife lived a short drive to the north. Also nearby was a man called Akohomen Ighedoise, who was the lead money man for Black Axe in North America.[21] An associate of Alaumary's told me that he started developing links with African underworld contacts around Toronto during his early card fraud career, and further developed these connections when he moved to Mississauga from Montreal. These links, combined with his existing career in business email compromise, gave Alaumary a powerful network of contacts, especially among the laundering gangs emanating from Nigeria. And so when Sweet asked him for bank accounts through which to wash hundreds of millions of stolen Maltese euros, Alaumary knew exactly who to ask, someone he knew of via his laundering contacts in Mississauga: a man listed in his iPhone contacts book only as 'Hush'. Thousands of miles away in Dubai, Ramon Abbas's phone pinged into life.

*

'I sleep good at night. When something good happens to me, I know it's because I did good. Not because somebody promised me money that I did not work for, or money that I don't deserve.'

This was Ramon Abbas, speaking in a video recorded in his lavish Dubai apartment in 2019. Given that he was at that point already knee-deep in fraud and about to embark on a succession of multi-million-dollar criminal schemes, it's hard to know what to make of it. The obvious answer is that he's just flat-out lying – he knows what he's saying is bullshit and he just doesn't care. But looking closely at the quote, there's another, more subtle explanation. Maybe Abbas was delusional enough to convince himself that the words were true. After all, he *was* working for his money: admittedly, the work was in perpetrating scams and laundering cash, but it was hard, skilled work nonetheless. And maybe he felt he deserved the income, because it was payback for all those years of grind and poverty back in Lagos. Maybe he was using the phrase 'did good' in a morally neutral sense, 'good' meaning effective, rather than ethical behaviour. If such an interpretation of Abbas's words seems a stretch, consider this: Abbas by now had millions of followers on social media, scrutinizing the hundreds of photos which he gladly shared with them. In one sense, he was living life in the goldfish bowl of Instagram. Yet this same individual was able to go home each day, close the door, sit down at the laptop and perpetrate crimes that, if he got caught for them, would destroy his carefully curated life in a moment, and scandalize many of those who idolized him online. Someone with the mental fortitude to live that kind of double life strikes me as someone eminently capable of Orwellian double-think when it comes to ethical behaviour.

And so on 16 January 2019, when a message from Alaumary arrived on Abbas's phone asking if he could provide two European bank accounts that could receive and layer 5m euros each from the impending raid on the Bank of Valletta, Abbas didn't hesitate. He replied the same day with details of an account in Romania which he said could be used for 'large amounts'.[22]

It wasn't the first time that Abbas and Sweet had worked together.

Apparently Sweet was a regular visitor to Dubai, flying out twice a year. He would party and hang out on private yachts. Perhaps it was inevitable that he would run into Ramon Abbas, who was also living the Dubai high life under his Hushpuppi Instagram persona. Sweet first met Abbas and his accomplices in Dubai back in 2013,[23] and it seems it was Abbas who introduced Sweet to Alaumary. It was to become a highly lucrative but ultimately ruinous triangular relationship.

As the hit on Bank of Valletta was being planned, Alaumary was in regular contact with Sweet. Perhaps remembering the challenges posed by the Bangladesh job, Sweet warned Alaumary that the stolen money had to move through the laundering account quickly, so it could not be recalled. Alaumary dutifully told Abbas to rinse the money through the Romanian account fast: '[m]y associates want u to clear as soon it hits . . . Cuz a recall can be.' He told Abbas they intended to take the bank for everything they could get: 'if they don't notice we keep pumping,' he wrote.[24]

By then, Sweet had a date set for the heist: 12 February. Alaumary was furiously trying to line up laundering accounts in time. He wanted six, each capable of handling 5m euro, for a total take of 30m. It would not have been easy – they're big sums of money, and as we've seen, banks were increasingly on the lookout for suspiciously large transfers. But the more Alaumary could wash, the higher his potential fee. He went back to Abbas on 10 February: 'Brother tonight is my dead line to submit anything more . . . Do u want add one more or just stick to that one u gave me?'

Abbas fired back the next day with details of a second account, this time in Bulgaria.[25] Alaumary went back to Sweet. He had managed to muster four accounts: three to handle euros (two of which were from Abbas), and one that would accept dollars. The escape routes for the money had been lined up – Alaumary and Abbas had to simply sit and wait for the hackers to do their work.

Sure enough, on Tuesday, 12 February 2019, shopkeepers in Malta started experiencing problems taking card payments with the

machines issued by Bank of Valletta. In an increasingly cashless society, many people were reliant on card payments and didn't have any
cash. Shopping trolleys full of food were abandoned in supermar-
kets. Then Bank of Valletta customers' cards stopped working. And
when they phoned the bank to complain, they couldn't get through.[26]
The bank's systems were grinding to a halt. The hackers' viruses had
accessed its networks and pulled out money via SWIFT transfers,
but they were inadvertently causing financial chaos as a result.

Meanwhile, Alaumary had good news for Abbas, texting: 'Wire is
completed. We did it. 500k euro. Should be on ur side by now.' It
was nowhere near the 5m euro they were planning for, but the hack
wasn't over yet. Alaumary texted: 'Brother, we still have access and
they didn't realize, we gonna shoot again tomoro am.'

But by the next day, the bank had discovered the hack. 'Today
they noticed and pressed a recall on it.' Alaumary then sent Abbas a
screenshot of an online article, writing: 'Look it hit the news.'

Abbas's reply was brusque: 'damn'.

'To[o] bad they caught on or it would been a nice payout,' wrote
Alaumary (*sic*).[27]

Clearly, the money-laundering duo were disappointed with their
take from the hack. Somewhere in the midst of the cybercrime,
things had fallen apart, at least as far as Alaumary and Abbas were
concerned. But they weren't seeing the full picture. It seems they
weren't the only collaborators Sweet and his pals were working
with. The hackers had been sending stolen Bank of Valletta money
to other launderers too, including in the UK. And one year after the
hack, events would give a fascinating insight into the street-level
laundering tactics the hackers' accomplices used to wash the cash.

In January 2020, the UK's National Crime Agency arrested six
people in London and Belfast in an investigation named Operation
Weldment. The agency said the arrests were 'linked to a cyber heist
on a bank in Malta' in February 2019 in which 13m euro was targeted. Clearly, the NCA was mopping up the UK end of the Bank
of Valletta hack.

The NCA claimed that £800,000 of the stolen money was transferred to bank accounts in the UK. Thanks to the bank's efforts to stop the attack, some of that money had been blocked before it could be withdrawn. But the hackers' accomplices had managed to pull out £340,000 of it, some via cash withdrawals, some via card transactions. 'They included payments to high-end stores such as Harrods and Selfridges in London, around £110,000 spent on Rolex watches at a store in London, and payments for a Jaguar and Audi A5 from a car dealership,' the NCA claimed.[28] In other words, the money had been successfully withdrawn and integrated.

It's no surprise that those in the UK laundering the stolen money should spend it this way: expensive cars and jewellery are an ideal way to turn hot money into movable funds. From London you can drive your flash Jaguar into Europe wearing a Rolex on each wrist, at which point you've successfully moved hundreds of thousands of pounds' worth of stolen funds over the border. Sure, you could do the same with cash, but as we discovered in Chapter Two, carrying around stacks of unexplained banknotes gives the police an ideal reason to stop you. Cars and trinkets are much less suspicious.

Partly thanks to police action like this from the NCA, Bank of Valletta was able to recover 10m euros of the stolen money, and hoped to claw back the remaining 2.9m, having traced it to Hong Kong. Alaumary, however, was undaunted. As the Malta job petered out, he messaged Abbas: 'Next one is in few weeks will let U know when it's ready.' The Canadian clearly felt that, despite the Bank of Valletta disappointment, his relationship with Abbas might open up a whole new world of possibilities. With Abbas's accounts able to wash millions, Alaumary could open the taps, working with his fraudster accomplices to target more victims for greater profits. In April 2019 he messaged Abbas to say he'd lined up four UK fraud targets and believed he could squeeze them for between $1m and $5m twice a week. He asked Abbas to provide 'open bene' accounts – slang for 'open beneficiary'. The name on such accounts can be changed repeatedly, making the victim less suspicious about transferring money into it; exactly the kind of tactic I'd encountered in my chats with the Instagram mule recruiter running the Money Plugs account.

The following month, Alaumary messaged Abbas again, showing him what seemed to be an incoming payment of £1.1m from a fraud victim, which he needed to launder. His messages have a desperate edge. 'I have other companies ready to swap bro pls help me out I am losing millions.' At one point, Alaumary tells Abbas of a plan to defraud a Premier League football club of £100m, plus another victim in Edinburgh whom they plan to target for £200m. But Abbas pushes back: too many of Alaumary's schemes are failing to take off. Abbas is getting sick of lining up laundry accounts (or 'houses', to give them the slang name), for which he has to pay accomplices (or give 'feedback' in slang). He messages Alaumary (*sic*): 'Bro I can't keep collecting houses n not give them a feed back n keep asking for more. This things cost a lot of money now to open.'[29]

All the while, Abbas continued his double life as Hushpuppi. At the same time as Alaumary was hounding him for accounts, Abbas was photographed hitting the shops with Manchester City footballer Benjamin Mendy, then flying off to Paris Fashion Week to attend a Louis Vuitton show.

And despite his frustration, Abbas clearly saw the potential in his burgeoning criminal relationship with Alaumary. The Canadian's long history in business email compromise spoke volumes. And, after all, he'd been kind enough to loop Abbas in on the Bank of Valletta raid, which could have been a lucrative endeavour. So towards the end of 2019, the pair get together to pull off what should have been a nice, neat job. This time there would be no North Koreans, no complicated bank hacking, no international accounts. Instead, it would be a small crew, hitting a juicy target with a straightforward BEC scam for a fat sum of money, with the profits all laundered through North America.

But it would not be so simple. Unknown to Abbas and Alaumary, this would be their final job together. Law enforcement was circling, and Alaumary was about to fly right into their net.

*

In October 2019, a law firm in New York state was working with a client who wanted to set up a refinancing deal for their property. The deal was almost done, and one of the final tasks for the law firm was to send almost $1m of the client's money to their bank. But unbeknownst to the law firm, they had been targeted by scammers working with Abbas and Alaumary. The criminals had tricked one of the law firm's employees. She thought she was emailing the bank, but in fact she was corresponding with the fraudsters, who were using an email address very similar to the bank's. So when she asked for the account details into which to transfer the client's $1m, they gave her the details of an account controlled by the scammers. You might be sighing as you read this at the ease with which yet another BEC fraud was executed, but to give the law firm credit, it did have procedures in place to stop such cons. All bank transfers had to be confirmed via both fax and a phone call. But these layers of protection proved achingly easy to subvert. When the law firm employee emailed what she thought was the bank's address to request a faxed confirmation, she was of course emailing the fraudsters themselves, who dutifully sent the confirmatory fax. And when she phoned to confirm, she was phoning the number given on the fax – which had of course been sent from the fraudsters. So it was their number she ended up calling. The crooks had fixed it so all communications led back to them.

And with that, the employee pressed send on a $922,857 payment.

Alaumary and Abbas were, as ever, braced for the speedy laundering work required when the payment finally dropped. One of their co-conspirators had flown from Toronto to Los Angeles to withdraw a chunk of the money.

'Did the big hit?' Alaumary messaged him. 'Yessir,' came the reply. A minute later Alaumary is texting Abbas with the good news:

'Sup bro,' asks Abbas.

'Conf[irmation] sent me today,' writes Alaumary.

Finally, after all the snags and misfires, this was a successful collaboration for the laundering duo. The money had been extricated from the victim and now all that remained was to move it quickly through their network. Alaumary messaged Abbas to say that he was on a plane and had just landed. A few seconds later, Abbas was chasing: 'Money came in?'

'Yes,' replied Alaumary.

'Give me a screenshot,' demanded Abbas.[30]

Alaumary said he couldn't because his Wi-Fi signal wasn't strong enough, but promised to send a confirmation soon. So Abbas waited, patiently biding his time for news of another big payday, perhaps contemplating which expensive car he might buy with the profits, or which designer outlet he could splurge in. But the screenshot never came. Because mere minutes after his plane landed, Alaumary was standing in Atlanta airport, his wrists cuffed, surrounded by Secret Service agents. The agency's years-long waiting game had come to an end, and Alaumary's laundering past had caught up with him.

Ever since they'd first exposed Alaumary as the real face of Ockie back in 2017, the Secret Service had been painstakingly tracking his movements, trying to build up a picture of their suspect. They ended up knowing a lot about the ins and outs of his life – his wife, his kids, his business ventures, both legitimate and illegal. The Service was hunting for a way to get him on to US soil so they could make an arrest. One option that's sometimes used is to lure a suspect to America on some very plausible or irresistible pretence (like the fake wedding ruse that undercover US Customs agent Bob Mazur plotted in Chapter One). But that's only allowed in cases where the suspect isn't in a country from whence the US can extradite them. After all, if you can legally drag someone to the US, what's the justification for using subterfuge? But the Secret Service had decided not to extradite Alaumary from Canada because they wanted to convince him to collaborate. They feared extradition would take so long he would lose his underworld connections, and therefore be useless as a covert source. So the Secret Service team – including agents Glen Kessler and Matt O'Neill and financial analyst Christine Pellerin – had to think outside the box.

This is where their insight into his lifestyle came in handy. They knew he generally took a holiday in the Bahamas a couple of times a year, staying at the lush Atlantis resort. If they could work with the Bahamian authorities, maybe they could seize Alaumary when he arrived there? Shortly after starting negotiations with the country's law enforcement, the team discovered something helpful: the Canadian was planning a Bahamian break around his birthday at the end of 2019. It offered the perfect opportunity to capture him. As Alaumary was scheming with Abbas to defraud the New York law firm, the Secret Service was making hasty preparations in the West Indies, desperately trying to get the local authorities on side. Shortly before Alaumary was due to arrive, Pellerin flew to the islands with a small team of colleagues. They waited nervously. While the resort's guests splashed in the pool and sipped cocktails, the Secret Service team spent hours strategizing for every eventuality, spending hours coordinating between US law enforcement and the Bahamian authorities. Despite all the preparations, no one was quite sure how it would go down. Meanwhile, Kessler was getting ready to fly in from Atlanta airport. He felt he stood a good chance of 'rolling' Alaumary; convincing him to work with the Secret Service. If he could manage it, they'd get right into the heart of the crime gang.

Alaumary's family arrived at Grand Bahama International Airport. And then, finally, the man himself. He was almost within their grasp. But there was a sudden and unexpected turn of events. Bahamian immigration wouldn't allow him to enter the country because they'd been tipped off by the Secret Service about his criminal background. After months of planning, the team's chances of success were fading fast. At this point, it was possible that Alaumary would just be put on a plane home to Canada, leaving the Secret Service back where they'd started. And if that happened, Alaumary might be even more cagey about travelling in future, offering even fewer opportunities to snare him. But the agents had a stroke of luck. Alaumary had missed the last flight of the day back to Canada by forty-five minutes. The next one wasn't until the following day, and with Alaumary unable to enter Bahamian territory, he faced spending a night in the airport jail. However, there *was* one flight he could catch which was leaving that night. By total coincidence, the flight was heading to Atlanta – the very same place from where Glen Kessler was waiting to depart for the Bahamas. Alaumary had friends in Atlanta, so he booked himself a seat – inadvertently buying himself a one-way ticket straight into the hands of US law enforcement.

Pellerin and her colleagues scrambled to get seats on the same flight, while also making hurried calls to Kessler in Atlanta telling him to stay put. As she made her way through the airport, Pellerin finally came face to face with the man they'd spent years tracking. She'd accumulated immensely detailed knowledge about his life. He, of course, didn't even know who she was. But as she passed him, Pellerin struggled to contain herself.

'It was amazing walking by him in the airport,' she remembers. 'I was holding my breath, not able to make eye contact with him. If I had, I wouldn't have been able not to smile, like, "Finally . . ."'

Pellerin and her colleagues sat nervously a few seats away from Alaumary during the two-hour flight to Atlanta. When he crossed the airport threshold, he was immediately placed in handcuffs, his phone was confiscated and he was guided to an interview room where Kessler was waiting.

But the meeting did not go the way Kessler expected. 'I showed him my entire PowerPoint presentation that I had shown to the United States Attorney's Office, all the evidence linking him to a variety of international cybercrimes. I offered him the opportunity to go to work for the Secret Service immediately. Even after this entire presentation, he looks at me and he leans back in his chair and says, "It's been a very long day. I need you to put me up at the Ritz Carlton tonight in Atlanta. Then you come by at ten o'clock tomorrow morning, and then you and I can discuss what's going to happen to me and how I'm going to help you out."'[31]

It seems, even in this dire situation, Alaumary still felt he was the Big Boss. Kessler had news for him.

'I just started laughing and said, "You don't understand. I'm about to throw you in the Atlanta City jail with some of the worst criminals on the planet." '32

Putting Alaumary into such an institution might seem a satisfying conclusion given his extensive criminal career, but it also presented Kessler with some problems. The agent wanted to push ahead with his plan to roll Alaumary. He says that by this time Alaumary had long known that Sweet was actually a front for North Korea's hackers, but had kept working with him anyway. Kessler now wanted to exploit that connection, keeping Alaumary in contact with the mysterious Sweet, so he could try to glean more about the shadowy hackers, and where they might strike next.

So once Alaumary was in prison, Kessler gave him a laptop and set him to work. But by this point, Alaumary had been offline for several days. It seems Sweet had grown suspicious. He hit Alaumary with a canny request: he wanted Alaumary to turn on his webcam to check his location. Clearly, if Alaumary revealed his current home – a cell in an Atlanta jail – it would be game over for their collaboration. So Kessler got hold of furniture, pictures and plants and turned an empty office in the jail into a convincing-looking apartment from where Alaumary could work. Every time Sweet requested webcam footage, the agents would have to leave the room while Alaumary gave the North Koreans a virtual tour.

Despite these considerable efforts, Kessler says they never managed to truly roll Alaumary. They got valuable info, but most of it was historical and not the live feed of real-time data so vital in derailing crimes before they happen.

It seemed the hiatus in communication after Alaumary's arrest had spooked the North Koreans, and they weren't alone. Rumours of Alaumary's capture had spread quickly among his accomplices. They must now have realized that their activities were being closely watched by US law enforcement. Abbas should have been particularly wary. Officers had analysed Alaumary's iPhone and quickly discovered a contact stored under the name 'Hush' – short for Hushpuppi – and a Snapchat contact called 'The Billionaire Gucci Master!!!' The FBI had already been working closely with the Secret

Service, and were well aware of Abbas's interactions with him. And they didn't have to look very hard to work out who Hushpuppi was and where he was living – one glance at Instagram would have told them everything they needed to know. According to Kessler, the Secret Service flew to Dubai and began briefing law enforcement on what they knew about Abbas thanks to Alaumary's arrest. The net was closing in on Hushpuppi.

But if Abbas was worried by the sudden disappearance of his close collaborator, he didn't show it on social media. A couple of weeks after Alaumary's arrest, he updated his Instagram: 'Tell the pilot get the chopper ready to take me to the Abu Dhabi F1 Grand Prix. My driver already waiting with my Rolls Royce, and some bad bitches in my Ferrari too. #AbuDhabiGrandPrix #Dubai'.

In fact, far from pulling his neck in, Abbas was about to perpetrate one of his most brazen scams yet; an extraordinary long-con which would net him hundreds of thousands of dollars.

In December 2019, Abbas began working with a fellow scam artist in Kenya, who'd hit upon a scheme to defraud huge amounts of money out of an unsuspecting victim. The target in this case was a Qatari businessman seeking a $15m loan for an international school. Abbas joined the fraud gang, and perhaps thanks to his wealth of experience he was given a key role. Abbas was to play the part of 'Malik' – pretending to be an employee of Wells Fargo bank in the US, and offering to help the Qatari businessman open an account into which the $15m loan would be paid.

'Malik' (aka Abbas) told the businessman that in order to set up the account, he would have to transfer $330,000 to cover various costs. What Abbas and his accomplices were now doing was simply a vastly larger-scale twist on the basic advance-fee scams covered in Chapter Seven – tricking the victim into paying a little money now with the promise of big money later. Remarkably, it worked. On 26 December, the Qatari businessman sent the funds.

What happened next was, even by Abbas's standards, a jaw-dropping piece of money-laundering bravado. Somehow, he managed to convince the victim to send $230,000 of the money directly to the account of a luxury watch seller. The seller used it as payment for a Richard Mille RM11-03 watch. Abbas then had one of his accomplices courier the watch back to him in Dubai. A week later, he's posting photos of himself wearing it on his Instagram account.[33] It's an echo of the integration tactics used by those who laundered the Bank of Valletta money in the UK. When you need to move hundreds of thousands around the world, using a fabulously expensive watch looks a lot less fishy than a thick bundle of banknotes.

Any good con artist will tell you: once you've got your hooks into a victim, you don't let go. Even after this audacious theft, Abbas and his accomplices went back to the Qatari and convinced him that in order to release the $15m loan, he needed to pay a further $300,000 in Kenya to cover taxes. The following month, March 2020, Abbas managed to trick the man into sending yet another $180,000.[34] This was all happening at the same time that he was welcoming Oyemykke into his Dubai home, giving his fellow influencer advice and telling him how success depended on working hard on his brand and his social-media presence. And yet, even while saying those words, Abbas knew it was all a lie. Every time he looked down at the gleaming watch on his wrist, the ugly truth shone back up at him.

In hindsight, Hushpuppi's last Instagram post is poignant in lots of ways. 'May success and prosperity not be a once upon a time story in your life. Thank you, Lord, for the many blessings in my life. Continue to shame those waiting for me to be shamed,' it reads. Abbas's pious gratitude is ironic enough. But the post also featured a photo of a shiny white Rolls-Royce Cullinan. It's worth around $300,000 – the same amount he'd first conned out of the Qatari businessman. In a final act of self-deceit, Abbas accompanies the photo with the comment '#AllMine'.

Just three days later, on 9 June, Dubai Police launched Operation Fox Hunt 2, a series of six simultaneous raids across the city targeting Abbas and twelve of his alleged accomplices. Late at night, an armed police team wearing black balaclavas, helmets and fatigues arrived at the Palazzo Versace. They were escorted up to number 1706, Abbas's residence, by hotel staff.

'A close friend of mine who used to work as security there, he opened the door with the master key to his apartment,' says Nedim Medunjanin, who was assistant chief concierge at the hotel at the time. 'The police came in, like, boom, "Police! Hands in the air!" It was like in the movies.'

Appropriately enough for a man who documented much of his life online, the drama of Abbas's arrest was all caught on camera by Dubai Police and later released on YouTube. The video is spectacular. Clearly someone at headquarters had discovered extra budget for special effects and production. Over a backdrop of green code from *The Matrix* movies and animations of computer screens, there's footage of the raid on the Palazzo Versace and a breathless voice-over which details how a team of highly trained police officers spent months accumulating evidence against the gang. The video ends with a *Fast and Furious* movie-style tracking shot of the vehicles they seized – including a brand-new white Rolls-Royce Cullinan.[35]

Three weeks later, Abbas arrived in the US to face charges. It was an ignominious end to the career of a man who started life hustling in the backstreets of Lagos and worked his way to the penthouses of Dubai. In prison awaiting trial, Abbas worked cleaning windows and showers. He also studied in a number of education classes including, hilariously, 'Intro to Navigating the Internet'.[36] News of his arrest and incarceration spread like wildfire, especially in his native Nigeria. Many there had long suspected that he never abandoned his criminal Yahoo boy roots, and his downfall was greeted by some with an outpouring of *Schadenfreude*. Bloggers gleefully wrote about his comeuppance. On social media, his arrest seemingly did little to dent his popularity – quite the opposite. His Instagram account stayed live for more than two years following his capture, and in the wake of his detention his account gained half a million followers, even without his constant updates.[37]

And so, with both Abbas and Alaumary behind bars, the long process of prosecution began. Abbas's lawyers argued that he was never the instigator of any of the crimes. They pointed out that Alaumary was the one chasing Abbas for help with the crimes, not the other way round, and they claimed Abbas had no idea North Korea was involved in the Bank of Valletta job. In a handwritten letter to the judge, Abbas described himself as 'erudite, kind, funny, selfless'. He claimed he only ever made $300,000 from the various frauds, but offered to pay $1.7m in restitution – even volunteering to sell two Rolls-Royces and a Ferrari to help.

Alaumary, too, was shoring up his counterarguments. His father wrote to the court to argue that the actual amounts gained from many of the thefts were far lower than the original amount targeted. It's a valid point. In the case of the Bank of Valletta, for example, it's often reported as a 13m euro theft. The fact that the bank retrieved most of the money is conveniently brushed over.

Nonetheless, even by Alaumary's father's own reckoning, his son was still connected to more than $18m of losses both in the US and internationally. That's a hell of a sum.

In the end, both men pleaded guilty. On 8 September 2021, Ghaleb Alaumary admitted two counts of money-laundering conspiracy and was sentenced to eleven years eight months in prison. Just over a year later, Ramon Abbas got eleven years three months for one count of money-laundering conspiracy. (There was also a fifty-seven-month sentence for Kelvin Desangles, the fraudster whose identity-theft shenanigans helped lead police to Alaumary, and six months for Jennal Aziz, the bank worker whose information helped him.)

In an odd twist of fate, at the time of writing both Alaumary and Abbas are imprisoned in Federal Correctional Institution Fort Dix in New Jersey, where their fellow inmates include Ikechukwu Amadi, the money launderer who worked with the Black Axe. One can only imagine what the dinner-table conversations are like. It's possible that prison was the first ever place Alaumary and Abbas met. Alaumary told Secret Service agent Glen Kessler that he never went to Dubai to meet Abbas – although Kessler says there's evidence to the contrary.

My attempts to interview them have so far failed. That's probably no surprise, particularly in Abbas's case. The story of a Nigerian Instagram celebrity who laundered money for North Korea is, as you can imagine, catnip for the world's media. There are multiple documentaries apparently in various stages of production (some may even have been released by the time this book comes out), and with money being splashed around, there's an ugly mercantile tinge to it all. When I approached one potential interviewee who claimed to have worked with Hushpuppi, he immediately asked me for a $10,000 upfront payment (which, considering I wanted to talk to him about his potential links to a man who conned victims using advance-fee fraud tactics, was an entertainingly ironic response).

Having never met either of the principal characters, I find myself in a strange position. Thanks to Hushpuppi's Instagram feed, I feel like I almost know the guy – or at least, his carefully curated public persona. As regards Alaumary, I've discovered a lot of information about his life from court records and interviews with the Secret Service, along with nuggets from sources like the Château Olivier website. But a sense of the man himself remains frustratingly elusive. There are hundreds of self-authored photos of Hushpuppi, but owing to Alaumary's paranoid secrecy, despite all my research I have only one picture of him – a grainy, low-resolution mugshot from which he stares out, expressionless and inscrutable. To fill in the blanks I sometimes picture him in Fort Dix prison, wearing the clichéd, Hollywood-movie orange jumpsuit, chatting to Ramon Abbas, comparing notes about their radically different upbringings and trying to work out where it all went wrong.

The ones who aren't behind bars, of course, are the North Koreans who are accused of hacking into Cosmos Co-Operative Bank,

Bank of Valletta, and a host of other financial institutions, and using the likes of Abbas and Alaumary to help them wash the money. The Lazarus Group's hackers and fixers – including Kim Il, who posed as Sweet in his dealings with Alaumary – are under North Korean protection and almost certainly safely back in the capital, Pyongyang.

If the accusations against them are correct, the hackers would have been working with dozens of money launderers around the world, of whom Alaumary was just one. It's likely they knew very little about his real life, and in fairness they had little reason to care so long as he performed the job effectively. By contrast, Sweet would have gained a vivid insight into Ramon Abbas's over-the-top lifestyle in Dubai, if it's true that the North Korean flew into the Emirate on multiple occasions. Nonetheless, when news of the arrests broke, Sweet probably faced a heck of a job explaining to his most senior bosses the kind of people they'd been relying on to launder the money from their attacks on the Cosmos and Valetta banks, and others. Merely explaining the concept of Instagram to a high-level North Korean government apparatchik could be a recipe for bafflement – let alone the idea that it could be used to generate a massively lucrative income.

Who knows what the North Koreans made of it all. But we can make a good guess at one likely reaction: Pyongyang's hackers must have looked at the case of Abbas and Alaumary and wondered if there was a less messy way to launder money. As experts in computer crime, the idea of working with vulnerable and fickle meatspace money launderers like this duo must have felt frustratingly anachronistic. If only there was a way to use technology to keep things neater and more clinical; to use the kind of crypto-laundering techniques we looked at in earlier chapters, but make them more efficient and effective.

Conveniently for the North Koreans and other cybercrime gangs, the new world of digital finance is helping them to do just that. It's a zone of minimal laws and regulations, painfully easy to hack and free of the cumbersome laundering restraints of 'real world' crime.

It's enabling some of the biggest thefts ever committed – sums that dwarf even the largest of the cases so far covered in this book. And in a bizarre twist in an already bizarre tale, North Korea's crowning glory in this new criminal endeavour would come thanks to a group of cartoon salamanders – little Tamagotchi-like creatures that, unknown to most of us, were the guardians of a colossal fortune.

10.

Tornado Cash

On the afternoon of 12 May 2017, Sky News began reporting on a cyberattack on a hospital in the north of England. Inside a nondescript building behind Vauxhall underground station in London, staff were turning up the volume on the TV and paying very close attention to the Sky coverage. The building is home to the UK's National Crime Agency (NCA), where it was rapidly becoming clear to the cybercrime unit that the hospital attack was far from a one-off. Organizations across the country were phoning in to the NCA to report similar attacks – not just hospitals, but mobile phone companies, car factories, local councils and more. In every case, workers' computers had been locked and were displaying a frightening on-screen message: 'Ooops, your files have been encrypted', alongside a timer ticking steadily down and a demand for a payment of Bitcoin worth $300.

It was an outbreak of ransomware. The contents of the computers had been scrambled by hackers, who were now extorting money to unscramble the files. By 2017, ransomware had become a highly evolved industry. It was the dominant cash-cow for many cybercrime gangs and the scourge of IT security departments worldwide. But this attack was far more deadly than anything that had gone before, thanks to a new and terrifying evolution in tactics.

Previously, any criminal wishing to stage a ransomware campaign faced a series of key challenges. First, they had to send the victim a message containing the ransomware virus that would scramble the target's files. They then had to somehow convince the victim to act upon that message – to click on a link or open an attachment. What the cybercrime fraternity had been seeking was the Holy Grail of ransomware: a virus that would spread itself automatically and trigger without any interaction from the victim. And in early 2017 they got it, courtesy of the US government. Several years earlier, its National Security Agency (NSA) had discovered a flaw in Microsoft's Windows operating system that allowed a virus to spread from computer to computer and detonate automatically. The NSA opted to keep the discovery secret so they could use it against adversaries. However, in 2017 this incredibly powerful cyber weapon somehow leaked from the NSA and was picked up by hackers, who made it available on the dark web.[1]

Soon enough, one innovative group of crooks had the brainwave of using the NSA's tools to spread ransomware, and that's what led to the 12 May outbreak. In order to scramble the victims' files, the hackers made use of Windows' built-in encryption tool. Once encrypted, the scrambled files were appended with the extension .wincry (rather than .doc or .jpg, for example). The May 2017 virus utilized the same tool to encrypt the files, and in a darkly humorous twist on the wincry name, it became known as WannaCry.

Prior to the attack, Microsoft had found out about the flaw the NSA had discovered, and the company released a software update to fix it. But many people didn't install it. So when WannaCry broke out, they were sitting ducks.

The virus tore a path of devastation around the world. Within twenty-four hours, 230,000 computers were infected in 150 countries.[2] The damage was particularly bad in the UK's National Health Service (NHS) for a number of reasons. It's one of the world's largest employers, with severely constrained IT security budgets, and interlinked computers spread across thousands of locations, some of which are so critical that they could not be turned off to have the Microsoft Windows update installed. As a result, WannaCry caused enormous problems in hospitals and other NHS facilities across the country. Accident and Emergency departments were forced to close and divert patients elsewhere, and almost 7,000 appointments had to be rescheduled, including more than a hundred urgent cancer cases.[3]

Given WannaCry's remarkable origin story and its stunningly rapid global success, it is perhaps appropriate that the story of its demise was equally surprising. A young security researcher working from his parents' house in a seaside resort in south-west England discovered a 'kill switch' hidden inside the code. Marcus Hutchins realized that the virus was programmed to check a particular website before scrambling a victim's files. If the website was up and running, the virus would stop before doing any damage. When Hutchins checked the site, he discovered that no one owned it. So he bought the domain for less than £10, activated it, and instantly brought the WannaCry outbreak to a crashing halt. (In yet another bizarre twist to the story, Hutchins was later arrested and convicted in the US, when it turned out he'd assisted cybercriminals when he was much younger. He was spared a prison sentence, and the judge noted that he had long since abandoned malware to work on legitimate security research.)

As the dust settled on the WannaCry outbreak, investigators looking into it found some troubling evidence. Elements of the virus were linked to previous cyberattacks attributed to North Korea's elite hacking unit, the Lazarus Group – the same team suspected of recruiting Big Boss and Hushpuppi to launder cash stolen from the attacks on Bank of Valletta and Cosmos Co-operative Bank, among others.

The US and UK – along with many other security analysts – believe that the Pyongyang regime unleashed the WannaCry ransomware attack on the world, harnessing stolen NSA cyber weapons to do so (claims denied by North Korea, which says it has nothing to do with this hack or any of the many others attributed to it).

On the one hand, it was a terrifying turn of events: North Korea is an unpredictable pariah state on the path to nuclear armament, and now it stood accused of causing worldwide chaos. Its attack had closed hospital emergency departments and denied urgent medical treatment to cancer patients. Hospitals had occasionally been targeted by hackers before, but never on anywhere near this scale.

WannaCry had also caused havoc in commercial companies and brought factories to a standstill. And its hackers had allegedly done it all from behind their keyboards, thousands of miles away from their victims.

From a financial standpoint, however, WannaCry was an epic failure. Very few victims paid the ransom – probably because researchers publicized the fact that even if you paid, you wouldn't get your scrambled files back. In all, the attack earned only a few hundred thousand dollars in ransom money despite its swift global spread. Contrast that with the revenue from just one strain of ransomware from one of the leading cybercrime gangs, which made $325m in a single month.[4] For professional virus gangs, making less than a million dollars is laughable; barely enough to buy a Lamborghini.

But those mocking WannaCry's profit margins were missing the point. Firstly, from a propaganda point of view, the attack spread fear and panic around the world and put the global powers on warning at how easily North Korea could strike at the heart of the digital systems that underpin most of modern society. Secondly, and more importantly in the context of this book, the attack taught North Korea's alleged hackers an incredibly valuable set of financial skills: how to launder cryptocurrency. And they would use these skills in criminal campaigns that were far more profitable.

During the WannaCry outbreak, victims had been told to pay the ransom money into one of three Bitcoin wallets. On 3 August, three months after the attack, at around 3 a.m. UK time, those three wallets were suddenly emptied. Thanks to the blockchain, people could watch in real-time as the funds were moved from wallet to wallet. What happened next looked like classic layering tactics: the money would be divided up, moved into different wallets, combined with other funds, then moved on. But, like a magician's cups-and-ball trick, if you kept diligently following the flow, you could just about keep up with where the money was moving. Within forty-eight hours, more than half of the original ransom money ended up in one wallet. I was one of the people tracking the transactions, and I got quite excited when I saw the journey end at this one destination. I believed if I could find out who owned that wallet, I'd at least find a collaborator of the Lazarus Group, and perhaps even Lazarus themselves.

But I was disappointed. The wallet belonged to a company called HitBTC. It's a large cryptocurrency exchange, which according to its website is incorporated in the British Virgin Islands.[5] This was where much of the WannaCry ransom money ended up. Given that HitBTC describes itself as 'one of the oldest crypto exchanges in existence' and offers contact details on its site, one would imagine that the global investigative agencies hunting the WannaCry hackers would have swiftly called HitBTC, requesting that it freeze the WannaCry funds. But it seems that didn't happen. Unlike in other crypto-tracing cases, there was no big public announcement from any law-enforcement agency confirming that the illicit funds had been seized. When I contacted them to ask where they are headquartered and whether they did indeed own the wallet through which the WannaCry money flowed, HitBTC replied with a boiler-plate response, not answering either question, but stating that they

> have developed the Anti-Illegal Activity policy which describes the basis of the multi-level procedure we implement on our platform. We constantly work on monitoring the environment, improving the procedures and instruments which protect our community, and, being an international company, collaborate with law-enforcement agencies from across the world on a regular basis to contribute to making crypto trading a safe and civilized market.[6]

This procedure clearly didn't hold up very well in the case of the WannaCry money, though. In the absence of any concrete evidence to the contrary, it is reasonable to assume that the WannaCry ransom payments went into HitBTC, and were then somehow extracted by the hackers, leaving the investigators in the dust. Effectively, HitBTC had unwittingly been used to layer the stolen funds, allowing the cybercriminals to integrate them at their leisure.

If indeed it was North Korea's Lazarus Group behind the Wanna-Cry attack, this would have taught them a valuable lesson. Think back to the story of Big Boss and Hushpuppi. Finding, recruiting and managing this pair of co-conspirators was a big job for the North Koreans. Through his pseudonym 'Sweet', Kim Il and his hacker colleagues were sending scores of messages to Big Boss, aka Ghaleb Alaumary. It took weeks, sometimes months, to coordinate the laundering of the money from attacks on banks like Cosmos and Valletta. And after all that, Big Boss and Hushpuppi got busted, exposing critical information about how the North Koreans operated. Added to which, the pair were just two among what would likely have been a global network of accomplices, all of whom needed managing and paying off. Money laundering in meatspace for such hacks is a lot of effort. By contrast, the digital washing of the WannaCry ransom money took place inside forty-eight hours and could all be managed online, with no capricious, greedy, fallible humans to deal with. WannaCry may not have earned megabucks for North Korea, but it almost certainly opened their eyes to the money-laundering benefits of crypto crime. Over the next few years, they began targeting more and more crypto firms, making ever larger amounts of money and steadily becoming ever more skilful in washing it.

Then came the global catastrophe that pushed North Korea even further into this space. The coronavirus pandemic closed off international travel and forced entire populations to stay indoors. Street-level money muling suffered, as did the launderers' ability to move cash and valuables across borders. Already isolated from the outside world, thanks to coronavirus North Korea found itself bereft of many of its global methods of making and moving illicit money. But its government showed no desire to rein back its belligerent pursuit of missile and nuclear technology. And so, to top up the regime's coffers and pay for the weapons, North Korea's hackers are accused of doubling down on their crypto-crime spree. It would lead them to carry out perhaps the biggest hack of all time – a heist of truly eye-watering proportions. It would also push them into the cutting edge of money-laundering tactics and, in a stunning turn of events, spark a raging debate about freedom of speech at the heart of the US financial system. And it all started with a video game based on salamanders.

Steven Tan was at work one day in early 2020 when a colleague told him about an incredible new money-making opportunity. Tan was twenty-seven at the time and working as a software developer on the outskirts of Manila, capital of the Philippines. He was doing OK career-wise, but like many people, he was also looking for a chance to make some extra cash on the side. His colleague's story sounded amazing. Apparently, ordinary people in the Philippines were making big sums simply by playing a video game. It sounded too good to be true. But then Tan saw it being covered on television. A documentary programme showed people playing the game, some of whom reckoned they were making $1,300 per month, just by fiddling with their mobile phones for a few hours a day.

'That's really big money in the Philippines,' Tan tells me. 'Earning that kind of amount, you could survive four to five months. I felt like it was legit, because it was aired on national television. Because of that TV news segment many people joined, including me. I was really interested.'

The game was called Axie Infinity. At heart, it was a pretty simple concept. It revolved around little virtual characters called Axies, which were loosely based on axolotl animals, a type of amphibious salamander. Players could create a team of Axies, personalize them, train them, and then use them to stage battles against other players' teams. If your Axie team won the battle, you'd be rewarded with in-game tokens called Smooth Love Potion (SLP). This would allow you to breed Axies together, creating more effective fighting teams. It was a bit like a cross between

Tamagotchi (the keyring-sized digital pets that became wildly popular in the late 1990s and early 2000s) and WWF wrestling.

And if that was all there was to it, Axie Infinity might well have remained a niche pastime for gamer geeks. But the company behind it, Sky Mavis, had an ambitious vision. Rather than simply selling a game to players as other companies had traditionally done, they wanted to create an entire industry around it – one which would share the financial benefits with the players. Instead of just buying the game as a one-off purchase, players would buy their Axies, which could then be traded between players. SLP tokens could also be bought and sold. Even the virtual world in which the game took place, Lunacia, was parcelled up into plots of land that could be bought and sold. The whole thing was a giant marketplace, and Sky Mavis took a cut of every transaction. It wasn't a totally new concept – other games had pioneered similar tactics – but Axie Infinity would push the model to new heights.

To make the marketplace work, Sky Mavis based the entire enterprise on cryptocurrency. Players could use their bank accounts or credit cards to buy a currency called ether, which is one of the world's most popular, ranking second only behind Bitcoin. They could use their ether to buy Axies, SLP tokens or Lunacia land, which they could trade with other players. They could then swap these in-game assets back into ether and thence back into real money. The more people played, the more valuable the in-game assets would become and the more money they could earn. At least, that was the theory.

This use of crypto technology was pivotal in Axie Infinity's success. It took the feverish obsession of video gaming and combined it irresistibly with the Wild West gold rush of crypto hype that was reaching its peak in the years after the game launched. Steven Tan was keen to get in on the action. He took about $1,000 worth of his savings money and purchased a team of three Axies (the minimum amount needed to fight a battle). It was the cause of some arguments with his wife, who questioned what he was doing, throwing his hard-earned money into such a weird endeavour. But he reassured her. From what he'd seen on TV, he expected he'd make the money back within three months and then start earning profit. He might even be able to give up his job and play full-time, just as he'd seen people doing in the TV news reports.

He wasn't the only one. Axie Infinity exploded in popularity, partly fuelled by booming valuations for cryptocurrencies (Bitcoin soared to an all-time high of more than $60,000 per coin in mid 2021). It's no coincidence that Tan had heard so much about the game among his peers around Manila. The Philippines accounted for something like 40 per cent of the game's estimated two million daily users.[7] And as the coronavirus pandemic kicked in, its popularity soared even higher. Deprived of traditional sources of income, many in the Philippines and elsewhere were tempted in by the prospect of being able to make cash just by playing games.

As the game boomed, prices spiked. In the end, a single Axie cost upwards of $300 – something Tan could just about afford, but well outside the reach of many in countries like the Philippines. This led to the creation of a shadow economy. Players or groups who could afford the Axies formed 'guilds' that would effectively rent out teams to players, called 'scholars', who in turn would play with the Axies, splitting the profits with the guild.

For some, this was an economic revolution in the making. The idea that people around the world could support themselves through a share of the gaming industry's immense profits seemed radical. For others, it was a modern version of serfdom, in which desperate gamers would eke out a bleak living bashing their phone for hours a day, while those higher up the chain raked in a disproportionate share of the cash.

It's fair to say, all this came as a bit of a surprise to the game's creators, Sky Mavis. One of them was a Norwegian named Aleksander Leonard Larsen. A veteran of the e-sports world (in which professional gamers compete, sometimes in giant arenas for huge prize money), Larsen saw the potential for a crypto-based game to share profits with players. He got together with five others to create Sky Mavis. The company is incorporated in Singapore but headquartered in Vietnam, where three of its co-founders are based. They watched Axie Infinity's meteoric rise with pride, but also some concern.

'Obviously, we were looking very closely at what was happening,' he tells me. 'Our goal as developers is always to make sure that the game economy is stable. It's hard to make a game economy stable when there are many, many outside factors that come in, and there are massive speculators.'

The crypto hype boom was rocket-fuelling Axie's growth. In the online forums in which Axie Infinity was discussed, the conversations sometimes became less about the game and more about pure crypto profiteering. People who'd started out earning a little extra cash now found themselves sucked into the febrile, heady world of speculation in a completely unregulated market.

All of this drove prices ever higher. At one point, Sky Mavis was valued at $3bn.[8] A single plot of land in the virtual game world was sold for a record-breaking $2m.[9] And it seems this didn't escape the attention of the Lazarus Group's gifted and crafty hackers. They set out to target the game and its extraordinary profits, in what would become perhaps the most lucrative cyber heist in history.

By March 2022, Steven Tan had been playing Axie Infinity for more than two years. The game hadn't lived up to his lucrative expectations, and things were about to get worse. He logged in to one of the game's discussion groups on Discord, a social media platform popular with gamers, to find some deeply worrying news. Players were talking about a hack on Axie Infinity's creator company, Sky Mavis. Details were still sketchy. No one quite knew what had happened, or what the consequences might be for players' money.

People inside Sky Mavis were already scrambling to answer those very questions as the problems came to light. Co-founder Aleksander Leonard Larsen had just flown back to his native Norway from the Game Developers Conference in San Francisco when a colleague told him they'd had a report from an Axie Infinity player who'd struggled to withdraw his ether currency from the game's systems. At first, Larsen didn't think it was a huge problem, and that it was probably just a glitch in the code. But when his tech team started to investigate, they uncovered something that would shock the company to the core: someone had sneaked into Sky Mavis's networks and stolen huge amounts of the players' money. As they totted up the damage, the picture got worse and worse. The hole in the game's finances was vast.

The hack had begun months before. Employees at Sky Mavis had been contacted by someone claiming to be a recruiter, who was eager to poach them for a well-paid job at another company. Such head-hunting isn't unusual in tech circles, says Larsen: 'Our employees are always high in demand because we have a lot of good people.'

One employee, a senior engineer, took the bait. They were interviewed for the job (reportedly over several rounds, conducted online), before finally being offered the position. But the job offer was fake; it was all a ruse to manoeuvre the employee into a position where they could be tricked into downloading the hackers' malware. The employee was sent a PDF document about the role which contained a virus. Once activated, it allowed the hackers into Sky Mavis's systems.

'It turned out that the person who they were interviewing and who downloaded this file had certain deep access levels [to Sky Mavis's network],' says Larsen. 'Once [the hackers] have access to the system, they go really, really deep.'

Thanks to this level of infiltration, the attackers were able to spot a weak point lurking at the heart of Sky Mavis. It would be the key to the theft of hundreds of millions of dollars.

As we know, Axie Infinity players could use the cryptocurrency ether to buy Axies, SLP and so on. But there was a snag. Anyone transferring money using ether is required to pay 'gas fees' – a cut of the transaction – that goes to support the Ethereum network which makes the transfer happen. The fees vary according to how busy the network is. Not only does this incur an extra cost for users, but dealing with all the gas fees can slow down the speed at which the whole network can run. Sky Mavis wanted to get round these problems for Axie Infinity users, enabling them to trade their Axies faster and avoid gas fees. They created a separate, internal blockchain to keep a record of all the trades going on within the Axie Infinity world. But, since players were still using ether to top up their Axie accounts and make purchases, Sky Mavis needed a piece of software that could match up the transactions on the internal blockchain with those on the external Ethereum one, and make sure everything was reconciled. This software was called the Ronin Bridge.

In order to match up the transactions, the Ronin Bridge relied on nine 'validators' – effectively, nine computers that crunched all the numbers, made sure the incoming and outgoing ether matched the trading activity inside Axie Infinity, and signed off on the transactions. As Larsen admits, Sky Mavis's decision to run its own blockchain had some risks. 'We could reduce all the gas fees, but . . . you take some trade-offs on security.' It was these security trade-offs the hackers would exploit. With their deep access to Sky Mavis, the hackers saw and understood the cryptocurrency set-up the company had created. They realized that if they could take over five of the nine validators, they'd be able to 'outvote' the other four, giving them effective control over any incoming and outgoing money.

Sky Mavis understood the risk of this type of attack, and had taken steps to prevent it. The company controlled only four of the validators. The others were run externally. When the hackers broke in, they were able to take over Sky Mavis's four machines. But it wasn't enough to hijack the network; they needed one more. Thankfully for the hackers, Sky Mavis had made a slip-up. The company that controlled one of the other validators had given Sky Mavis temporary control over it a few months before the hack. But that access had never been revoked, so now the hackers could use their infiltration of Sky Mavis to exert control over the vital, fifth validator. With that, the hackers had majority control. Axie Infinity's bank vaults were blown wide open, along with all the crypto that its players had deposited. It was time to steal.

'They sent a message to the validators to authorize a withdrawal,' says Larsen. 'The Ronin Bridge recognized that this is a legit trans-action because it has all the required signatures from the [majority of] validators. So they basically were able to drain the entire bridge.'

At 1.30 p.m. UK time on 23 March 2022, the hackers went to work, transferring hundreds of millions of dollars' worth of crypto out of Axie Infinity.

'You feel violated, in a sense,' Larsen says of his reaction at the time. He says he had to bottle up his emotions while they scrambled to deal with the fallout. But as each long day came to a close, he couldn't shut it out. 'It was hard to sleep because that's really [when] the emotions come up.'

During its period of rapid growth, Sky Mavis had done extraordin-arily well in raising money from investors, at one point being given $150m.[10] I ask Larsen why they didn't spend more of that money on security. 'That's kind of an easy argument to make in hindsight,' he counters. 'When you're building a company, you're scaling fast. It's quite hard to actually catch everything that you need to do.'

As word of the hack spread, worried Axie users logged in to check on their in-game accounts. But when they did so, they saw their balances were unchanged: they still had all their Axies, SLP tokens and so on, valued at the current market rates. On the sur-face, everything looked fine. But the reality was that the Sky Mavis accounts full of cryptocurrency that stood behind those assets had been cleaned out. It's a bit like logging into your online bank account and seeing a healthy balance, when in fact the bank's vaults are empty of cash.

Sky Mavis quickly understood the disastrous consequences this might have for players' confidence. It created a blog giving rolling updates on what had happened and worked hard to backfill the losses. The company did so using its own profits (which they'd kept separately from the players' own funds and which hadn't been affected by the hack), and also raised $150m from investors keen to see the company stay afloat.[11] They reassured players that their in-game assets were secure.

That was true, but it didn't mean that players didn't lose out, as

Steven Tan discovered. He'd invested in Axie Infinity at the peak of the market, paying $1,000 for his three-strong team of wrestling Axies. But the values had started to fall, even before the hack happened. Crypto prices slumped heavily from the tail-end of 2021. Tan had tried hard to stem the losses, playing his team of Axies and trying to make back his money by earning Smooth Love Potion tokens that he could then sell. But he was still down on his initial investment. Now, in the wake of the hack, he watched the values plummet even further, and remain steadfastly flat. He reckons he got back only about 20 per cent of what he put in – a loss he eventually just wrote off. 'I feel like I made the biggest mistake,' he tells me.

But it seems this didn't put him off. When I spoke to Tan in 2023 while researching this book, he was on the Discord chat boards, trying to return to Axie Infinity in order to make back a little of his money. But this time, he said he couldn't afford to buy his own team. Instead, he was applying to be a 'scholar' – to play with others' Axies and split any resulting profits. 'It's really tiring,' he says. 'You just have to play at least eight to ten hours a day. You have to compete to reach the top and then you will earn maybe $20 to $30 for a month.'

There are certainly those whose lives were changed for the better by Axie Infinity's 'play-to-earn' model, especially if they got in early. But like any fast-rising craze, there are untold numbers of others like Tan who joined later on and invested time and/or money in the hope of big gains, only to receive precious little in return.

But the biggest winners in all this were the hackers. Their raid on Sky Mavis and their cunning manipulation of the Ronin Bridge had seen them escape with 173,600 ether and 25.5m of another cryptocurrency called USDC.[12] At the time, that was worth an astonishing $625m.

That's a strong contender for the title of the biggest hack of all time. Certainly, there are hacking teams who've made far more than that (the revenue of some ransomware gangs is measured in the billions, for example), but that's thanks to criminal campaigns that ran over a period of time, with multiple victims rather than a single target. There are also hacks on individual victims from which the profits have increased over time to exceed the Axie job. For example, in August 2023 Heather Morgan and Ilya Lichtenstein were convicted in connection with the laundering of money stolen from a crypto exchange called Bitfinex.[13] The case got a lot of publicity, not least because of Morgan's side-hustle career as a 'cringe rapper' under the pseudonym Razzlekhan. Also grabbing headlines was the amount of money involved – approximately $3.6bn. At first blush that seems to massively exceed the Axie Infinity haul. But at the time it was stolen from Bitfinex back in 2016 it was only worth $72m. In terms of a single hack, carried out on a single victim, valued at the time of the theft, I've struggled to find anything bigger than the Axie Infinity job. And even if there is a bigger incident, it'll be hard to beat Axie on speed: the entire $625m theft took one minute and fifty-five seconds. In terms of dollars per second, it's almost certainly the fastest crime in history.

Regardless of whether the hack tops the charts, perhaps the more worrying aspect is the question of who was behind it. As various investigators examined the heist, they claimed the clues led to one suspect: North Korea. On 14 April 2022, several weeks after the attack, the FBI publicly added the Axie Infinity hack to its growing list of Lazarus Group activity. It became yet another entry in the global crypto crime spree that the Hermit Kingdom is accused of running in the years since the 2017 WannaCry attack. The total amount reportedly stolen by the North Korean state has been spiralling dizzily upwards. In recent years, every time a headline reported Lazarus's 'most audacious heist', the group would go on to pull off something even bolder. The Japanese exchange Coincheck was robbed of $534m in 2018. The Singaporean exchange KuCoin was hit in 2020, in which $275m was stolen. And now $625m from Axie – at the time of writing, the biggest yet (but at this rate it may have been exceeded by the time of publication). Through these heists, North Korea is believed to have stolen more than $2bn worth of crypto since the WannaCry attack of 2017. That's almost certainly an underestimate: the figure comes from the United Nations (UN) and is based mainly on public reporting, so it fails to take into account other crypto heists allegedly perpetrated by North Korea that haven't hit the news.[14]

What's more worrying is where this money is ultimately spent. North Korea has recently been heavily ramping up its missile-testing programme, and its regional neighbours are experiencing frightening consequences. Within a six-month period between 2022 and 2023, residents in northern Japan were twice warned by their government to take shelter as Pyongyang's missiles flew over their airspace.[15] Analysts fear the country is frighteningly close to mounting a nuclear weapon on top of a long-range ballistic missile, capable of reaching the US. All of this needs to be paid for and, according to analysts, the crypto thefts are funding a large part of it – up to half, according to the US government.[16] Within this context, the huge sum stolen from Sky Mavis represents a serious chunk of income for the regime, and therefore a big worry for the rest of the world.

But to spend the money it allegedly stole from Sky Mavis, North Korea first had to launder it. Thanks to their experiences from attacks like WannaCry and others, the Lazarus Group have become increasingly adept at this. But as their skills have grown, so have those of the defenders. As we've seen, crypto can be traced, and if the criminals try to launder it at a legitimate exchange, law enforcement can contact the exchange and get the funds frozen before the thieves can extract it. That's exactly what happened to the money from the KuCoin attack in 2020. In the end, about 80 per cent of the haul from KuCoin was recovered via this track-and-freeze method.[17]

In the case of the stolen Sky Mavis crypto, the Lazarus Group's hackers initially tried to use above-the-board exchanges to launder some of the money – around $16m.[18] But the exchanges in question publicly announced that they would work with law enforcement to prevent the stolen funds being moved. The hackers realized that using legitimate exchanges wasn't going to be an option. The clock was ticking and they needed a solution, fast. They had to find a layering option that could outfox those pursuing the money. Where on earth could they launder half a billion dollars, no questions asked?

The answer to their prayers came thanks to a group of crypto devotees half a world away from Pyongyang. This small group of talented coders dreamed of a new, better world shaped by innovative financial tech. But thanks to the Lazarus Group, their dream would turn into a nightmare, pitching them into a running battle with some of the most powerful financial forces in the world.

Ameen Soleimani's long association with all things cryptographic began in college, when he went on to the legendary dark web drug emporium Silk Road and used Bitcoin to buy magic mushrooms. Since then he's been involved in a range of projects utilizing crypto technology in everything from news coverage to energy markets. Like many in the field, Soleimani believes such schemes can make fundamental improvements to society. Specifically, he's interested in tackling what he terms 'coordination failure' – put simply: the human struggle to make good decisions at a global level. 'We lack the coordination tools,' he says. Soleimani and his peers believe technology can provide them, and 'will allow us to coordinate at scales previously unprecedented, transcending borders and faiths. That's what we believe. That's our religion. We believe in coordination.'

One such tool is called a 'DAO' – a Decentralized Autonomous Organization. The idea is to create an entity capable of making decisions and acting upon them, when there is no one central person or group in overall control.

The decentralization trend is taking off in other areas of technology. WhatsApp, for example, is one of many 'end-to-end encrypted' chat apps – meaning that only the senders and recipients of the messages can read them. WhatsApp's owners have no magic button that can allow them to look at users' communications, and so if law enforcement demands access, WhatsApp can tell them 'sorry, we can't help you'. The idea is to have no one person or group sitting at the centre with access to everyone's messages. But, of course, that doesn't mean that these apps are immune to requests for surveillance. For example, WhatsApp is owned by Meta, parent company of Facebook. So if a government wants to put the squeeze on WhatsApp to introduce ways to open up communications, it can apply that pressure on Meta.

The idea of a DAO is to get around this by going one step further: creating organizations that are truly autonomous, and where there's no central point upon which governments and law-enforcement agencies can put pressure. Crypto technology is a pivotal element in making DAOs a reality, and to understand why, we have to look a bit more deeply into what this tech actually is.

Throughout this book, we've looked at crypto in quite basic terms, as a simple payment method; one person sends a Bitcoin to another, and that's that. But there's more to it. Cryptocurrency innovations like Ethereum offer the chance to set conditions around the transfer of the money, via a system called 'smart contracts'. For example, say I want to run a lottery. In the meatspace world, I'd need to gather in money from people who want to take part, issue them with tickets, draw the winning number and then hand the pot to the lucky number holder. But with Ethereum and smart contracts, the entire process can be automated. Lottery entrants can send their payments via Ethereum, and built into the code behind the transfer of their money is a contract which states that, on a given date, the total pot will be automatically sent via the blockchain to one randomly chosen winner.

These smart contracts are at the heart of how a DAO works. Anyone who interacts with the DAO is given a voting token, issued via the blockchain. Anyone can make a suggestion as to how the DAO should be run. Suggestions are then put to the vote and, thanks to smart contracts, if the suggestion gets majority support, it's automatically put into practice.[19]

Soleimani believes such DAOs can help solve the 'coordination failure' problem, by creating truly autonomous organizations that can make good decisions regardless of borders and religions. 'It's sort of like you're giving birth to a thing that exists on its own,' he says.

As well as DAOs, Soleimani is also passionate about solving a conundrum that's been evident throughout this book – making crypto transactions truly private. 'Have you ever used the block-chain? It's entirely public, right? It's really, really annoying. We wanted privacy,' he says.

His solution was to help create a crypto mixer. But as we've seen, in the past, such mixers have proved fatally vulnerable to investiga-tion by the authorities. In the case of Helix, for example, US authorities were able to track down the man behind it, arrest him and gain full access to the inner workings of the tech that was sup-posed to anonymize Bitcoin transactions. The problem was that there was a single point of failure – in that case, Helix's creator Larry Harmon. Soleimani wanted to avoid this hazard, and this is where his work on DAOs came in very handy.

Soleimani set to work helping to raise funds for the creation of a new mixer – one that would offer true privacy by using DAO tech-nology to make an autonomous service with no central authority. It was called Tornado Cash and, according to Soleimani, it was developed by three coders – Roman Storm, Roman Semenov and Alexey Pertsev – under a company called PepperSec. But having allegedly written the code, they did not remain in charge. In Sep-tember 2021, two years after launching the service, they 'burned their keys' – meaning they irrevocably revoked their ability to make changes to or control the running of the service. This would make the service 'unstoppable', Storm said.[20] It seems that as far as they were concerned, they had done their job by developing the code, and it was now up to the community of users to decide how it would be applied. From now on, Tornado Cash was running, pilot-less, on the choppy waters of the crypto seas.

If that was all that had happened, most of the world might never have heard anything more of Tornado Cash. It might have remained an innovative new service mainly of interest to the folks living on the edge of the emerging crypto space. But that wasn't to be its destiny. Instead, Tornado Cash came to the attention of the Lazarus Group. Thanks to Lazarus, Tornado Cash would now be thrust into the full glare of the global media, and spark consequences far beyond anything Soleimani and his peers could have predicted.

The Lazarus hackers had been trying desperately to launder their illicit money, running it through various crypto exchanges and systems in a bid to stymie foreign authorities' attempts to freeze and recover the money. But no matter where they turned, the blockchain meant the funds could be tracked and, if the exchanges were prepared to play ball with the investigators, those funds could be frozen inside the exchange. Between $40m and $60m was clawed back in this way.[21] What the Lazarus Group was seeking was a method to launder the remaining money in a way that would evade recovery efforts, and that's what led them to Tornado Cash.

Soleimani and his colleagues did not create their mixer to encourage criminal activity. But nonetheless, according to Chainalysis the Lazarus Group funnelled $455m of the stolen Axie funds into Tornado Cash.[22] The fact they were using a mixer wasn't surprising – during that year, evidence has shown that North Korea's cyber teams were the biggest single user of mixers.[23] Thanks to their experience with crypto heists like WannaCry, Coincheck, KuCoin and others, North Korea's techies had become adept at using these innovative new services to launder. But Tornado Cash would be their biggest and arguably most effective to date: a masterpiece of digital money laundering. The Brink's-Mat of cyberspace.

Tornado Cash's autonomous software did what it was programmed to do: it took the $455m, mixed it with other users' crypto and disbursed it back to the hackers as clean funds.[24] Soleimani says this came as a big surprise. 'That blindsided everybody in the space, us included,' he tells me. 'Tornado Cash was meant to be a public good. We made this for ourselves and for our friends.'

Thanks to the blockchain, everyone could see that the bulk of the Axie money had been sent to Tornado Cash. But thanks to the mixer's software, they faced a big struggle to trace it beyond the mixer. The stolen funds had been layered very effectively.

Nonetheless, the authorities could trace the money as far as the mixer, and they set about rounding up the individuals they say are behind it. On 10 August 2022, the Dutch financial crime unit arrested 29-year-old Alexey Pertsev, one of the people who allegedly created the original code behind the mixer.[25] They'd been investigating Tornado Cash since June 2022, and now they pounced, stating that the Dutch Financial Advanced Cyber Team suspected that the service had been used to conceal 'large-scale criminal money flows', including from North Korean hacks. They accused Pertsev of being involved in concealing those flows. Pertsev denies the charges and has been given permission by the court to question Chainalysis about how it analysed the crypto data that helped get him arrested.

And on 23 August 2023, the US Department of Justice charged Roman Storm and Roman Semenov, accusing them of sanctions violations, operating an unlicensed money-transmitting business and laundering more than \$1bn via Tornado Cash, including the Lazarus Group's stolen Axie Infinity crypto.[26] Storm was living in the US and at the time of writing is out on bail. He pleaded not guilty to the charges against him, which his lawyer called a 'novel legal theory' with 'dangerous implications for all software developers'.[27] Semenov was reported to be in Russia and did not respond to my requests for comment.

But despite these high-profile arrests and charges, the authorities pursuing the Axie hackers still had a problem. When they'd taken action against mixers in the past – for example, identifying Larry Harmon as the man behind Helix and successfully prosecuting him – they had managed to close down the mixer as a result. But in this case, thanks to Tornado Cash's existence as a DAO, that wasn't an option. There was no one apparently in charge. So they took a different tack: the US Treasury sanctioned Tornado Cash, accusing it of assisting in laundering the money for North Korea, itself the subject of rigid sanctions.[28]

What this meant in practice was that any US citizen or organization using Tornado Cash could now be prosecuted for interacting with a sanctioned entity. The US couldn't shut Tornado Cash down, but that didn't necessarily matter. Instead, the goal was to send out a warning message in a bid to freeze out the mixer, turning it into a pariah in the world of crypto. The idea was that, thanks to the sanctions, people would be so worried about using Tornado Cash that it would eventually wither on the vine.

The sanctions must be seen in the wider context of America's decades-long conflict with North Korea. The two countries are still technically at war (a truce was signed between them, but never a peace treaty). And as North Korea is increasingly accused of resorting to cybercrime to keep its regime afloat, the US government has turned the financial flows into an active battleground, targeting the regime's money-laundering activities. North Korea's alleged push into crypto crime has expanded that battle to the crypto space, and sanctions have become a key weapon in the fight.

The arrests of Pertsev, Storm and Semenov, and the sanctioning of Tornado Cash itself, sent shock waves through the crypto community, which quickly rippled out into the wider tech world. Not only was it a challenge to the concept of a DAO as a leaderless entity, but it also raised the prospect that those who created innovative technology could be held personally liable for its misuse.

Soleimani sums it up thus: 'Are you responsible for every unintended downstream use of a product that you make?' As he points out, the authorities tend not to prosecute gun manufacturers when their products are used in anger. 'Just because somebody goes and buys a weapon that's intended for self-defence and then uses it to attack somebody else, that doesn't mean you should be liable for it as somebody who simply creates the tools to promote self-defence. And that's really what privacy is,' he says.

The backlash against Pertsev's arrest didn't just happen online. There were protests on the streets in the Netherlands, as some in the country's tech industry spoke out against what they felt was the thin end of an extremely worrying wedge. At the time of writing, Pertsev has recently been released on bail, pending trial. He's still living in the Netherlands, his movements monitored thanks to an ankle tag.

A sizeable section of the crypto community increasingly felt that the actions of the US and Dutch authorities betrayed a deeply worrying ignorance of how crypto tech works, and a dumb, heavy-handed approach to policing it. One group set out to prove just how stupid they felt the whole exercise was – and to illustrate their point, they set up a stunt. It would target some of America's biggest celebrities, and bring one of them toe to toe with the US government in an epic civil liberties battle.

Like Ameen Soleimani, Dave Hoffman is someone with a profound belief in the power of crypto systems to transform society. Thanks to these tech innovations, he believes we're on the cusp of an entirely new social order. At the heart of his thinking is the idea of getting out from under the sway of traditional financial institutions – or 'TradFi' as it's increasingly being called in the crypto industry. Hence the title of Hoffman's popular podcast: *Bankless*. Naturally, Hoffman has an Ethereum wallet, and the address is public, so that his podcast listeners and other supporters can make donations and take part in competitions.

Then one day in August 2022, Hoffman logged on to Twitter (now renamed X) to find some surprising news: someone, somewhere, had made a payment to his Ethereum wallet. Normally, that might be a welcome contribution, but in this case it was a big headache, because whoever had sent the money had wired it to him via Tornado Cash.

Hoffman had used the mixer himself in the past, prior to the Axie Infinity hack. He believed it was a neat privacy-preserving tool, and says he had no idea North Korea might be accused of laundering hundreds of millions of dollars through it. But now he potentially had a very big problem on his hands. Thanks to the US Treasury sanctions, anyone interacting with Tornado Cash could be prosecuted. And here was Hoffman, who had been very publicly revealed as someone receiving funds sent via the mixer. There was nothing he could have done to stop the payment being made to him: any user of Tornado Cash can send funds to the mixer and specify any recipient address, with or without the permission of its owner.

'Because of the way Tornado Cash works, anybody can end up the recipient of money from it,' he says.

And that was the whole point. Whoever had sent him the money was trying to show how foolish the US Treasury had been in sanctioning the mixer, by sending innocent people money through Tornado Cash. 'That really exposes the lunacy of this,' says Hoffman.

He says he has no idea of the identity of the prankster who sent the money, but Hoffman was far from the only target. It seemed that anyone with a big Twitter following and a public Ethereum address had been pulled into the stunt. Accounts connected to comedian Jimmy Fallon and basketball legend Shaquille O'Neal had also been hit, among dozens of others. It's called a 'dusting' attack: sending a small amount of money to a multitude of people to embroil them in a controversy. The sums weren't exactly enormous – just a few hundred dollars' worth for each recipient – but whoever was behind the activity was seemingly prepared to spend a total of $52,000 dollars to prove a point: that the sanctions were a waste of time and impossible to police.

Hoffman's initial reaction was one of amusement: 'It was comical,' he says. 'I just "broke" one of the worst laws of all time. That's hilarious to me as a law-abiding individual. It's a farce.'

But as the laughter died down, Hoffman realized the consequences were potentially very serious. Technically, he could be accused of sanctions-busting. It seemed unlikely the US authorities would go after him, of course, but the whole territory was so new that no one could be sure. Hoffman's lawyer warned him that he needed to send a formal communication to the Treasury making it clear he disavowed the payment, and he placed the money in a separate Ethereum wallet which he doesn't touch. And as far as Hoffman is concerned, this isn't a one-off. He's been told he needs to update the Treasury every year. Hoffman's reaction was predictably blunt: 'I don't intend to waste my time like that,' he tweeted. And so now, Hoffman is suing the US Treasury. He's part of a joint legal action involving cryptocurrency think tanks, exchanges and other individuals. They argue that the Treasury, via its sanctions branch, the Office of Foreign Assets Control (OFAC), is overstepping its powers.

'The OFAC sanctions list has historically always been for people or entities,' says Hoffman. 'This is a neutral piece of technology that I previously used as a consumer to access privacy. It's authoritarian and against the will of the people to ban smart, neutral pieces of technology. As a believer in Western liberal values, when I see our nation state banning its citizens from accessing neutral pieces of technology, I'm like, "That's too far, back up." '

The debate has spilled out of the crypto community and into the political sphere. A few weeks after Hoffman was pulled into the dusting attack, Republican Congressman Tom Emmer joined those expressing concern about the Tornado Cash sanctions. He wrote a public letter to Treasury Secretary Janet Yellen, supporting OFAC's overall goals, but questioning – as Hoffman and others have done – whether it was right for the Treasury to take action against a piece of computer code.

OFAC says that any US citizens affected by the sanctions can extricate their money, but to do so, they will need to apply and go through an OFAC process. Critics point out that this would involve users de-anonymizing themselves to the US government, which runs completely counter to the idea of using a privacy-preserving crypto mixer in the first place.[29]

Given that Tornado Cash was used to launder hundreds of millions of dollars stolen from Sky Mavis allegedly by North Korea and, according to the Dutch authorities, hundreds of millions more from other crimes, you might well wonder why any law-abiding citizen would use it. But in a world of near-ubiquitous surveillance, there are some very strong arguments in favour of such privacy tools, and recent world events have only served to strengthen them.

For example, when Russia re-invaded Ukraine in February 2022 there was a global outpouring of support. Many of Ukraine's sympathizers around the world wanted to make financial contributions to help the country's government and citizens. Crypto became a vital financial lifeline as the country faced down the Russian forces; the country became the third-biggest adopter of crypto in the world in 2022.[30]

But given Russia's tendency to target its critics, and the very public nature of the blockchain, would-be donors to Ukraine might worry that making a sizeable crypto payment would put a target on their backs. So, some of them turned to mixers like Tornado Cash to anonymize their payments.

One notable donor to Ukraine was Vitalik Buterin, the founder of Ethereum. In the wake of US sanctions on Tornado Cash, as debate raged about the mixer's use in laundering criminal money, the multi-millionaire revealed that he'd used its services to donate money anonymously to Ukraine.[31] Ironically, by doing so he of course de-anonymized himself. But Buterin clearly felt strongly enough that the arguments in favour of mixers like Tornado Cash needed to be voiced, regardless of the consequences.

What's emerging in the debate and legal actions surrounding Tornado Cash is a potential battle royale, pitting crypto ideologues, privacy campaigners and libertarians against the regulatory forces of financial control. It's a fight over principles that are as fundamental as it gets. As Hoffman puts it: 'Tornado Cash is code. Code is words. Code is speech. They're trying to silence speech, and that is why I have decided to sue them.'[32]

What Hoffman's comments reflect is a sentiment written deep into the DNA of many in the crypto community. The dream of folks like Hoffman and Soleimani is to build something new – something that can stand outside the traditional power structures that no longer seem to be capable of solving our big global problems. The world of crypto innovation they're creating hasn't come from the big banks, or governments, or military institutions – it was built by technologists. And whatever you think of it, it's been remarkably successful in gaining ground and disrupting the old order. Think how far Bitcoin and the blockchain have come in just over a decade.

And now these young crypto disruptors are watching as what some of them regard as the old, fusty forces of TradFi – including bodies like OFAC – finally catch up and try to rein in and regulate. The argument from a swathe of the crypto industry is clear: 'We built this new world of crypto. You don't get to come in here and tell us how to run it.' Many people like Hoffman and Buterin believe crypto is the key to all our futures, and as far as they're concerned, the outcome over Tornado Cash and other such disputes will determine the destiny of humanity. Within this context, they believe the pursuit of privacy trumps all, including the fight against money laundering.

Crypto is now a battle for freedom of speech and privacy, and money laundering is the front line.

But while, on the one hand, the legal action being taken against the US Treasury is massively important, in another way, it barely matters at all. As Hoffman says, at heart, Tornado Cash is a piece of code, and as such, it is a genie that can never be put back in the bottle, no matter how much the authorities try. That's because, while the public-facing Tornado Cash website has been shut down, and while US citizens risk prosecution for using the service, the code itself is freely available. It has been replicated on dark web channels and re-uploaded by free speech advocates.[33] Anyone who wants to use it and has the technical skills can still do so at any time, and they are doing so. It's true to say that the sanctions have put a dent in its activities, and its usage has fallen heavily since the Treasury's actions, making it a less effective mixer.[34] But as Soleimani points out: 'Tornado Cash is on track to process $250 million a year, despite being sanctioned by OFAC.'

In Tornado Cash we have reached (for now at least), the zenith of the tech/money-laundering relationship that we have traced throughout the course of this book. As a piece of unstoppable code, it sits beyond the reach of any government or law-enforcement agency in the world. It provides financial privacy, certainly, but it equally enabled the laundering of almost half a billion dollars allegedly stolen by one of the world's most dangerous regimes – which may well now use that money to build weapons of mass destruction that endanger everyone on the planet.

Welcome to Money Laundering 2.0.

II

Future Money

I love telling people the story of the hack on Axie Infinity. I like seeing the look on their faces when I reveal the vast size of the theft. I take a guilty pleasure in unveiling the unprecedented speed with which the crime was carried out. I encourage them to take out their phone and calculate how many dollars per second it adds up to. When they finally comprehend the enormity of it, some are shocked and surprised that such a giant crime could have been committed, and yet so few people have heard of it. Why, I ask them, did they not know about it? Why wasn't it headline news? Why are heists like the Brink's-Mat theft and the Great Train Robbery part of common language, but this jaw-dropping story is barely acknowledged? When you search online for 'biggest thefts of all time', Axie is nowhere to be seen.

The answer is obvious when you think about it: whereas other crimes involve tangible, traditional assets like cash, gold or high art, the Axie job was about a type of cryptocurrency many people have never heard of, stolen from a video game most people have never played. It all sounds like 'funny money', only relevant to geeks operating somewhere in cyberspace. It doesn't seem real.

North Korea's alleged hackers, of course, don't feel that way at all. For them, money is money, it doesn't matter where it comes from. Perhaps you don't care much about North Korea, because you feel that the goings-on in this peculiar pariah state seem a long way away from your daily life. But, as we discovered after Russia's re-invasion of Ukraine in 2022, events in seemingly far-away places can have a direct and profoundly damaging impact on the world's economy. With that in mind, now think of where

North Korea sits in the world. The countries in that part of the globe – including China, Taiwan, South Korea and Japan – are powerhouses of our modern, tech-dependent global economy. Many of our most beloved gadgets were either made there or contain components that were. Any destabilization in this region would have an immediate and immensely detrimental impact on all our lives. If, as the US claims, North Korea is now funding half its missile programme from cyber heists, the half-billion dollars of stolen Axie money could even now be paying for rockets and nuclear weapons material that will ramp up tensions in an already-fraught world. None of this would have been possible without the hi-tech laundering tools available to the hackers. Without systems like Tornado Cash, it's possible that the stolen Axie money would still be sitting, unusable, in crypto wallets.

The fact that this crime and the subsequent laundering took place in a weird niche of cyberspace – the fact that so many of the crimes covered in this book are happening in hard-to-grasp, hi-tech areas – is not a reason to ignore them. In fact, it's the opposite: it's an absolutely key aspect that we need to grasp. That's because today's criminals and the launderers who serve them are looking for precisely these seemingly remote, cutting-edge areas of the economy in which to steal and launder giant sums of money away from prying eyes.

Fundamentally, money launderers are seeking environments that have four key attributes. Firstly, they want there to be lots of trading, so they can hide among the crowds of legitimate customers as they wash the money. Secondly, they want the asset prices to be highly flexible, so they can move big sums without arousing suspicion. Thirdly, launderers are looking for industries with little or no regulation, so there's less chance of authorities or law enforcement sniffing around. And fourthly, they're looking for a global industry, so they can easily move stolen funds from one jurisdiction to another.

Think of those four attributes: high volume, flexible asset prices, lack of regulation and global scale. That's *exactly* the kind of territory many tech innovators are desperate to inhabit. Think of the world of cryptocurrency: the occasionally wild swings in the value of Bitcoin, the frantic trading that accompanies it, its creation as a deliberately borderless currency, and the fact that governments are wrestling with the regulation of it – it's got all the attributes the launderers want.

Video gaming is another example. Hackers are not just raiding these companies for money, as happened to Axie Infinity, they're also using them for laundering. One of the most popular titles is Counter-Strike: Global Offensive (CS:GO) made by a company called Valve. The gameplay revolves around butch plots involving bomb threats, kidnapping, terrorists and lots and lots of guns. But the competition isn't just about body count, there's an aesthetic element too. Players can add a bespoke look to their weapons by earning 'loot boxes' which allow them to make cosmetic improvements to the guns, knives and so on. In order to open the boxes, players must buy a key using the in-game purchasing system. A marketplace for these keys quickly emerged as players vied to have the 'coolest' weapons. Given that Valve claims there can be up to 29 million people playing the game every month, there is a febrile trade in loot box keys and high trading volumes as a result – which ticks the first box for the launderers.

Next, the launderers are looking for flexible asset prices. Again, the CS:GO marketplace starts to look very attractive. For example, how much is the key to a CS:GO loot box worth? For most of us, nothing at all. We probably don't care a jot if we can upgrade our in-game AK-47 assault rifle with the iconic Fire Serpent design. But for some avid players of the game, that upgrade is worth as much as $5,000.[1] For launderers, this is very handy indeed, because it means they can potentially wash large amounts of money quickly through things like loot box keys. If the authorities ever investigate, they might question the size of the transaction. But the launderer can respond by saying 'Well, that's how much it was worth', and it's very hard for the authorities to prove otherwise. If I pay an outrageous sum for a loot box key, people just assume it's part of the crazy world of tech prices.

Next on the launderer's laundry list is an environment where there is little or no regulation. Again, video gaming is useful territory – unlike banks and other financial institutions, there's no dedicated regulator tasked with keeping the money flows clean. Lastly, launderers are seeking global economies so they can move money internationally. CS:GO is an international franchise – something that its makers almost certainly pursued with gusto.

Given all these factors, it's perhaps no surprise that launderers saw an opportunity to wash their criminal proceeds via CS:GO's in-game marketplace. They used fraudulently obtained money to buy CS:GO keys, then sold the keys on the marketplace and extracted the profits as clean funds. Over time, it seems they took over almost the entire economy. In October 2019, Valve put out a remarkable statement: 'Worldwide fraud networks have recently shifted to using CS:GO keys to liquidate their gains. At this point, nearly all key purchases that end up being traded or sold on the marketplace are believed to be fraud-sourced.'[2] Valve took action, preventing the keys being traded, and continues to crack down on launderers attempting to use its services. There was no estimate as to how much money had been washed via CS:GO keys. But with tens of millions of people playing the game, and keys changing hands for $10 or more, it's not hard to conclude that hundreds of millions of dollars could have been laundered via this game alone.

It's not just video gaming. Anywhere that the tech industry creates an economy with these four attributes, it's likely money launderers won't be far away.

Take Non-Fungible Tokens, or NFTs, for example. You may have seen the headlines swirling round this new technology as prices boomed in 2022. There were stories of people apparently paying thousands of dollars for cartoons of apes. It all seemed a bit mad, but behind it was something potentially very powerful.

NFTs were created to solve a growing conundrum: how do you protect value in digital art? For example, there's only one master copy of da Vinci's *Mona Lisa* – any duplicates will never rival the original. But more and more artists are now creating digital works, and these can be screen-grabbed, downloaded and photographed repeatedly with almost no loss of quality. So how do you stop people just ripping them off, in the same way people used to illegally burn CD copies? NFTs are the answer. An artist can create an NFT of their work – in reality, a unique string of letters and numbers – and sell that alongside the digital artwork. The transaction history of these NFTs is stored in the digital amber of the blockchain, and anyone who owns the NFT can use that record to prove they own the rights to the original work.

Trade in NFTs sky-rocketed as artists and celebrities hopped aboard the bandwagon. In the first few months of 2021 the value of all NFTs on the market increased by an astonishing 1,785 per cent. Once again, it provided perfect conditions for money laundering: feverish trading, wildly flexible asset prices and a global marketplace operating way outside any regulatory regime.

Sure enough, it didn't take analysts long to turn up evidence that these criminals are starting to exploit the headline-grabbing NFT phenomenon. In April 2021, a user logged on to one of the big NFT trading websites to make a sale. From the outside it looked like any other NFT trade – everything went without a hitch, with the sale being made for 0.4 ether (then worth around $800). But when investigators at Chainalysis looked more closely at the deal, they discovered something suspicious. Like any crypto transaction, NFT trades are publicly recorded on the blockchain. In this case, the NFT trading website listed the buyer and seller's Ethereum wallet addresses, and so, using the blockchain, Chainalysis could see the transaction history of both parties to the trade. They found that, shortly before the sale, the seller had sent the buyer an Ethereum payment for almost exactly the same amount that the buyer had subsequently paid for the NFT. It wasn't the only example. Chainalysis found hundreds of other instances of this particular seller sending money to other accounts, apparently funding them to make a subsequent purchase. It seemed like the seller was paying people to buy. Things got even weirder when Chainalysis totted up how much the seller had actually made from all these mysterious trades.

Including gas fees (the small percentage paid to conduct an Ethereum transaction), this seller had *lost* $8,383.[3]

It was a perplexing state of affairs – why would an NFT seller pay people to buy their NFTs, and make a loss while doing it? If you're a money launderer, however, it all makes perfect sense. The first thing to realize is that, in this case, the seller and the hundreds of buyers are all one individual. The person who created this scheme had set up all these many persona accounts on the NFT trading website in order to wash illicit money. They would send some of the money to one of their buyer persona's Ethereum wallets. Then they would list an NFT for sale, and use the buyer persona's money to buy it, before extracting the funds from the buyer persona's account. They did this hundreds of times. Yes, they'd lost a few thousand dollars on the trades, but by rinsing the transactions through all their buyer accounts, they'd achieved the primary goal of money laundering – to break the connection between the dodgy incoming money and the clean outgoing money. Setting up those hundreds of accounts and managing the trades between them may seem an immense effort, but it's very possible that much of it was done via automated software.[4]

This wasn't an isolated case. Chainalysis found evidence suggesting $1.4m had been rinsed via NFTs in the last three months of 2021. That's obviously a very low figure compared to many of the laundering operations covered in this book, but it needs to be seen in the context of how new NFTs are – the year before, Chainalysis found almost no evidence of laundering at all

High volume, flexible asset prices, lack of regulation and global scale: from Airbnb to OnlyFans to Uber to Bitcoin and more, tech has boomed by setting up shop in spaces where those four aspects are present. As we've seen throughout this book, technologists have a conspicuous habit of creating innovations that inadvertently have precisely the kind of attributes money launderers crave. Launderers and techies may be distinct groups, but they often end up inhabiting the same territory. If you want to understand the symbiotic relationship between tech and money laundering – the relationship that's driven much of the activity covered in this book – this is the underlying explanation.

On the plus side, it seems that the forces of the traditional financial world are getting increasingly wise to this emerging realm of wrong-doing. As this book was being finished, the news was dominated by two massive criminal prosecutions that rocked the world of cutting-edge finance, and thrust hi-tech money laundering into the headlines.

November 2022 saw the collapse of FTX, one of the world's biggest cryptocurrency exchanges. Revelations emerged that its founder, Sam Bankman-Fried – an idiosyncratic tech guru emblematic of the new breed of 'crypto bros' spearheading the industry – had used the company's immense wealth to fund his other firm, Alameda Research, as well as to make personal investments and political campaign donations. A year later, Bankman-Fried was found guilty on multiple charges including – perhaps inevitably – money laundering. At the time of writing, he was due to be sentenced in early 2024.[5]

During the FTX mayhem of late 2022, there was talk of a potential white knight who could save the business: fellow crypto behemoth Binance. In the end, Binance did not ride to the rescue. Instead, it became the second high-profile casualty of the US government's crackdown on crypto. The company had already been accused by journalists of laundering money from the darknet marketplace Hydra, and just a few weeks after Bankman-Fried's conviction the company pleaded guilty to engaging in money laundering and sanctions violation. It agreed to pay an eye-watering fine of $4.3bn. Its founder and chief executive, Changpeng Zhao – who had also previously been considered a crypto titan – stood down and agreed to a personal fine of $50m. In the wake of the conviction, the comments from the prosecutors left little doubt as to their view of the free-wheeling world of crypto and its lax approach to money laundering. Attorney General Merrick Garland summed it up: 'Using new technology to break the law does not make you a disruptor, it makes you a criminal.'[6]

But despite the US authorities' growing attempts to be sheriffs of the Wild West of financial innovation, the reality is that we can't stop tech creators from pushing at the boundaries – and, arguably, we wouldn't want to. Not only is it an innately human drive, but it also has important benefits for growing our global economy and (quite often) improving our lives. In fact, tech is being used to fight back against some of the laundering tactics described in this book; artificial intelligence systems are being trained to spot suspicious transactions and block them, for example. But the flip-side of tech's constant, restless evolution is that every innovation potentially throws up new opportunities for launderers to do their work.

The more tech-savvy the launderers become, the greater ability they have to work across the criminal spectrum: pulling in money from traditional, street-level crimes like drug dealing and prostitution, as well as washing the money from cutting-edge cybercrime and fraud. And every new avenue for the money launderers helps enable the kind of addiction, theft and abuse that has damaged so many victims featured in the preceding chapters of this book, from Melanie Thompson – who was kidnapped and advertised on Backpage – to the romance fraud victims of the Amadi brothers. The criminals who conduct these heinous crimes rely on a shadow financial industry to enable their work, and technology is proving pivotal to their profits.

Acknowledgements

The list below is incomplete for a number of reasons: firstly, my endlessly fallible memory; secondly, for safety reasons I've omitted the names of the friends and family members who gave feedback on the book – thanks to all of you; thirdly, I've had many conversations with wise people at conferences and events during the course of researching the book which have guided and informed me, but the specifics of which have eluded me. If you're not on this list and feel you should be, please feel free to claim your free drink and my apology when next we meet.

First thanks go to my literary agent, Luigi Bonomi of LBA Associates, who helped get the book on the go, and then my editor at Penguin Business, Celia Buzuk, who steered it through with characteristic calm and competence, and to her colleague Claire Collins who did a great job stepping in to oversee it during Celia's absence. Thanks as well to the innumerable others at Penguin Business who worked to make the book everything it is.

Also thanks to: Nicolás Escobar, Juan Carlo Giraldo of Red+ Noticias, and Simone Bateman for her tremendous help arranging and translating Escobar's interview, Ken Rijock, Bob Mazur, Thomas Brewster and Susan Radlauer at *Forbes*, Roger Smethurst, Lisa Ward and colleagues at Greater Manchester Police, Melanie Thompson, Jason Amala of PCVA Law, Bassem Banafa, Moira Kim Penza of Wilkinson Stekloff, Andy Greenberg at *Wired*, Lucy Sneddon and Matt Sutton at the UK National Crime Agency, Christine Stafford, Nick Carlsen and Ari Redbord at TRM Labs, Phil Larratt, Madeleine Kennedy and colleagues at Chainalysis, Sam Bent, George Butiri, Ricky Patel at US Homeland Security Investigations, Lili Infante, Nicholas Smart at Crystal Blockchain, Sebastian Zwiebel and Carsten Meywirth of Germany's Bundeskriminalamt, Priyanka Goonetilleke, Alex Knorre, Artem Kuriksha, Andrey Kaganskikh, John Omoruan, Gary Warner of University of Alabama, Crane Hassold, Tom Cronkright and Claudia Lee of CertifID, Patrick Scruggs of the US Attorney's Office, Mike Kelly of Toronto Police, Steven Meighan, Sean Sheehan and Michael Cryan of Ireland's Garda, Kenoly Ugbodu, Mike DeBolt of Intel471, Matt O'Neill and Christine Pellerin and colleagues of the US Secret Service, Glen Kessler, Olukoya Abisoye ('Oyemykke'), Steven Tan, Aleksander Leonard Larsen of Sky Mavis, Kalie Moore of High Vibe PR, Ameen Soleimani, David Hoffman, Don Smith, Rafe Pilling and Ben Drysdale of Secureworks, and Charles Brown of Blackdot Solutions.

Plus all those who read chapters of the book and offered sage feedback: Hugh Levinson and Carl Johnston of the BBC, Alex Pillow of Moody's, Tom Mackenzie of Bloomberg, Tom Keatinge and Allison Owen of RUSI, Steve Brown and Paul Trueman of Mastercard, Toni Sless of the Fraud Women's Network, Dilara Bogut, Catherine Winter, Tara Annison of Twinstake, Erica Stanford, and David Mapstone of Sky News.

And, of course, my mum and my wife, without whose love and support this book (and much else in my life) would not have been possible.

Notes

1. Pablo's Problem

1 Norman A. Bailey, 'La Violencia in Colombia', *Journal of Inter-American Studies*, Vol. 9, No. 4 (October 1967), p. 562.
2 Roberto Escobar and David Fisher, *The Accountant's Story: Inside the Violent World of the Medellín Cartel* (Grand Central Publishing, 2010), p. 30.
3 Ibid., p. 18.
4 It's often written that Escobar was named the seventh richest man in the world by *Forbes* during the 1980s. This is untrue. At that time, *Forbes* did not rank billionaires, but listed them by valuation category ('over $10bn', etc.). Escobar was listed from 1987–1993. Eerily, his 1993 entry ended with the following: 'Escobar will soon leave this list. Perhaps, this earth.' He was killed in December that year.
5 Escobar and Fisher, op. cit., pp. 45–60.
6 Ibid., p. 66.
7 Ibid., p. 70.
8 Ibid., p. 76.
9 James Kelly, 'South Florida: Trouble in Paradise', *Time*, 23 November 1981.
10 'Anguilla', The CIA World Factbook, www.cia.gov, accessed 12 December 2022.
11 Ken Rijock, *The Laundry Man* (Penguin Books, 2013), pp. 38–40. (It appears that financial advisers still see the same advantages in Anguilla today, see: 'International Offshore Jurisdiction Review – Anguilla as a Tax Haven', Offshore Protection, 25 October 2022, www.offshoreprotection.com, accessed 12 December 2022.)
12 Ibid., p. 49.
13 Ibid., p. 39.

14 Ibid, p. 65.

15 Ibid, p. 169.

16 While modern interpretations have emphasized the characters of individual Smurfs, in the original cartoons they were imagined as a communal, homogeneous group of creatures living in a patriarchal, all-male society (Peyo, 'La Flûte à Six Trous', *Spirou*, 8 May 1958).

17 Robert Mazur, *The Infiltrator: The True Story of One Man Against the Biggest Drug Cartel in History* (Transworld, 2016), p. 27.

18 Ibid., p. 29.

19 Ibid, p. 229.

20 Escobar and Fisher, op. cit., p. 200.

21 Ibid., p. 3.

2. From Bury to Bitcoin

1 Neil Robertson, 'Drugs Worth £1 Million Found at Bury Woman's Home', *Bury Times*, 17 October 2014.

2 Sarah Marshall, 'Doncaster Dealer Found With Loaded Gun and £100k Drug Stash is Jailed for Over a Decade', *Doncaster Free Press*, 3 April 2019.

3 Danny Shaw, 'Hundreds Arrested as Crime Chat Network Cracked', BBC News, 2 July 2020. There was subsequent controversy over whether the law-enforcement operation was legal and therefore whether evidence from the EncroChat hack was admissible in court, which at the time of writing was still being resolved in the UK.

4 Marshall, op. cit.

5 Neal Keeling, 'Shocking Moment Two Women Gangsters Do Cash for Drugs Swap in Doncaster Prison Car Park While Holding a Baby', *Examiner Live*, 5 December 2020.

6 This explanation is inevitably incomplete and brushes over much of the detail, because this is a general readership book and is not specifically about Bitcoin and cryptocurrency. The behind-the-scenes explanation as to how Bitcoin and the blockchain really work is quite complex, but I recommend starting with 99Bitcoins, 'Bitcoin

Transactions – from "Send" to "Receive" ', YouTube, 21 September 2017, and then Khan Academy, 'Bitcoin – Transaction block chains', YouTube, 2 May 2013.

7 Chainalysis, 'DeFi Takes On Bigger Role in Money Laundering but Small Group of Centralized Services Still Dominate', 26 January 2022.

8 Greater Manchester Police, 'Jailed For Nearly 140 Years: Final Offenders in Multi-Million-Pound Cross-Pennine Drug Bust Sentenced', 4 December 2020.

9 Chainalysis, op. cit.

10 HMRC, 'Tax Criminal to Spend Further 10 Years In Prison', 4 March 2013.

11 'Midland Gang Jailed for £170 Million VAT Fraud', *Sunday Mercury*, 23 October 2012.

12 HMRC, op. cit.

13 Neal Keeling, 'The Yorkshire Drug Dealer and His "Beauty Booth" Used as a Front for Major Heroin and Cocaine Trafficking Plot', *Examiner Live*, 4 December 2020.

14 Ibid.

15 Matthew Sparkes, 'UK Police Forces Have Seized More Than £300 Million in Bitcoin', *New Scientist*, 5 January 2022.

16 Sean Seddon, '£180,000,000 of Cryptocurrency Seized in Biggest Ever UK Crime Sting', *Metro*, 13 July 2021.

17 John Collins, Chief Legal and Regulatory Officer, Santander UK, giving evidence to House of Commons Treasury Committee, reported in 'Economic Crime', Eleventh Report of Session 2021–22, 26 January 2022, p. 54.

3. Crypto Pimps

1 Melanie Thompson's contributions are a combination of quotes she gave to me in interview and quotes she gave in an interview with Women's March Global (Women's March Global Dialogues Sex, Lies, and Classifieds—Dialogue #3, www.medium.com, 11 May 2018). I am indebted to her for telling me her story.

2 FrontPageConfidential, 'About Us', www.frontpageconfidential.com, accessed 1 November 2022.

3 Christine Biederman, 'Inside Backpage.com's Vicious Battle With the Feds', *Wired*, 18 June 2019.

4 Mark Jacobson, 'The Voice from Beyond the Grave', *New York Magazine*, 3 November 2005.

5 Biederman, op. cit.

6 Jacobson, op. cit.

7 United States Senate Permanent Subcommittee On Investigations, 'Backpage.com's Knowing Facilitation of Online Sex Trafficking', p. 43.

8 New York Penal Law, Sec. 130.00 Sex Offenses; Definitions of Terms; Sec. 230.00 Prostitution.

9 United States Senate Permanent Subcommittee On Investigations, op. cit., p. 20.

10 Ibid., p. 44.

11 Ibid., p. 44. By taking payment, Backpage could argue it was trying to deter illegal behaviour on the site because those placing the ads often handed over credit card details, allowing an element of vetting and record-keeping by its staff.

12 United States Senate Permanent Subcommittee On Investigations, op. cit., p. 43.

13 'Sales Director for Backpage.com Pleads Guilty to Conspiracy', Associated Press via NBC News, 18 August 2018.

14 Maggy Krell, *Taking Down Backpage: Fighting the World's Largest Sex Trafficker* (New York University Press, 2022), p. 74.

15 Trafficking Victims Protection Act 2000, 22 U.S.C. § 7102(11)(A), www.justice.gov, accessed 1 November 2022.

16 Email from Yiota G. Souras, Senior Vice President and General Counsel, National Center for Missing and Exploited Children to Permanent Subcommittee on Investigations, 5 January 2017.

17 Amicus Curiae Brief of the National Center for Missing and Exploited Children, in the case of J. S., S. L. and L. C., Respondents Village Voice Media Holdings, L.L.C., d/b/a Backpage.com; Backpage.com, L.L.C.; New Times Media, L.L.C., d/b/a Backpage.com, Supreme Court of the State of Washington, 4 September 2014, p. 10.

18 Ibid., p. 8.

19 James C. McKinley Jr, 'Bands and Pop Singers Join Fight Against Backpage.com Ads', *The New York Times*, 26 April 2012.

20 Nicholas Kristof, 'Not Quite a Teen, Yet Sold for Sex', *The New York Times*, 18 April 2012.

21 Krell, op. cit., pp. 1–5.

22 'Woman Admits Prostituting Runaway', *St Louis Today*, 2 September 2010.

    M.A., a Minor, by and through her Natural Mother and Next Friend, P.K., v Village Voice Media Holdings, Llc., D/B/A Backpage.Com, and Backpage. Com, Llc, United States District Court, Eastern District of Missouri, Eastern Division, 15 August 2011.

23 *Jane Doe No. 1 et al., Plaintiffs, Appellants v BACKPAGE.COM, LLC et al., Defendants, Appellees*, United States Court of Appeals, First Circuit, 14 March 2016. The case later featured in the documentary *I Am Jane Doe*.

24 Krell, op. cit., p. 99.

25 *People v Ferrer et al.*, Sacramento County Superior Court, Ruling of Judge Bowman, 9 December 2016.

26 *Backpage.com, LLC v Dart*, United States Court of Appeals, Seventh Circuit, Exhibits B & C, 30 November 2015.

27 *USA v Lacey et al.*, United States District Court for the District of Arizona, 28 March 2018, p. 36.

28 *People v Ferrer et al.*, Superior Court of the State of California, 23 December 2016, p. 3.

29 *USA v Lacey et al.*, op. cit., p. 40.

30 Ibid., pp. 40 and 41.

31 *People v Ferrer et al.*, Sacramento County Superior Court, Ruling of Judge Bowman, 9 December 2016.

32 Krell, op. cit., p. 119.

33 Melanie Thompson requested that I not publish his name.

34 Krell, op. cit., p. 120.

35 *People v Ferrer et al.*, Sacramento County Superior Court, filed 23 December 2016.

36 United States Senate Permanent Subcommittee On Investigations, op. cit., p. 31.

37 Ibid., p. 26.

38 Ibid., p. 2.

39 Krell, op. cit., p. 143.

40 Richard Ruelas, 'Backpage Never Knowingly Posted Prostitution Ads, Defense Attorney Argues', *AZ Central*, 8 September 2021.

41 Joe Duhownik, 'James Larkin, Phoenix New Times Co-founder, Dies At 74', Courthouse News Service, 2 August 2023.

42 Internal Revenue Service, 'Backpage Principals Convicted of $500m Prostitution Enterprises Promotion Scheme', 17 November 2023. Lacey's co-defendants were found guilty of charges related to facilitating prostitution, in addition to money-laundering offences.

43 The Texas Human Trafficking Prevention Task Force Report, December 2018.

44 Krell, op. cit., p. 121.

4. Welcome To Video

1 'Onion Routing, Brief Selected History', www.onion-router.net, accessed 4 December 2022.

2 *United States of America v Eric Eoin Marques*, Amended Criminal Complaint, 8 August 2013, p. 6.

3 '#OpDarknet – To Catch a Predator', www.pastebin.com, 18 October 2011.

4 Patrick Howard O'Neill, 'The Darkest Net', *The Daily Dot*, 28 September 2014.

5 Ibid.

6 Max Daly, 'Inside the Repulsive World of "Hurtcore", the Worst Crimes Imaginable', *Vice*, 19 February 2018.

7 *United States of America v Eric Eoin Marques*, Amended Criminal Complaint, 8 August 2013, p. 12.

8 Ibid., p. 13.

9 Department of Justice, 'Dark Web Child Pornography Facilitator Sentenced to 27 Years in Prison for Conspiracy to Advertise Child Pornography', 16 September 2021.

10 For understandable reasons, almost no one who knew Falder has ever spoken publicly about him. I am deeply grateful to his former colleague for agreeing to talk to me anonymously.

11 Richard Vernalls and Rachael McMenemy, 'Warped Paedophile Began His Sick Campaign of Abuse While at Cambridge University', *Cambridge News*, 20 February 2018.

12 Andy Greenberg, *Tracers in the Dark: The Global Hunt for the Crime Lords of Cryptocurrency* (Doubleday, 2022), p. 243. Published in the UK as *Lords of Crypto Crime: The Race to Bring Down the World's Invisible Kingpins* (Octopus, 2024).

13 *United States of America* v *Eric Eoin Marques*, Amended Criminal Complaint, 8 August 2013, pp. 15 and 16.

14 *United States of America* v *Jong Woo Son*, Indictment, 9 August 2018, p. 5.

15 Greenberg, op. cit.

16 Ibid.

17 'Chainalysis in Action: DoJ Announces Shutdown of Largest Child Pornography Website', www.chainalysis.com, 16 October 2019.

18 Greenberg, p. 244, op. cit.

19 *United States of America* v *Jong Woo Son*, Indictment, 9 August 2018, p. 4.

20 Greenberg, op. cit.

21 Ibid.

22 Ibid.

23 Department of Justice, 'South Korean National and Hundreds of Others Charged Worldwide in the Takedown of the Largest Darknet Child Pornography Website, Which was Funded by Bitcoin', 16 October 2019.

24 Greenberg, p. 257, op. cit.

25 Julia Hollingsworth, 'How Bitcoin Transactions were Used to Track Down the 23-Year-Old South Korean Operating a Global Child Exploitation Site from his Bedroom', CNN, 20 October 2019.

26 Jun Ji-hye, 'Public Anger Growing Over Child Porn Site Operator's Annulment', *Korea Times*, 5 May 2020.

27 Department of Justice, 'Dark Web Child Pornography Facilitator Sentenced to 27 Years in Prison for Conspiracy to Advertise Child Pornography', 16 September 2021.

28 Chris Johnston, 'Lux captured: The simple error that brought down

the world's worst hurtcore paedophile', *Sydney Morning Herald*, 14 May 2016.

29 The National Crime Agency, 'Depraved "Hurt Core" University Academic Jailed for 32 Years', 19 February 2018.

30 Chris Johnston and Nino Bucci, 'How Matthew David Graham's "Hurtcore" Paedophile Habit Began on the Dark Web', *The Age*, 7 September 2015.

5. Dark Gold

1 Amanda Garrett, 'Bath Man Pleads Guilty, Forfeits More Than $200 Million in Bitcoin Money Laundering Case', *Akron Beacon Journal*, 18 August 2021.

2 I've changed Tom Dodd's name, as he still works in the tech industry and was only allowed to speak by his current employer on condition of anonymity.

3 *United States of America* v *Larry Dean Harmon*, 10 August 2021, p. 3.

4 'Frequently Asked Questions', www.grams.link, accessed 8 December 2022.

5 'Introducing Grams Helix: Bitcoins Cleaner', DeepDotWeb, 22 June 2014.

6 Ibid.

7 *United States of America* v *Alexandre Cazes*, 19 July 2017, p. 8.

8 Andy Greenberg, *Tracers in the Dark: The Global Hunt for the Crime Lords of Cryptocurrency* (Doubleday, 2022), p. 148. Published in the UK as *Lords of Crypto Crime: The Race to Bring Down the World's Invisible Kingpins* (Octopus, 2024).

9 Chainalysis, Crypto Crime Report, February 2022, p. 102.

10 'After the Breach: The Monetization and Illicit Use of Stolen Data', testimony by Nicolas Christin Ph.D., Carnegie Mellon University, before the Subcommittee on Terrorism and Illicit Finance, US House of Representatives, 15 March 2018.

11 Chainalysis, op. cit., p. 109.

12 FinCEN, *United States of America Financial Crimes Enforcement Network*,

Department of the Treasury in the Matter of: Larry Dean Harmon, Number 2020–2 (undated).

13 *United States of America* v *Larry Dean Harmon*, op. cit., p. 5.

14 FinCEN, op. cit., p. 7.

15 Greenberg, op. cit., p. 158.

16 Ibid.

17 Greenberg, op. cit., p. 195.

18 Ibid., p. 204.

19 *United States of America* v *Alexandre Cazes*, 19 July 2017, p. 19.

20 'Massive Blow to Criminal Dark Web Activities After Globally Coordinated Operation', www.europol.europa.eu, 20 July 2017.

21 'So Long, and Thanks for All the Fish', www.reddit.com, 15 December 2017, accessed via www.archive.org, 10 December 2022.

22 Greenberg, op. cit., p. 173.

23 David Voreacos, 'Millions in Cryptocurrency Vanished as Agents Watched Helplessly', *Bloomberg*, 3 October 2022.

24 *United States of America* v *Gary James Harmon*, 28 June 2021, p. 3.

25 In its action against Larry Harmon, US Treasury states Coin Ninja had a crypto mixing service, but does not link this to use by darknet markets. Instead, it states that Harmon failed to register Coin Ninja as a money services business.

26 Leigh Cuen, 'US DoJ Calls Bitcoin Mixing "a Crime" in Arrest of Software Developer', *CoinDesk*, 13 September 2021.

27 US Department of Justice, 'Man Sentenced for Stealing Over 712 Bitcoin Subject to Forfeiture', 27 April 2023.

28 US Department of Justice, 'Ohio Resident Pleads Guilty to Operating Darknet-Based Bitcoin "Mixer" that Laundered Over $300 Million', 18 August 2021.

29 DEFCONConference, 'DEF CON 30 – Sam Bent – Tor – Darknet Opsec by a Veteran Darknet Vendor', YouTube, 20 October 2022.

30 Bent claims he was eventually caught via different means. He says an accomplice made mistakes that led to one of his packages being intercepted and illegally opened. His accomplice was then arrested and pleaded guilty, implicating Bent himself.

31 US Department of Justice, 'First Nationwide Undercover Operation

Targeting Darknet Vendors Results in Arrests of More Than 35 Individuals Selling Illicit Goods and the Seizure of Weapons, Drugs and More Than $23.6 Million', 26 June 2018.

32 You can see more about Bent's story at www.doingfedtime.com

6. The Hydra

1 Flashpoint and Chainalysis, 'Hydra: Where the Crypto Money Laundering Trail Goes Dark', Flashpoint, 25 May 2021.
2 Andrey Kaganskikh, 'Эйфория Cargo', www.cargo.baza.io, undated.
3 Priyanka Goonetilleke, Alex Knorre and Artem Kuriksha, 'Hydra: A Quantitative Overview of the World's Largest Darknet Market', University of Pennsylvania, European University at Saint Petersburg, 22 September 2022.
4 Ibid., p. 5.
5 Flashpoint and Chainalysis, op. cit.
6 Ibid.
7 Goonetilleke, Knorre and Kuriksha, op. cit., pp. 1 and 2.
8 Department of Justice, 'Justice Department Investigation Leads to Shutdown of Largest Online Darknet Marketplace', 5 April 2022.
9 Flashpoint and Chainalysis, op. cit., p. 4.
10 Anna Baydakova, 'Russia's Largest Darknet Market is Hawking an ICO to Fund Global Expansion', *CoinDesk*, 12 December 2019.
11 Flashpoint and Chainalysis, op. cit., p. 11. I am grateful to the report's authors, Vlad Cuiujuclu and András Tóth-Czifra, for further explaining Hydra to me, in addition to Nicholas Smart of crypto-tracing firm Crystal Blockchain.
12 *United States of America* v *Dmitry Olegovich Pavlov*, Indictment, 5 April 2022, p. 6.
13 Andy Greenberg, 'Shutdown of Russia's Hydra Market Disrupts a Crypto-Crime ATM', *Wired*, 5 April 2022.
14 Angus Berwick and Tom Wilson, 'How Crypto Giant Binance Became a Hub for Hackers, Fraudsters and Drug Traffickers', Reuters, 6 June 2022.

15 'The Crypto Money Laundering Myth and the Machine Working Overtime to Sell a False Narrative', Binance, 6 June 2022.

16 This explains why the figure from Crystal Blockchain is much lower than the US Department of Justice's figure for the amount of Hydra money exchanged through Bitzlato. The DoJ's estimate of $700m factors in money exchanged 'either directly or through intermediaries', whereas the Crystal Blockchain figure assesses direct transfers.

17 Remarks by Deputy Secretary of the Treasury Wally Adeyemo on Action Against Russian Illicit Finance, US Department of the Treasury, 18 January 2023.

18 US Department of Justice, 'Founder and Majority Owner of Bitzlato, a Cryptocurrency Exchange, Charged with Unlicensed Money Transmitting', 18 January 2023.

19 US Attorney's Office, Northern District of California, 'US Charges Russian FSB Officers and their Criminal Conspirators for Hacking Yahoo and Millions of Email Accounts', 15 March 2017.

20 Intelligence and Security Committee of Parliament, 'Russia', 21 July 2020.

21 Edward Wilding (ed.), *Virus Bulletin*, January 1990.

22 Geoff White, 'How the Dridex Gang Makes Millions from Bespoke Ransomware', Forbes.com, 26 September 2018.

23 Chainalysis, Crypto Crime Report, February 2022, p. 40. As the report notes, the rise in the number of strains may be linked to Russia's re-invasion of Ukraine that year. In response to the invasion, the US became more aggressive in sanctioning ransomware groups, making it harder for victims to pay. The ransomware gangs responded by rebranding, allowing victims to argue that they were not paying a sanctioned entity.

24 Kartikay Mehrotra and William Turton, 'CNA Financial Paid $40 Million in Ransom After March Cyberattack', *Bloomberg Business*, 20 May 2021.

25 Marco Figueroa, Napoleon Bing and Bernard Silvestrini, 'The Conti Leaks, Insight into a Ransomware Unicorn', BreachQuest, 9 March 2022.

26 Chainalysis, op. cit., p. 41.

27 Figueroa, Bing and Silvestrini, op. cit.

28 John Fokker, Jambul Tologonov, 'Conti Leaks: Examining the Panama Papers of Ransomware', Trellix, 31 March 2022.

29 At the time of writing, the leaker's identity is unknown. It was initially suspected to be a Ukrainian member of the Conti gang, but many now claim it was a Ukrainian security researcher.

30 Chainalysis, op. cit., p. 39.

31 Ibid., p. 123.

32 Scott Mlyn, 'Photos Show the Impact at the Pumps from the Colonial Pipeline Hack', CNBC, 12 May 2021.

33 Colonial Pipeline, 'Our Company', colpipe.com, accessed via archive. org 11 February 2023.

34 Chris Isidore, 'American Airlines Has to Add Fuel Stops after Pipeline Shutdown', CNN Business, 11 May 2021.

35 Chainalysis, op. cit., p. 51.

36 US Department of Justice, 'Department of Justice Seizes $2.3 Million in Cryptocurrency Paid to the Ransomware Extortionists Darkside', 7 June 2021.

37 Chainalysis, op. cit., p. 52.

38 Mary-Ann Russon, 'US Fuel Pipeline Hackers "Didn't Mean to Create Problems"', BBC News, 10 May 2021.

39 Fabiana Batista, Michael Hirtzer and Mike Dorning, 'All of JBS's US Beef Plants were Forced Shut by Cyberattack', Bloomberg, 31 May 2021.

40 BBC News, 'Meat Giant JBS Pays $11m in Ransom to Resolve Cyber-Attack', 10 June 2021.

41 US Treasury, 'Treasury Sanctions Russia-Based Hydra, World's Largest Darknet Market, and Ransomware-Enabling Virtual Currency Exchange Garantex', 5 April 2022.

42 BBC News Russian Service, https://t.me/bbcrussian/26316, 6 April 2022.

7. Black Axe

1 Oseo John Omoruan, *My Campus Cult Diary* (self-published, 2019).

2 Ogaga Ifowodo, quoted in Selena Ross, 'Shadowy Black Axe Group Leaves Trail of Tattered Lives', *Globe and Mail*, 12 November 2015.

3 Michael Peel, 'Nigeria-Related Financial Crime and its Links With Britain', Chatham House, November 2006, p. 2.

4 Oludayo Tade and Ibrahim Aliyu, 'Social Organization of Internet Fraud Among University Undergraduates in Nigeria', *International Journal of Cyber Criminology (IJCC)* ISSN: 0974–2891, July–December 2011, Vol. 5 (2), p. 868.

5 Eugène François Vidocq, 'Memoirs of Vidocq' (E. L. Carey and A. Hart, 1834), p. 58. The scam outlined by Vidocq, of course, occurred in France (in Bicêtre, specifically). Reportedly, it became known as the Spanish Prisoner Letter fraud due to its later use during the Spanish–American War.

6 Steve Lohr, ' "Nigerian Scam" Lures Companies', *The New York Times*, 21 May 1992.

7 'National Manpower Stock and Employment Generation Survey', Nigeria National Bureau of Statistics, 2010.

8 Tade and Aliyu, op. cit., p. 873.

9 Detective Constable Mike Kelly of Toronto Police, quoted in Ross, op. cit.

10 The Cheshire Cat, 'The Ethics of Scambaiting', www.419eater.com, accessed 31 January 2023.

11 Peel, op. cit., p. 7.

12 '2008 Internet Crime Report', Internet Crime Complaint Center, 'Top Ten Countries by Count: Perpetrators', p. 8.

13 Richard Uku, a counsellor in the Nigerian Embassy in Washington, quoted in Lohr, op. cit.

14 Hank Hyena, 'When Things Fall Apart', *Salon*, 2 August 1999.

15 Sean Williams, 'The Black Axe', *Harper's Magazine*, September 2019.

16 Brian Williams, 'University Professor Helps FBI Crack $70 Million Cybercrime Ring', NBC News, 21 March 2012.

17 *United States* v *Muhammad Naji*, Criminal Complaint, 14 January 2015, p. 6.

18 Ibid., p. 7.

19 Ibid., p. 9.

20 Department of Justice, 'International Money Launderer Pleads Guilty to his Role in Defrauding Law Firms and Other Scams', 7 May 2015.

21 *United States of America* v *Dana Marie Jewesak*, Criminal Complaint, 9 March 2016, pp. 2 and 3.
22 'Toronto "Romance Scam" Linked to $5B FBI Fraud Probe', CBC News, 22 October 2015.
23 'International Fraud and Money Laundering Scheme', FBI, 19 January 2018.
24 Internet Crime Complaint Center, 'Federal Bureau of Investigation Internet Crime Report 2022'.

8. Smurfing on Snapchat

1 Aine McMahon, 'Nigerians were Largest Group of New Irish Citizens in 2013', *Irish Times*, 1 July 2015.
2 Boboye received seven years, with the final two suspended. Olanyian received four with the final year suspended.
3 I checked this with an anti-fraud expert at a major bank, who told me that in order to open the business account, the man behind the Money Plugs Instagram account would still need to provide ID in my name, as the director of the company. However, with banks increasingly offering online account creation, the anti-fraud expert suspected that his plan was to create a fake ID for me in order to open the account in my company's name.

9. Hushpuppi and Big Boss

1 Biographical information on Abbas's early life comes from a combination of court documents and Abbas's Instagram account.
2 'Hush Money', *File on Four*, BBC Radio 4.
3 Biographical information on Alaumary's early life comes from court documents.
4 Details of Château Olivier from www.chateauolivier.ca
5 Records from Soquij, dossier 2803-01, 31 May 2018.

6 *United States of America* v *Ghaleb Alaumary*, Document #80, 26 January 2022, p. 12.

7 Research by Intel471 conducted for *The Lazarus Heist* podcast, BBC World Service.

8 *United States of America* v *Ramon Abbas*, Defendant's Sentencing Memorandum and Motion in Support of Variance and Exhibits, 7 August 2022, p. 14.

9 'Hush Money', *File on Four*, BBC Radio 4.

10 Interviewed for *The Lazarus Heist* podcast, BBC World Service, Season 2, Episode 3, 'Hushpuppi'.

11 Colin Freeze, 'Canadian Linked to North Korea was Part of MacEwan University Cyberheist', *Globe and Mail*, 20 March 2021.

12 Ibid. MacEwan University did not respond to my request for comment.

13 *United States of America* v *Jennal Aziz*, 18 February 2019, and *In the Matter of the Criminal Complaint Filed Against Kelvin Desangles, aka 'Kelvin Desanges'*, Affadavit in Support, 7 December 2017.

14 This information is from my interview with former US Secret Service Agent Glen Kessler.

15 *United States of America* v *Ghaleb Alaumary, aka 'Canada', aka 'Ockie'*, 8 May 2019, p. 4.

16 'Oman's Bank Muscat Hit by $39 mln Prepaid Card Fraud', Reuters, 26 February 2013.

17 ANI News Official, 'Cosmos Bank Cloned Card Heist Planned in Thane', *Times of India*, 12 December 2018, and *United States of America* v *Ghaleb Alaumary, aka 'G', aka 'Backwood', aka 'Big Boss'*, 17 November 2020, p. 9. There are differing figures for exactly how much was taken from Cosmos Co-Operative Bank, as well as from other victims of Alaumary and Abbas. I have opted where possible to take the amounts from the plea agreements reached between the defendants and US prosecutors, on the basis that this represents a figure upon which there is at least some consensus from multiple parties.

18 *United States of America* v *Ghaleb Alaumary*, Plea Agreement, 17 December 2020, p. 13.

19 Brijesh Singh, interviewed for *The Lazarus Heist* podcast, BBC World Service, Season 2, Episode 2, 'Big Boss'.

20 Nadeem Inamdar, 'Pune Court Convicts 11 Accused in Cosmos Bank Cyber Fraud Case', *Hindustan Times*, 23 April 2023.

21 US Attorney's Office, Middle District of Florida, 'Canadian Leader of Complex Nigerian Fraud and Money Laundering Ring Sentenced', 20 January 2023.

22 *United States of America* v *Ramon Olorunwa Abbas, aka 'Ray Hushpuppi', aka 'Hush'*, Criminal Complaint, 25 June 2020, p. 19.

23 Details of Sweet's activities in Dubai come from my interview with former US Secret Service agent Glen Kessler, who was given them by Ghaleb Alaumary during his post-arrest interviews.

24 *United States of America* v *Ramon Olorunwa Abbas*, Document #11, 29 July 2020, p. 6.

25 Criminal Complaint, op. cit., p. 20.

26 Interview with Abigail Mamo, Chief Executive Officer, Malta Chamber of Small and Medium Enterprises, speaking to *The Lazarus Heist* podcast, BBC World Service, Season 2, Episode 3, 'Hushpuppi'.

27 Criminal Complaint, op. cit., p. 21.

28 'Arrests in Belfast and London in Cyber-Heist Money Laundering Investigation', National Crime Agency, 30 January 2020.

29 Criminal Complaint, op. cit., pp. 22–4.

30 Ibid., pp. 16–18.

31 From the author's interview with Kessler.

32 Ibid.

33 *United States of America* v *Ramon Olorunwa Abbas, aka 'Ray Hushpuppi', aka 'Hush'*, Plea Agreement, 27 July 2021, pp. 15–17.

34 Ibid., p. 17.

35 Dubai Police, 'Dubai Police take down "Hushpuppi", "Woodberry", ten international cyber criminals', YouTube, 25 June 2020.

36 *United States of America* v *Ramon Abbas*, Defendant's Sentencing Memorandum, Document #66, 7 August 2022, and Document # 66-6.

37 Ibid., Government Sentencing Position, Document #65, p. 3.

10. *Tornado Cash*

1 Ellen Nakashima and Craig Timberg, 'NSA Officials Worried About the Day its Potent Hacking Tool Would Get Loose. Then It Did', *Washington Post*, 16 May 2017.

2 Foreign and Commonwealth Office, 'Foreign Office Minister Condemns North Korean Actor for WannaCry Attacks', 19 December 2017.

3 William Smart, 'Lessons Learned Review of the WannaCry Ransomware Cyber Attack', Department of Health and Social Care, NHS Improvement, NHS England, February 2018, p. 5.

4 'Cyber Threat Alliance Cracks the Code on Cryptowall Crimeware Associated with $325 Million in Payments', www.cyberthreatalliance.org, 28 October 2015.

5 'Legal Information', www.hitbtc.com, accessed 13 May 2023.

6 Geoff White, 'The Wild Hunt for the WannaCry Hackers', www.geoffwhite.tech, 13 December 2018.

7 'Axie Infinity Live Player Count', www.playercounter.com, accessed 13 May 2023. John Joseph Benares, 'Axie Daily Active Users Dip Below 1m, First Time in 8 Months', United Gamers, www.unitedgamers.gg, 13 May 2022.

8 Miles Kruppa and Tim Bradshaw, 'Crypto's Hottest Game is Facing an Economic Maelstrom', *Financial Times*, 26 November 2021.

9 Camomile Shumba, 'A Plot of Digital Land Just Sold for $2.3 Million on Axie Infinity, as the Real-Estate Race Heats Up Across the Metaverse', *Business Insider*, 25 November 2021.

10 Kruppa and Bradshaw, op. cit.

11 Ronin Network blog, 'Community Alert: Ronin Validators Compromised', 29 March 2022.

12 Ibid. The ether stolen was Wrapped Ether, or WETH, which is compatible with smart contracts.

13 US Department of Justice, 'Husband and Wife Plead Guilty to Money Laundering Conspiracy Involving the Hack and Theft of Billions in Cryptocurrency', 3 August 2023.

14 United Nations Security Council report S/2023/171, 7 March 2023, p. 74.

Giving a total dollar amount for the crypto allegedly stolen by North Korea is difficult, partly due to the considerable fluctuation in crypto-currency exchange rates. For example, Bitcoin's value halved between November 2021 and May 2022, so the dollar value of any funds stolen during late 2022 would now be much lower. However, Bitcoin's price went up sixfold between September 2020 and March 2021, therefore any funds stolen prior to late 2020 would have massively increased in value.

15 Justin McCurry, 'North Korean Missile Launch Sparks Evacuation Confusion in Japan', *Guardian*, 13 April 2023.

16 Sean Lyngaas, 'Half of North Korean Missile Program Funded by Cyberattacks and Crypto Theft, White House Says', CNN, 10 May 2023. The US official quoted in the report had previously stated the estimate at a third, but CNN confirmed with a White House spokesperson that the updated figure was accurate.

17 *The Lazarus Heist* podcast, BBC World Service, Season 2, Episode 8, 'Bitcoin Bandits'.

18 Elliptic Blog, 'North Korea's Lazarus Group Identified as Exploiters Behind $540 Million Ronin Bridge Heist', 14 April 2022.

19 In reality, DAOs currently aren't as decentralized and democratic as their proponents might wish. Research by Chainalysis found that, among the top ten DAOs, 90 per cent of the voting token power was held by just 1 per cent of the token holders. Chainalysis, 'Dissecting the DAO: Web3 Ownership is Surprisingly Concentrated', 27 June 2022.

20 William Foxley, 'Developers of Ethereum Privacy Tool Tornado Cash Smash their Keys', CoinDesk, 14 September 2021.

21 This is according to Sky Mavis's Larsen, who says legal actions are now under way to return it to his company.

22 Chainalysis, 'Understanding Tornado Cash, its Sanctions Implications, and Key Compliance Questions', 30 August 2022.

23 Chainalysis, 'Crypto Mixer Usage Reaches All-time Highs in 2022, with Nation State Actors and Cybercriminals Contributing Significant Volume', 14 July 2022.

24 According to researchers from crypto-tracing company Elliptic, this took place over a period of forty-five days. This is because, in order to effectively launder such a large sum via Tornado Cash, the hackers

needed to ensure there was a sufficient amount of assets moving around inside the mixer ('liquidity' to use the technical term). Tornado Cash needed to combine the incoming money with other users' funds. Depositing a huge sum like $455m would have made this very difficult.

25 FIOD, 'Arrest of Suspected Developer of Tornado Cash', www.fiod.nl, 12 August 2022.

26 US Department of Justice, 'Tornado Cash Founders Charged with Money Laundering and Sanctions Violations', 23 August 2023.

27 X.com, @brianeklein, 24 August 2023.

28 US Department of the Treasury, 'US Treasury Sanctions Notorious Virtual Currency Mixer Tornado Cash', 8 August 2022.

29 Anna Baydakova, 'Crypto 2023: It's Sanctions Season', *CoinDesk*, 12 December 2022.

30 Chainalysis, 'The 2022 Global Crypto Adoption Index', 14 September 2022. First and second were Vietnam and the Philippines, respectively, further bolstering the case that Sky Mavis had found the perfect marketplace for its crypto-based game.

31 Andre Beganski, 'Ethereum Cofounder Says He Used Now-Blacklisted Tornado Cash to Donate to Ukraine', *Decrypt*, 9 August 2022.

32 At the time of writing, the applicants had lost their lawsuit against the US Department of the Treasury, with the court ruling that the US government had acted within its rights in sanctioning Tornado Cash. The crypto community behind the lawsuit has announced its intention to appeal.

33 Andrew Throuvalas, 'Professor Republishes Tornado Cash Code Following GitHub Takedown', *Decrypt*, 24 August 2022.

34 Chainalysis, 'How 2022's Biggest Cryptocurrency Sanctions Designations Affected Crypto Crime', 9 January 2023.

11. *Future Money*

1 Calum Patterson, '11 Most Expensive CSGO Skins in 2023: Knives, AK-47, AWP & More', *Dexerto*, 4 May 2023.

Notes

2 'Key Change', blog.counter-strike.net, 29 October 2019.

3 Chainalysis, Crypto Crime Report, February 2022, p. 33.

4 Chainalysis listed this activity as 'wash trading' – in which a trader artificially inflates the price of an asset by posing as both seller and buyer, and gradually increases the asset price through a series of sales. However, given the losses incurred by this individual, money laundering seems a more likely explanation.

5 Department of Justice, 'Statement of U.S. Attorney Damian Williams on the Conviction of Samuel Bankman-Fried', 2 November 2023.

6 Department of Justice, 'Binance and CEO Plead Guilty to Federal Charges in $4B Resolution', 21 November 2023.

Index

Index